MEMOIRS

MEMOIRS

Israel Sieff

WEIDENFELD AND NICOLSON
5 Winsley Street London W1

© 1970 by Israel Sieff

All rights reserved. No part of this publication may be reproduced, stored in a retrieval system, or transmitted, in any form or by any means, electronic, mechanical, photocopying, recording or otherwise, without the prior permission of the Copyright owner.

SBN 297 00234 1

Printed by C. Tinling & Co. Ltd., London and Prescot.

Contents

	FOREWORD	ix
1	My Family and its Origins	1
2	My Childhood in Manchester	17
3	My Youth, and Simon Marks	29
4	The Beginnings of Marks and Spencer	52
5	Secretary to Chaim Weizmann	66
6	The State of Israel is Born	94
7	As Weizmann's Man in Israel	122
8	Simon Reshapes Marks and Spencer	141
9	The Thirties: PEP	162
10	War and Post-War	177
11	Thinking it Over	191
	INDEX	207

List of Illustrations

between pages 30–31

1 Schooldays at Manchester Grammar School
2 Dr Chaim Weizmann, his sister Gita and Lord Sieff in Palestine about 1918
3 One of the original Marks & Spencer stalls in Manchester
4 Lord Sieff and Lord Marks as young men

between pages 78–79

5 Rebecca Sieff in the early days of her marriage
6 An informal photograph in Palestine, early 1930s
7 Wedding-day picture of Israel and Rebecca Sieff
8 A recent picture of Lord Sieff

between pages 126–127

9 Dr Weizmann at the opening of the Daniel Sieff Research Institute
10 A four-generation picture
11 Edward Sieff, present Chairman of Marks & Spencer
12 The Board of Directors of Marks & Spencer when Lord Sieff was Chairman
13 An informal picture taken while Granada were doing a tape-recording of Lord Sieff's life
14 Lord and Lady Marks
15 and 16 Two informal family group photographs taken on the occasion of Lord Sieff's 80th birthday

Foreword

Many a man on whom has been bestowed the gift of a long and happy life may feel, as he enters his old age, like recording for his own and the interest of his loved ones, some of the events and reflections which, for him at any rate, have made his own years memorable. So it is with me now. I see no importance in these personal annals: they are simply an affectionate account of things and people I have loved.

I hope my family and my friends will like to read what I have recalled, and will look over my shoulder at these pictures in the gallery of mind which they have helped to paint.

I want not only to register events, but to record debts, those unpayable debts of gratitude, to beloved colleagues – especially to my brother-in-law Simon Marks and my brother Edward Sieff. I have drawn freely on their unpublished notes and on our discussions and conversations. I also want to record my grateful thanks to my old friend and ally, my brother-in-law, Harry Sacher, on whose unpublished history of Marks & Spencer I have generously been allowed to draw. In this way, to some extent, I hope, our two families will live on in these imperfect pages. I wanted also to record my gratitude to my beloved wife, my children, my children's children, and theirs too, giving thanks in the words of the prophet Isaiah for '... a joy of many generations...'.

Acknowledgements

I am grateful to the *Observer* for permission to quote from an interview, and to my secretary, Gail Owen, for her assistance in preparing the manuscript.

1
My Family and its Origins

The story of my life, and of the people who gave me life, is a story of chance and coincidence, of actions taken on impulse, of the faith and hope of the Jewish people, and of the goodness of God. It is a story of the comfort and inspiration of human relationships: the love of my parents, of my wife and children; and comradeship over almost the whole of my lifetime with my dear friend, Simon Marks.

The family of Sieffs, Ziffs, Zievs, and there are many other ways of spelling the name, are scattered all over the earth, a diaspora within a diaspora. To find the first of them, so family legend has it, one must look back a thousand years to Pum-beditha, a city of Babylon. When in AD 70, under the Emperor Titus, the Romans suppressed a great rebellion of the subject Jewish people, destroyed the Temple of Jerusalem, and banished the survivors unto the ends of the earth, the Jews streamed, stricken in body and spirit, into many and various parts of Europe and Asia for refuge. The task of their leaders was to try and preserve and reconstruct Jewry out of the psychological and social ruins to which the Romans had reduced it. In the succeeding centuries, under the rule of the new Persian kingdom of the Sassanides, the Jews patiently and painfully built up many centres of culture and learning in Asia Minor. A Babylonian Talmud, or commentary on the law (Torah), evolved that was different from the Palestinian, or Jerusalem Talmud, though mutual visits of rabbis from both centres kept the two bodies of law and wisdom in contact. And it was on the Babylonian Talmud that the social, legal and religious life of the Jews came to be based. By the end of the third century community life and religious organisation in Babylonia was far more highly developed than it was in Palestine. Some great cities like

Nehardea, the 'Jerusalem of Babylon', were entirely Jewish. When Nehardea was destroyed in AD 261, Pum-beditha rose to take its place. It became a great centre of Jewish life and learning. It was the seat of the head of the Babylonian Jewish community, the *Rosh Ha-Golah*, or Exilarch. Around the year AD 900 at Pum-beditha the works and wisdom of a certain Rosh Ha-Golah shone out like a guiding light. He was learned, and he was holy: a *Tzaddik* or 'most right righteous man', *Chasid* or 'most pious man', a *Talmid chachem*, 'the wisest of the wise' – of such spirituality, it was said, that he communed directly with the great spirits of the Jewish past. His teaching and example were so luminous that he was given the name of 'Shining Light'. The Hebrew word for this is *Zief*. All of us Sieffs, Ziffs, Zievs, are said to be descended from him. When I was a child I was warned by my great grandfather that if I did not do well in life I would bring shame not only on myself, my family and my friends but on the name of a great and holy ancestor.

I remember my great-grandfather very well. He came from his home in Lithuania when he was in his nineties to spend a week in Manchester and see how his émigré grandson, my father, was getting on. He stayed about a week, and then went back, and shortly after died. I was most impressed by his beard. Like his hair it was bushy and white; it came well down his chest. Here and there red strands showed that in earlier life it must have been a luxuriant red. He was a rabbi, and wore a round hat and a long black kaftan. I thought at first that a rabbi was a kind of priest. But he explained to me what I dimly grasped then but properly understood later: that a rabbi is a teacher and pastor, not a priest: that a rabbi is an interpreter to man of God, not an intermediary, having no extra power, no hierarchical status. And though the rabbi may preach, in Orthodox worship the *chazzen* (cantor) usually conducts the service. The Hebrew word for priest is *kohen*, anglicised to Cohen. Priests did not exist after the first great Jewish society was broken up by the Babylonian Exile. All this impressed me, but what I recall most vividly about him was that he told me that as a little boy he had seen Napoleon riding by on his horse in the distance at the head of a column of men, head sunk on chest as the paintings depict him, leading the retreat back from Moscow across the plains of what had been Poland.

My great-grandfather also added a little to my knowledge of our family history. He explained to me that in the city of Vilna, in

MY FAMILY AND ITS ORIGINS

Lithuania, then part of Poland, in the eighteenth century lived a great and good Jew called Elijah Ben Solomon Zalman. He was famous throughout Europe for his knowledge of the Torah and the Talmud. Vilna was one of the greatest Jewish centres in Europe, and Elijah Ben Solomon Zalman became its Gaon, Gaon meaning the supreme authority. The Vilna Gaon, my great-grandfather told me, had a brother called Joshua, and it was from Joshua that our branch of the Sieff family was descended. We should be very proud to be part of the family of the Vilna Gaon.

The Sieffs certainly come from Lithuania, that part of what is now a territory of the Soviet Union, lying on the European mainland at the south-eastern corner of the Baltic sea, marching with what we used to know as Prussia. Though the greater part of the land is flat or gently undulated, it is a hard unfriendly land, with marshes and peat lands, the most common type of soil being boulder-clay. The coast lands are half dunes and half lagoons. There are two thousand lakes. The climate is harsh; temperatures are below freezing point for a third of the year. It was and is a predominantly agricultural area: about seventy-five per cent of the population drew their livelihood from farming, and many from the trade in timber.

The Sieffs used to live not far from the city of Kovno, which was at one time the capital of Lithuania, its Lithuanian name being Kaunas, an ancient city, of commercial and strategic importance, standing on the confluence of the rivers Niemen and Vilia, about 133 miles east north-east of the great city of Koenigsberg across the German border, and about the same distance, as the crow flies, east of the curving coast of the Baltic Sea. Around the year 1900 its population would probably have been about two hundred thousand. Most of the Sieffs lived in the tiny, predominantly Jewish, township of Siady, on the border between Lithuania and Courland, not far from Kovno, their names on the stones in the cemetery going back to the beginning of the sixteenth century. Oddly enough, however, it was my mother, who is not a Sieff, who came from Siady, while my father came from another small town, or large village, Eiregola, a few miles away. From what my great-grandfather told me I imagine Eiregola as a cluster of wooden houses with a church and a synagogue also made of timber – timber was plentiful, stone was not – unpaved roads which were dusty in summer and muddy in winter, and if not looking poor at any rate not looking prosperous.

We Eastern and Central European Jews were mainly Ashkenazic

Jews; very few were Sephardic. The Ashkenazim and the Sephardim are the two main branches of Jewry. The Sephardi Jews live in, and come from, Portugal, Spain and Southern France. Their vernacular is Ladino. The Ashkenazi moved from Northern France to German cities on the Rhine, centuries ago, mixed with Jews who had moved there long before from Palestine and Babylon, and on into Central and Eastern Europe. Their vernacular is Yiddish, a mixture of many tongues but mostly German and Hebrew. The Sephardi and the Ashkenazi are different in many ways – racially, religiously, culturally, and even in terms of class. The Sephardi have tended to be sophisticated, cosmopolitan, intellectual. They have reached high positions in letters, politics and finance throughout the centuries. The Ashkenazi have been pedlars, peasants, proletarians, with deep religious feelings for the other life, producing prophets rather than dons. The Sephardim have on the whole been middle and upper class compared with Ashkenazim, who have been working people. Sephardim have tended to assimilate in any country they found themselves in: not many of them have been Zionists. Most Zionist leaders were Ashkenazic Jews. But these are only illustrative generalisations.

The Sieffs came from well inside the Pale of Settlement, the areas acquired by Russia as a result of the partition of Poland, beginning in 1772. The Czars concentrated its Jewish citizens within the Pale. The Jews did not enjoy full civic rights. They were not allowed to leave the Pale without permission, and movement was discouraged. The ostensible reason was to prevent them dominating economically the backward Russian peasant, but since the Russian government made countless exceptions, and in many respects encouraged the *economic* activities of the Jews, it is more likely that the object of the restrictions was to limit the expansion of the Jewish religion. The Jewish centres of Lithuania had in the past suffered fewer restrictions than had many other Jewish settlements: and it was said that in consequence the Lithuanian Jews had a characteristic spirit of independence and enterprise. Other students have pointed out that the general personality of the Lithuanian Jews is in contrast to that of the Ukrainian Jews. The Lithuanian Jew lived in a forbidding countryside, and was anxious about his food. The Ukrainian Jew lived on fertile wheatfields. Lithuanian Jews, therefore, it is said, are religious to the point of being puritanical, basing their hopes on a life to come beyond the grave. Ukrainian Jews are happier. They produced *Chasidism*: that eighteenth-century Jewish protest against doom-laden orthodoxy, and affirmation of God's Will that we be happy in this world too. Certainly Lithuanian Jews came to have a special character in the eyes of other Jews, that character varying in the eye of the beholder, some regarding us as rather narrow and pedantic types, others as hard and sharp – 'What can you expect? He's a Litvak.' A kind of Scot in Jewry? Whatever the reason, many Litvaks led the way in emigration when the circumstances were most daunting.

My great-grandmother had a corn mill in the village of Eiregola; the villagers brought the corn to be ground, and my great-grandfather and his wife lived on the proceeds of the proportion of the corn they kept in exchange for rendering the service. The idea of a man who was a rabbi living partly off the community, partly off his wife's inheritance, was perfectly acceptable in an orthodox Jewish community. If it was thought that a potential son-in-law was a good man, likely to become a rabbi, who would devote himself to Talmudic study, the parents would promise to support the young couple. Such a son-in-law, or *aydem*, in those days was much sought after. My great-grandfather, therefore, because he lived on my great-grandmother's dowry was no slouch. His son, my grandfather, married when he was fifteen, and his bride was fourteen. My great-grandfather, whose marriage apparently was most fecund, realised that there would be too many children to share the inheritance of the mill, so he encouraged my grandfather also to become an *aydem auf kest*, 'a son-in-law who boards'. My grandmother, a girl from a family with whom my grandfather grew up, brought a sweets and sugar store by way of dowry.

My grandfather too became a rabbi, continuing to live in Eiregola, until late middle-age. My father, by then well established in Manchester, sent for him to come and join him, and they came over with enthusiasm. My grandparents were a considerable influence on me. Grandpa was kindly, gentle and tolerant, even submissive, whereas my grandmother was a strong, a dominant personality, critical of him sometimes to the point of being a scold. What they had in common was high regard for the orthodox Jewish religion, though Grandpa's respect for it exceeded his desire to conform to it in practice. There was something of a gap between my grandfather and my parents on this account: my grandmother knew my mother was not really religious, let alone orthodox, and that my father, too, though also a man of the highest principle, was not at all rigid in his attitude to his faith. Also, by this time he had become an English citizen, and was very proud of it: I remember the day his naturalisation papers came – he waved them in front of my mother's face, and kissed them – a picture of glee and gratitude. So, while my grandfather practised as a Jewish rabbi in Manchester my father made it clear that he was practising there as a British businessman. Moreover, he was the bigger, broader and certainly the more successful figure of the two. My grandfather, in fact, rather looked up to my father. This is contrary to the Jewish law, and it created a kind of tension between the two, a tension, I think which has existed between the two generations in many immigrant Jewish families: the son has made good abroad, has assimilated somewhat, and sends for his father: the new relationship cuts across the traditional one; sometimes in this situation the grandchildren, and the womenfolk suffer.

My father set up my grandparents in a small haberdashery business in Strangeways, not far from the prison, a little way up from the Victoria Station. I used to go straight there from school every Friday as a little boy and sit and listen to my grandfather patiently expounding the teaching of the Jewish law. He was discerning, clear-eyed and gentle hearted. He taught me, as nobody else has done, what were the essences of the greatest laws; which of the laws must be kept to the letter and without qualification, and which could be interpreted more liberally, be broken sometimes, to live a sensible as well as a good life. He made a deep impression on me of the reward as well as the duty of being kind, and treating all men with equal love and consideration. Sometimes my grandmother would scold him for lax interpretations, but my memory of those Friday nights is deep and warm and grateful. It was he who interested me in the Hebrew language – he even kept his accounts in Hebrew – and arranged for me to have Hebrew lessons. He was no puritan, and once I reproved him for ogling two pretty girls coming up Cheetham Hill Road towards us. 'I know them,' he said. 'Grandpa,' I said, 'they don't know you.' When my grandmother died, he – rather quickly we all thought – married a Polish Jewess, and took her back to Eiregola. I was deeply sorry to see him go, but I felt then as now that though he and my father were fond of each other in their way, there was no wrench when the day came for parting.

Now, I turn to my father. He was quite happy as a boy in Eiregola, but showed no bent for religion or his studies at the Jewish gymnasium, or at the High School of nearby Kovno. Academically he got no further than what we would nowadays call 'A' levels, though he read a great deal and was passionately fond of music. He had no wish to become a rabbi like his father and grandfather, and while still a youth his mind turned to business. At about the age of twenty, he had accumulated a little capital, about fifty pounds, and after some difficulty obtained permission to cross the frontier into Germany and live with an elder cousin of his, Dr Pinetti, who, I think, had a cloth business in Koenigsberg. With his cousin's help my father built up a small business of his own, buying hemp, flax and barley in Russia, and selling it in Germany. He also began to become interested, through his cousin, in textiles. He learned that there was profit to be made in buying waste or scrap by way of tailors' cuttings, sorting the wool from the hemp, and the linen from the cotton, grading each of the stuffs, and then re-selling. Patience, energy and a rigid sense of quality is required for this, and my father had them. He got a better price for his waste than his competitors because the buyers found that they could rely on his selections. In the end he saved them money, because they did not have to re-sift and re-grade the stuff he supplied them with. In a year or so he was doing very well. Then came the pogroms of 1882 and the great upheaval in the world of European Jewry, and my father's life, like that of millions of other Jews, was changed.

The causes of the great wave of anti-Semitism and the new nineteenth century diaspora which led to more than two million Jews leaving Eastern Europe mainly for America between 1881 and the early 1900s were manifold. The catastrophe was unexpected, for in most parts of Europe in the 1870s the general circumstances of European Jewry seemed to have been rapidly improving. In fact, however, a historically new kind of anti-Semitism was developing, and the incubator was Bismarckian Germany. The German 'anti-Semites' – the word anti-Semitism was coined in 1879 by a German pamphleteer called William Marr – propagated the view that Jews were not merely a different but – this was the *new* element – an *inferior* race, and that they were to blame for most of the social and economic ills from which modern society was suffering. In Germany at this time even some distinguished scholars began to express this view: the historian Treitschke, for example: he spoke of the Jews as 'Germany's misfortune'. The German anti-Semitic movement, originally academic in character, can be said to have become social in character in 1873 when over-speculation following the

Franco-Prussian war resulted in a financial crash. For this the Jewish financiers were blamed. In 1879 the anti-Semitic movement assumed a political aspect. Bismarck the German Chancellor, who had risen to power by exploiting the support of the Liberals, now allied himself with the reactionaries. For his own political purposes, he deliberately associated himself with the idea that the Jews were Germany's misfortune. Disfranchisement of the Jews was debated in the Prussian diet, as a matter of practical everyday politics.

German anti-Semitism spread to Austria, Hungary, and France. But it was in Russia that it erupted into fire and blood. Russians used German thinking and writing on the subject to fan popular prejudices. On 13 March 1881, the moderately-minded Emperor Alexander II, approved proposals for constitutional reform submitted to him by his minister Melikoff. On his way back from the Michael Riding School that same day the Emperor was assassinated by six young Social Revolutionaries armed with bombs. Three days later his successor, Alexander III, dismissed the proposals for reform, and reaction set in. Anti-Semitism in Russian society seized on the assassination as a pretext for an onslaught on the Jews. Alexander III himself was a bitter anti-Semite: the handful of terrorists of the Socialist Revolutionaries included some Jews. In May 1882, the infamous 'May Laws' were promulgated. Jews were excluded from all share in local government, even in towns where they contributed half the population and paid three quarters of the taxes. Only ten per cent of Jews were to be admitted to schools, almost entirely supported by Jewish taxes. Jews were forbidden to buy or lease property outside the towns, even within the Pale. They were debarred from agricultural pursuits, and from work in factories outside the towns. They were forbidden to live within a given distance of the frontier. Worse was to come. These laws, committing the Jews to a police state within a police state were followed by a wave of terrible persecution. Mob after mob in town after town attacked the Jewish population. In the next few years the greatest community of Jews in Europe, forming over one half of the Jewish population of the world at that time, was by deprivation of constitutional rights and frightful physical persecution hurled back into the worst days of the Middle Ages. Europe stood aghast. Russia added a new word to the vocabulary of the western world: *pogrom*, meaning 'devastation'.

These were the events which launched the great new exodus which added nearly two million Jews to the population of America and took the number of Jews living in Britain from about 60,000 to 180,000 between 1880 and 1904.

The point at which my father reluctantly made up his mind to leave home was the agreement made between Bismarck and the Czar that all Russian Jews living in Germany, who had not made application for German citizenship, should be instructed to return at twenty-four hours' notice to within the Russian Pale of Settlement, where they would be eligible for military conscription. Bismarck wanted no foreign Jews in German trade: the Czar wanted soldiers. My father had no choice but to leave Koenigsberg and return to Eiregola. He was forced to sell his promising new business overnight, for a fraction of its actual worth. But it was the prospect of military service which he found intolerable. He thought deeply about it on the journey back from Koenigsberg, and by the time he reached Eiregola had resolved not to serve in the army of a government which had treated his fellow Jews so cruelly. When he got back to Eiregola he told his parents that he proposed to get out of Russia as soon as possible. They tried to dissuade him. To attempt to get out was a dangerous business, for since he was liable for military service he would not be allowed to emigrate from Russia legally. First he would have to smuggle himself across the frontier into Germany. But when they realised he was resolved to go, come what may, they acquiesced. It was his mother who organised his escape. She would not allow his father to be involved, in case the plot failed, in which case her husband would suffer severely. There was a covered wagon belonging to the mill, which frequently carried sacks of corn across the German frontier. It was a familiar sight to the guards, and had dozens of frontier clearances chalked across it. My father filled the wagon with sacks of corn, the horses were harnessed, my grandmother took the reins. My father, with the equivalent of £40 upon him, hid himself in the furthest corner. When they reached the frontier they did not pass without notice, for it was known that Jews had used similar methods of escape. The guards climbed on to the wagon and thrust their bayonets into and between all the outside sacks. My father used to say that it was his cowardice that saved him: only because he had crept into the furthest corner did he avoid a most painful detection. The wagon was allowed to proceed. I do not think my father ever quite got over the nervous strain of his escape. He never liked to talk of it. He always became anxious when brought face to face with officialdom, and tried to avoid such contingencies. He did not like giving information about himself to officials. I believe he almost failed to be given his naturalisation papers because he did not supply all the answers to the questions. The marks of an early year spent under an autocratic and oppressive bureaucracy were on him faintly for life.

Once he left my grandmother he made for the port of Stettin, where he bought a one-way ticket to New York. There were relatives and neighbours there; they might give him a start. Some days later the ship made port, and he was told his journey had ended. It had been much shorter than he had expected, so he asked at what port the ship had arrived. He was told that it was Hull, an English port. 'But I'm going to America,' he said. 'You have no ticket for the United States,' the purser told him; 'your ticket takes you only as far as Hull.' Like thousands of other refugee Jews before him my father had been swindled by the German ticket dealer.

My father found himself on the quay in Hull, not knowing a word of English, knowing nobody, with a few pounds' worth of currency left in his pocket. He stood there, stunned, with no notion of what he should try to do. He had a stroke of luck. Hull was the port of entry for Russian immigrants intending to settle in Britain. Standing around, therefore, were a number of Jews from the countries around the Baltic who had settled in Britain, and had come now to the docks to meet friends and relatives disembarking. One of them saw this young man standing helpless and alone, guessed what had happened and addressed him in Yiddish. My father told him what had happened. The stranger took him home to his family and put him up for several days. They discussed what my father might do to start earning a living. My father's benefactor was a wholesaler of cheap imitation jewellery, and doing well. He advised my father to invest his few remaining pounds in cheap imitation jewellery, and hawk it around Hull on a tray slung around his neck as a pedlar.

It was rather a change from running a business in Koenigsberg, but the next day my father set out with his tray of wares in high hopes and good spirits. The first door at which he knocked was opened by a woman. She took one look at my father, and said, 'We don't want any dirty Jews around here,' and slammed the door in his face. He had only the sketchiest knowledge of the English language at the time, but he understood 'Dirty Jew' and saw the expression on her face. He was not so much upset as alarmed. His nerves had not recovered from the strain of his escape and the shock of the ticket swindle, of finding himself virtually stranded without friends in a country he had never intended to come to. The pogroms were fresh in his mind. He did not go to another house in Hull. He sat and thought for a few moments, went back to his would-be benefactor, and asked him where was the nearest place in which there was a large community of Jews. From what he was told he came to the conclusion that Manchester, where there were several thousand well-established Jews, might give him the physical and psychological security which he knew he was in need of. The next day he took the train due west across England's northern Midlands from Hull to Manchester.

This was a moment when the wheel of chance began to spin fast for Ephraim Sieff. When he got out of the train at Manchester, he stepped on to the platform in front of a man he had known back in Eiregola. They were amazed. They embraced, they talked, they walked down the platform together talking animatedly in Yiddish. 'What are you doing in Manchester, Ephraim?' 'I've come here to find work.' His old neighbour was surprised: he recollected my father as the up and coming son of a comfortably off village corn-miller; he could not understand that my father was virtually penniless; he thought he had come on a visit. But he was ready to help. My father used to say that though he wished nobody ever to be down and out, the experience of being suddenly uplifted when in that condition by a fellow creature who owed one nothing was the most wonderful thing that could happen to a man. 'You come with me,' his friend said. 'I am working for a master-tailor who is a very good man; he will find you something to do to get you going.'

Many Jewish immigrants had found themselves able to make decent livings in the cheap tailoring trade. Many English working men and their families could afford better clothes than their grandparents, but the British makers of clothes could or would not yet produce garments at a cost low enough for the mass buyer. Emigrant Jews could manage it. Many of them established themselves in big cities like Leeds, Manchester or in the East End of London. My father went with his friend to the house of the master-tailor. They knocked at the door. It was opened by a woman, who, the moment she beheld my father, gave a loud scream, and fell back in a faint. She thought she was seeing an apparition. She had worked in my grandmother's house in Lithuania as a girl and a young woman, and had seen my father grow up, baby, child and youth. She had emigrated to England only a year previously. She had come to Manchester, had met, and had subsequently married, another Litvak refugee, who by now had become a successful tailor. When she had recovered, she took my father to her husband, and then gave him a good meal. Then, with tremendous pride, the former domestic, showing off to her former mistress's son, took him all over her house to display her good fortune.

She even showed him the basement. When she threw open the door of one of the rooms he saw that the floor was covered with scraps and cuttings of cloth – pieces of woolcloth, pieces of linencloth, jute and lining material, cotton and here and there a little silk.

As he stood there looking at the piles of cuttings on the floor my father's mind flew back to his business at Koenigsberg. 'What do you do with these cuttings?' my father asked. 'Nothing. They are waste. We pay a man ten shillings to take them away. He collects them and sells them.' 'If I take them away without charging you,' said my father, 'can I have your cuttings?' 'You are a friend, you can have them on the same terms as he does.' 'Do you know the name of any firm that might buy them?' 'Yes. The man once left some papers here. There is a firm called Beaumont and Company, in this city.'

My father did not dally when his mind was made up. He took off his coat there and then and got to work. He worked long into the night. The next morning he enquired where he could get sacks and hire a hand-cart. He loaded his bags on to his barrow, and pushed them across Manchester to the warehouses of Beaumont and Co. He still knew only a few words of English, so he carried cards with him on which the master-tailor had printed in block letters the names of the streets en route for Beaumont and Co., and the prices of the various bags. When he pushed his hand-cart into Beaumont's yard the owner of the company was standing there. He saw my father's foreign dress, this good-looking yet somewhat disorientated youth, the barrow, the bags and the printed asking cards. He spoke a little Yiddish, and called across the yard to my father: 'What have you got there, young man?' My father replied in Yiddish: 'I have wool, cotton and jute, cuttings of the very best quality.' 'Who sorted them?' 'I did.' 'Oh, you did, did you?' 'Yes, very carefully.' 'Well, I would like to see them.' Mr Beaumont inspected the cuttings and was impressed by them. There was still, in spite of the Yiddish, a little difficulty in conducting negotiations, and my father had to make use of his printed price cards. They settled on a certain figure per bag. 'I will buy,' concluded Mr Beaumont, 'but only on condition that you will bring me more at a similar price.' He knew he was on to a good thing. On the way back to the master-tailor's house my father knew that he had made a profit but he did not sufficiently understand his own price cards to be sure how much. When he got back to the house and gave his report, the master-tailor and his wife were delighted. Their protégé had made a profit of fifteen shillings on his first day's work. 'Now,' said my father, 'Do you know of other tailors who will let me have their cuttings?' The master-tailor's wife was a woman of action. 'I shall put on my hat and coat' she said 'and take you to them now.'

That was how my father's business, and the fortunes of my branch of the Sieff family, began. In a year or two hand-carts had given way to horse-drawn vans, and my father had warehouses of his own, the first of them located not far from Victoria Station, Manchester. He went from strength to strength. Eight years after the day he had pushed his hand-cart there he bought Beaumont and Co. out at a price satisfactory to the owner. He went on and on, expanding and expanding, but, in essence, doing the same thing, hiring other people to do what he had done on the very first day on the floor of the master-tailor's cellar, choosing people he felt he could train and trust to sort and grade according to his own standards. He did nothing new; he did what other people were doing, but did it better. There is always room for people like him.

His business went on and flourished at a steady pace up to the outbreak of the first world war when it was turned into a private limited company, Sieff & Beaumont Ltd. Then it was given a tremendous impetus by the demand for gun cotton, for which my father supplied the cotton waste, and by the demand for white cotton waste as substitute for the cotton imports, cut off by the submarine blockade, needed for the manufacture of paper, including, incidentally, paper for bank notes. In 1921 there was a slump, and prices of fifteen pounds a hundredweight went down almost overnight to twenty-five shillings a hundredweight. But he was too well established to be damaged by this, and when he died in 1933, he was worth about four hundred thousand pounds. But it all began with the cuttings on the basement floor.

Beaumont and Co. had a great significance to me personally. When I was still a young man in my early twenties, just about making my way in my father's business, and, as the eldest son, being brought on, being trained for the day when I might take it over, I entered into a deal with another merchant, which ended in my losing my father's company a sum of about twenty thousand pounds. I will say in my own defence that I was defrauded, but it was a great blow to my pride and self-confidence, even though I knew that my father knew that I was not to blame. A few weeks after I had learned the worst my father called me into his office one morning, and said: 'Israel: I am handling too much for myself these days: you are growing older and more mature: from tomorrow you must conduct the business of Beaumont and Co. You must not think of yourself as being responsible to me for running it. It is now your company: it will depend on you, and you will depend on it.' I took it over, and things went well for me. Many years afterwards I discovered what I had come to suspect, though it did not occur to me at the time: he had given me Beaumont and Co. to run because he thought it would restore the confidence I might have lost by being let down. Years later when my father had died, and when my younger brother Teddy and I had become involved in the affairs of Marks and Spencer I felt that to try and retain control of Sieff & Beaumont Ltd. was not fair to the men who had helped us to build it up, some of them relatives of ours. So Teddy and I sold the company to the men who at that time were running it; the managers became the owners. We did this because it suited us; but other dispositions would have suited us better, and we chose this one because it seemed to perpetuate something of the spirit of the Sieffs' first acquaintance with the firm. I think if he had lived, my father would have liked to see what Teddy and I did.

So far I have said little about my mother. She was a remarkable woman, and I adored her. I know very little about her family background. She never wished to talk about it. This I know: she was born and grew up in Siady which, as I mentioned earlier, was very much a Sieff settlement. When she was fifteen, her father died, and her mother remarried. My mother did not like my step-father; she distrusted him. She was a beautiful woman, and as a girl must have been ravishing. From one or two remarks she made in later life I wondered whether some Russian army officer or local Czarist official might have started to pursue her. It would have been a common enough predicament for an attractive young Jewess in those days. When she was seventeen, without telling anybody she fled, and somehow made her way to Waterford, where her father's brother had gone a few years before and was a rabbi. After a few months she left Waterford. Once she spoke as though a male friend of her uncle, a furniture salesman from Dublin, had begun to embarrass her with his advances. I once asked her, 'But how many Jews were there in Waterford?' She said, 'Oh, a minyon.' A minyon means ten men, and a minyon of ten men was necessary to hold a service. A minyon, therefore, was a way of describing the smallest Jewish community possible. Too small a settlement of Jews aroused a sense of insecurity in refugees. Her uncle in Waterford had been visited by a Manchester rabbi called Dagutski, who when he left to return home said to her, 'Whenever you wish, come and visit me in Manchester. I have two daughters of about your age: they will be very glad to have you as their guest.' So to Manchester she went. The Dagutskis took her to their bosom: she must stay with them and become one of the family. She said she could not impose herself upon them; but she would be grateful to stay until she could earn her own living. My mother was apprehensive, but also independent; indeed, as I must say again later, the tension between these two traits was the key to an understanding of her character.

She had been in Manchester a few days, when one afternoooon she was sitting sewing at the window of an upstairs room of the house in Stocks Street, in the Jewish Ghetto. My father, too, had been in Manchester only a few days; he passed down this street on his way to a client, looked up to the window and immediately saw her. He was struck by her beauty. What happened must be incredible to anybody who did not know my father's peculiar blend of simplicity and decisiveness. He knocked at the door of the house. It was opened by Rabbi Dagutski. He saw a young man of good looks, refinement and dignified bearing, obviously from Eastern Europe. Dagutski had come from those parts himself.

'Good afternoon,' said my father, in Yiddish. 'Do you have a daughter?'

'I have two daughters.'

'I would be very grateful if I could be allowed to meet them.'

'Who are you, may I ask?'

'I am Ephraim Sieff, the son of Chaim Sieff of Eiregola,' said my father.

'You are Ephraim Sieff, the son of Chaim Sieff, of Eiregola?' exclaimed Rabbi Dagutski. 'And how are your father and mother? Are they here too?' The Rabbi had come from the same district of Lithuania only a few years before. He had studied at the same school of learning as my father's grandfather and knew him well. He took my father into the house, and sent for his wife and two daughters to come down and meet him.

The daughters came down and were introduced to my father. He greeted them, and said to the Rabbi: 'Have you another daughter?'

'No, these are my only daughters.'

'But there is another young lady in your house, I saw her sitting upstairs in your window!'

'Ah, that is a young friend who is staying here as our guest.'

'I would like to meet her too. She resembles a member of a family I know in Lithuania.'

This is the only occasion on which to my knowledge my father told a lie. My mother was brought down to meet him. A little over a week later they were married.

My mother outlived my father by many years. She lived to be eighty-six. Two months before she died, when she was ailing, she said to me, 'You know, Israel, I must tell you something. I didn't really love your father when I married him. It was an escape from what might have been misery. I didn't want to be dependent on anybody. I wanted to be independent. I wanted to be secure, and to be at rest. So I married your father. But when you were born I began to love him very much.' She paused, and then came the last and sweetest smile I ever saw on her beloved face. 'I think that is a good way of getting married,' she said. When I look back on her and her life and her personality I believe that it was somewhat on her conscience all through her married life that she had married not for love but for security, not material security, but for psychological and physical security.

2
My Childhood in Manchester

I was born on top of a chip shop. My father and mother occupied the first floor of two rooms of a house in Clarence Street, about a mile north of the very centre of Manchester. The house was owned by a family called Cohen, who made a living slicing up potatoes, frying them and calling them chips. The Cohens did very well, and diversified into cold tongue. The increased trade made the premises crowded and noisy. My father and mother got fed up with the din, and moved to the first house, a tiny place in Elsworth Street, the kind of house where, if you open the front door and take one step you are half way across the living room. Elsworth Street was just off the Cheetham Hill Road, very near Stocks Street where my father first saw my mother, and only a couple of hundred yards from Victoria Station and my father's warehouse. When I was five or six years old we moved half a mile further north to Heywood Street. Here we lived in a semi-detached house opposite a Welsh-speaking Methodist chapel. I can remember liking the minister because he let us play football on a piece of ground at the back of the chapel. It was at this time that my father's business began to prosper greatly. As his fortunes improved my father always wished to improve his status in the Jewish community, and the means of doing so was to live not only in a bigger house but in a better district. The social ascent could almost be equated topographically – almost in movement by yards north-west up the Bury New Road from Victoria Station. The station was in the Strangeways district, where the prison was, noisy and busy, with slummy back streets around. As you went up the Bury New Road, the lowest end of which was called Great Ducie Street, the business district gradually gave way to houses, first small ones, then further up larger ones with gardens. When I was twelve, my father decided to increase his status yet again, and we moved well up the scale to 408 Bury New Road. Number 408 Bury New Road was one of four houses joined together. The priest of the Greek Chapel a little further down the road lived in the first, we lived in the second, Mr Cohen, who manufactured raincoats, lived in the third, and a Rumanian Jew lived in the fourth. Opposite us was a line of a dozen or so small shops, the kind you strike in a residential area. There was a tram stop a few yards up the street, which was very convenient. Further north-west were the bigger and better houses, most of them detached – when I got married my father increased his status yet again and went and lived in one of them. In front of our house was a little garden – lawn and flowers – and a path ten yards long or so leading from pavement to front door. The furniture in the house was undistinguished – neither of my parents cared nor had much taste. It was good solid stuff. The only signs of affluence were a good set of Wedgwood, and two maids who lived in and looked after the family when it got large. This was a much better residential district, 'swish' by Elsworth Street standards. It was in the Borough of Salford, not the city of Manchester, and the particular section was called Higher Broughton. Cheetham Hill was immediately to its east. Bury New Road was the main artery of the area. The Sieffs had gone up in the world.

I was one of five children; I was seven when William was born, and I am sixteen years older than my brother Teddy. My sister, Miriam, who later married Simon Marks, the future Chairman of Marks and Spencer, is five years younger than me, and Pauline was born when I was eighteen months old. My earliest memories, in some curious way, seem to me to be those of an only child treated with great affection by loving parents only just saved – I hope – from being spoiled by the arrival of another offspring. In any case, I cannot recall feeling my life changed by the coming of the second child.

As a small child I went to the Board School in South Hall Street, and from then on, until I went to the Manchester Grammar School at the age of twelve, I went to the Collegiate School in Cheetham Hill Road. The pattern of my family life as child and teenager was secure and regular. Breakfast was an extremely 'healthy' meal – my mother believed, it seems to me looking back, that the best thing she could do for her children was to stuff them with as much rich food as she could get her hands on. Before I went to school, therefore, in the morning,

I breakfasted off two chops, and a dish of well cooked and seasoned vegetables. At lunch-time at school we were given fifteen minutes to go and buy food in the refectory, but Simon and I would always nip across the road to a small shop run by an Italian organgrinder, and stock up with ice cream and chestnuts and chocolate. I would get back from school at about three-twenty. There would be another appetising and generous mess of cooked food and vegetables, steak, or conceivably chops again, but cooked differently, with a pile of cakes, and, if I wanted it, a bottle of ginger beer. After this I would get on with my homework, working for an hour, or perhaps an hour and a half, frequently reading quite a bit on my own initiative, though doing both homework and private reading in the company of Simon Marks, by now my inseparable schoolboy friend. My father would come in from business about six to six-thirty. The first thing he would do, as she sometimes puts it today, was to see if my sister Miriam was alive. Miriam was delicate. 'I'm delicate,' she used to say to people, particularly when she wanted to avoid doing something she was being asked to do: her delicacy got her out of many visits to synagogue. My father would then have a wash, read the paper, and about seven to seven-thirty we would sit down, all of us, to a very good supper. Looking back on it our day's eating would not make very happy reading for a dietician: yet my mother lived to be eighty-six, I am still eating with gusto in my eighties, and the rest of the family also seem to have devoured their way into long and healthy lives.

There would be soup at every meal, including breakfast – a habit brought from Lithuania, I suppose. We did not eat much bread, though my father liked bread very much, his favourite dish being chops and vegetable, and plenty of bread with it. My mother did not give us butter when meat was on the table, since to do so would have been to break Jewish religious law. After the soup and meat there would be a good kosher pudding. My mother attached great importance to giving us what she considered was high quality food, and went to much trouble to get it. Her shopping expeditions, especially in the early days when money was a factor in the operation, were conducted with great energy and concentration. My sister Miriam, who often accompanied her, still talks about them, and of the eagle eye with which my mother would inspect each joint.

After supper the family would very frequently settle down to play cards. We played solo, whist, and bridge. On at least one evening in the week my father would go out to a concert, and when I got up to seven or so, he used to take me with him. He had a profound love of music, as a result of which Pauline learned the piano, and I learned the violin. On at least another evening my father would go down to the Jewish working men's club, where there would be lectures, debates, or discussions. As I've said, my father was a natural but undeveloped intellectual, and his evening listening to the Hallé Orchestra and his evening listening to a lecture on literature or the arts, were the occasions in the week when in his humble unassuming way he opened the door which took him to where his heart and mind belonged. Mother was a curious contrast: when my father went to a concert, she would go to the pictures. Yet it was she who bullied, badgered, and cajoled me into spending an hour and a half five days a week learning Hebrew. Looking back, it is a strange paradox that it was she the philistine, who put most educational pressure on her children, while my father, in his small way the practising aesthete and intellectual, was altogether more easy-going about the cultivation of our minds.

I would go to school by tram most mornings. Sometimes my father would take me in his pony and trap. This has a curious little history. It would never have occurred to us to have one, but when my father acquired Beaumont and Co. it was on the understanding that he assumed responsibility for a number of its commitments, varying from outstanding debts to dependent relatives. Among them was the pony and trap and the man who looked after it. The pony and trap were consequently lodged in a stables behind our house, and the man who had looked after them went on doing so.

Considering that we were Jews, and that my father was in his way religious, I cannot say that my childhood was particularly Jewish. We went to synagogue, of course, and as I said I studied Hebrew. But we were not devoutly orthodox. We observed the great feasts. In September/October we would observe *Yamim Noraim*, the Ten Days of Penitence, which ends with *Yom Kippur*, the Day of Atonement, when God wipes the penitent man's slate clean. We would celebrate the delivery of the Jews from the Egyptians at the Feast of the Passover. On the eve of this great day, the most cherished of Jewish holidays, called the *Pesach*, a great family *Seder* is held, Seder meaning 'an order of procedure'. It is a combination of banquet and religious ritual. The matzo, or unleavened bread, is on the table; grandfather, father, or oldest son leads the service; there are prayers and reading from the *Haggadah*, which tells the story of the Deliverance and gives the hymns and chants. It was a great night for us. It still is. We would observe Pentecost (*Shavuot*, in Hebrew) our harvest festival; and the third great pilgrimage festival, *Succoth*, or the feast of the Tabernacles, when Jews give thanks for being delivered from the Wilderness. These are the great celebrations when all Jewish males are supposed to go and give thanks in the Temple. Then there were the two post-Biblical festivals, of *Hanukkah* ('Dedication'), commemorating the victory of Judah the Maccabee over the Syrians in 167 BC and the subsequent re-dedication of the Temple: and *Purim* (Hebrew – 'Lots'), which commemorates the rescue of Persian Jewry by Esther when Haman threatened to annihilate them. Every Friday we stayed in and as a family celebrated the Jewish Sabbath. But we would not have been classed as great synagogue folk, even in our religious prime.

Indeed, looking back on my life, I must confess that I cannot do full justice to the question of what kind of a religious disposition it was exactly that I inherited from my parents. All I am sure of is that I inherited a profound one. My father, though not so doctrinally inclined as his father and grandfather, who, after all, were rabbis, had studied the Talmud and believed in the power of God to make his days happy if he so desired. He frequently quoted such sentences from the Talmud as 'All Jews are brethren'; 'No Jew must be allowed to go hungry'; 'God gives to him who gives'; I was the recipient of many of these Talmudical 'titbits', many of them, no doubt, taken out of context.

My mother, on the other hand, was an agnostic. She did not believe in prayer as a method of obtaining benefits. She possessed a tremendous sense of what she called 'rightness'. I remember asking her to explain what she meant by 'rightness' but she could not define it to me, and clearly did not think definition necessary. I think for her it meant relations with other human beings based on compassion and a sense of justice, virtues in which she personally abounded.

I am sure that my father worked hard to make me understand the value of good tradition. He saw in tradition a sort of anchorage which would never let him down, and I think he taught me that too, although I must confess I am not an *orthodox* traditional Jew. This emancipation I kept hidden for a short time as my father would have been disappointed and upset. He contributed a great deal to my understanding of human values, but above all he impressed on me the bounty of charity. He was one of the most charitable men I ever knew, spiritually and in material things. I often complained to him that he would give all his money away. His reply was always 'God gives to him who gives'. On looking back, I believe, however, that my mother had the greater influence over me because I was sympathetic to her idea of the need for 'rightness' in human relationships. Although she went to synagogue to please my father, I do not think it meant as much to her as it did to him. At the back of her mind was the notion that she believed she knew what was right and wrong without going to synagogue to be told about it by the rabbi, and she did not doubt that rightness always got the upper hand.

My father was much more conservative and conformist by nature than my mother. His motto was 'leave well alone'. Modest, reserved, generous to a fault, slow to anger, without passion, fearful of the strange and unconventional, he tried all his life to leave well alone. When his affairs were not going well, he laboured day and night to bring them back to the level where they could be left alone. He purposely avoided any situation which might disturb the even tenor of his day and way. He was a lovable being, yet tremendously shy of demonstrating his affection even to my mother. He lived to a routine, and was off balance when his routine was disturbed.

He disliked the strangeness of being away from home even for a short time. When this was inescapable, his luggage was always topped by a railway guide, with the time of his return carefully marked in it. He ate food cooked other than by my mother with a nervousness and anxiety, as if he expected a strange animal to pop out of his plate and jump into his mouth. He had no vanity except a liking for neatness in dress. His charming head, not too long, but well shaped with all his features in good proportion, always filled me with pleasure, and a certain satisfaction that he was such a good example of manly looks.

Deep down within him was an incorruptible core of willpower, which sustained him in difficult times, as well as a faith in his own capacity. He rarely wore these qualities on his sleeve, for this would have meant that he was drawing attention to himself. He hated attention being drawn to him. Perhaps this trait too went back to the days of pogroms, escapes and hurried journeys. He got me out of many scrapes, but I never knew what portion of it was due to paternal love, and how much to the desire to prevent me from drawing attention to the fact that he was, alas, my father.

He made himself completely aware, and kept himself so, humbly and frankly, of his so-called lack of knowledge. A phrase he frequently used was 'I never had a proper education like you'. I tried to discover what he thought was education. To him it meant a knowledge of historical facts, the names of authors and the books they wrote, quotations, tags and references. He failed to realise that a knowledge of facts was useful, but what was more important was the means one employed to live a beautiful, useful life. He saw education as something of a commodity, not as a process by which to get the best out of oneself and out of one's neighbours and friends, to help the community to lead a better, more decent, more human, more enlightened existence. In fact he behaved as the most perfectly educated person should: but if anybody had told him this he could never have believed it.

It is not my father who supplies the rail back to my childhood. He is someone who stood on the sidelines, and took an objective interest in what my mother was doing with us. If we were successful in school, or in other scholastic activities he was proud of us, and thanked God that he could give us a good education but he did not emotionally riot in his pride like my mother did. He took our successes as if doubtful of their reality. My mother was much more outwardly emotional yet still down to earth. She looked upon our success as natural to her children, and thought no more about it than to thank God they did not work so hard as to become ill.

I think I have mentioned that my father was fond of music, and regularly took me to concerts. Although he had no real knowledge of music, and composers, he knew what he liked, and liked it well. He insisted at a very early age that I should learn the piano and the violin, which I did without much success, though I believe that in the long run he was not sorry that I proved to be such an imperfect performer on these instruments, for otherwise my success would have drawn people's attention to him.

'People' to him did not include the members of his family or for that matter the members of his synagogue congregation. 'People' were the vast mass of strangers in whose midst he had perforce set his path. They were the potential aggressors, the anti-Semites, the xenophobists, the strangers to his speech and upbringing. Deep down within him there lurked always the fear of the pogrom. He had seen windows broken, and insulting anti-Semitic epithets written on the walls of his father's shop in Strangeways. Buried deep in his unconscious was the conflict between his way of life, and his Jewish past as represented by his relations with his father and mother.

There was a good deal of apprehension in his psyche. His fear would sometimes be released and to a degree out of all proportion to the occasion. I remember at the end of one trading year he came into the home looking very pleased with himself. 'Sarah', he said to my mother, 'this year I have made a profit of seven thousand pounds.' He was jubilant. Only a few months later he came into the house, his face as if in misery. 'Sarah! we are ruined. The income tax has gone up to one and sixpence in the pound!' 'But if you made a profit of seven thousand pounds last year, and income tax is only up by a small proportion, how can you be ruined, Ephraim, and in so short a time?' He was quite irrational for the moment: a disproportionately small setback had aroused his deepest insecurity: the long arm of government had reached him, and at the other end of the arm he apprehended not elected MPs in Britain but the tyrants of the massacres in Russia. I remember another occasion. One day he was driving us in the pony and trap through the streets not far from our home to his office. Four or five hooligan lads caught sight of us, and when we had trotted past, shouted 'Jews' at us and threw stones in our direction. There were no casualties, but my father's face went deathly pale, and he shook up the pony into a trot. He was still shaken and silent when we reached the office, and was not himself for many hours.

But those were rare occasions. When he had kissed his naturalisation papers he had kissed the seal of freedom and security. He never regretted the day he had come to the strength and stability of England, the adopted country he learned to admire and love.

I never heard him say that he loved his mother or admired his father, though he kept them in comfortable conditions as soon as he could afford to do so, and at all times was a dutiful son. In his own married life he was content because my mother studied his needs and wishes, and ministered to them with all possible care and speed. He thought he was in truth an orthodox Jew, and meant to observe all the required rites and ceremonials. When, however, as his business developed, he discovered that some of them prevented him from giving full play to his business skill, he shed them. I used to wonder how he justified these backslidings from the narrow path of orthodoxy. I sometimes tried to elicit the promptings which provoked this breach of tradition, but I never got – for me – a satisfactory reply. I believe he thought that his uprightness, transparent honesty, and profound moral sense, would be regarded by providence as ample compensation for his strayings from true orthodoxy. Yet I am sure that his decision for example to keep his business open on Saturday morning could not have been reached without a great deal of inner conflict. The first time this happened he left for his office in the clothes which he usually wore when he went to synagogue. He had to pass through the Ghetto and see his fellow Jews in their Saturday best, intent on reaching the House of Prayer. He hid his face in his morning newspaper. It was only towards the end of his life that he found renewed joy in the Saturday morning Synagogue service, because his sense of values made him change the emphasis from business to spiritual and emotional peace.

He was, I think, by leaning a Chasid. The Chasidim are a sect of Jews who believe in strict adherence to the Jewish law, are deeply and simply religious, but who react against the obscurantism of the old priesthood, are more democratic in their approach to the synagogue, and, above all, believed in overcoming the profound unhappiness of their history in this world by song and dance and gaiety. Chasidims went to their deaths in concentration camps, singing and dancing, praising God and rejoicing in life to the very threshold of their death. Each year on the day of the feast of Hanukkah my father gave a party to the local Chasidim in Manchester. He set a bottle of whisky before each guest to enable him to celebrate with a joyful evening. He was no Chasid himself, but he loved to give them a room in his house where twenty or thirty of them could sing and dance to the glory of God.

My father was very soigné in his dress. It was his only outward vanity. He never wore any ornament such as a tie pin or signet ring, both *à la mode* in his period. He eschewed any form of the bizarre or ostentatious in his clothes. He rarely departed from the blue and the grey. When he did, it was due to a temporary aberration, for which he atoned by very quickly giving the suit, the shirt or the tie away. His clothes were as modest and reserved as his own nature. Like his spirit and being they were of the finest quality, and announced their presence by their calm and simplicity. He used to quote a saying he had learnt during his unhappy residence in Koenigsberg.

> Kleider machen Leute
> O! das ist doch wahr

> Gold, Silber und Seide
> Traegt doch mancher Narr.*

This was at the same time an excuse for his modesty, and an arrogant avowal of his capacity. Had I suggested this to him he would have been shocked beyond measure, for whilst he was always prepared to 'leave well alone' – and dig no deeper than into the surface of his character in case he found something to which attention would be drawn – he could not help feeling from time to time, without being aware of it, that his ability to get on in life for example marked him out from the average. He would have denied this vehemently, and did indeed do so, pointing out that Jewish refugees from Eastern Europe had been responsible for the furniture industry, cap industry, clothing, etc., etc., and desiring me to infer that he possessed no special characteristics over and above the average intelligent Jewish immigrant.

Of course, to him the Jew was a being apart from the rest of mankind, marked out for suffering as well as for the endowment of special qualities and abilities. Amongst Jews he felt he was amongst his equals, and therefore could find repose of spirit and mind, for amongst them there was no need to prepare his defences against potential aggression. He did not understand the mentality nor the outlook of his non-Jewish friends and acquaintances. He would have liked to have got some glimpse of their motivations, and of their attitude of mind. He looked at their faces, and their grimaces determined for him whether they were friendly or hostile to him. Alas, too often he was equally misunderstood.

> Es ist eine Gerechtigkeit auf Erden
> Das die Gesichte wie Menschen werden.†

To my mother I owe more than to my father the inner security and self-confidence which my father did not ever really have. My mother was almost fiercely loyal to her children, and though she criticised and sometimes bullied us, and occasionally delivered an admonitory clout, nobody else was allowed to attack us. When I started to take Hebrew lessons, and did not show much enthusiasm for it, she was angry with me. She lectured me about not valuing what was being done for me

---

* The dress makes the man:
This is very true.
Gold, silver and silks
Are worn by many a fool.

† Alas! 'tis true on earth we find
That faces mirror oft the mind.

and wasting hard-earned money. But when I came home one day and told her that my Hebrew teacher had said I was lazy, she rose to my defence like an eagle. We all knew that whatever happened to us our mother's love and strength would never let us down.

By comparison my father was detached. He could see that my mother's love was totally adequate to her children's needs. So he worked at his business, was a good father, and a good husband. He was there if wanted, but never interfered or intruded. Through him I learned principle more by example than by precept, though a few simple precepts which he taught me stand out glowingly in my recollection. I suppose my most lasting single memory of him goes back to the day when I was Bar Mitzvah, which is a ceremony which corresponds, very roughly, with confirmation in the Christian church. According to Jewish law a young boy then becomes a man. When we came home from the service at the Synagogue, I wearing a silk hat and an Eton suit, long trousers for the first time and a big white collar and black tie, my father took me into his library. He said, 'Israel, there are two things I want to tell you that you must remember all your life and that is God gives to him who gives; it is from the Talmud; and the other is that the man who transforms a miserable man into a contented man merits a place on the right hand side of God. Remember these two things and you will never want and you will never be unhappy.'

In my final glimpse of my father through the deepening shadows of time I see him clearest not as a Jew but as an Englishman, this Ashkenazi Litvak from Eiregola. His naturalisation papers arrived at Heywood Street when I was six years old. If I had thought his ecstasy on that occasion was simply the result of feeling free and safe I had proof to the contrary a few months later. Queen Victoria was to visit Manchester to open a technical college or some other institution. My father spoke about it for weeks: I was to go and see with my own eyes the Queen of my country; my father was going to show her to me, and he for the first time was going to look at her himself.

We set out early in the day, the streets were crowded. As we approached the causeway along which she would ride the people were packed densely. Steadily, patiently, but perseveringly my father insinuated his way, row by row, until, with me holding his hand and pushing behind him, we had arrived almost at the front. There further progress, and all vision, was barred by the body of a huge man in a labourer's clothes. He felt us pushing and turned around.

'What are you pushing for?' he demanded. He was an Irishman. He towered over my father, a man of barely medium height.

'I wanted my little boy to see the Queen,' said my father, in what was at that time still a heavy foreign accent.

'What's the Queen to you?'

'She is my Queen. I'm a British citizen.'

'Well, she's my Queen too.' He moved to make a bit of room for my father, picked me up, put me on his shoulders, a little leg on each side of his muscular neck, holding my hands in gigantic fists.

I had a wonderful view of the Queen. But the view I shall remember longest is of my father's face, full of love and pride, and gratitude, looking at his first born son looking at the Queen of the country which had given him freedom and self-respect.

3
My Youth, and Simon Marks

Since I entered into a long and happy marriage with one member of the Marks family, had a life-long friendship with another and spent most of my business life working in the firm it established, I can say that the day I made my first acquaintance with the Marks family was the most consequential of my life. I remember it well. I was twelve. It was a Saturday; it was bitterly cold. As I turned into Cheetham Hill Road I saw in front of me three little girls walking in unison with military precision. They were obviously of the same family for they were identically dressed. This was sixty-eight years ago but I can see them as clearly today as I saw them then. Each wore a heavy coat made of a blue woollen cloth. The cuffs and broad low hem were of a dark fur. They wore hats to match. The difference between the height of the tallest girl on the end and that of the girl in the middle seemed to be exactly the same as that between the height of the girl in the middle and the shortest girl, walking on her left. It was as though they had chosen to walk in that order to show off each other's particular qualities, or perhaps so that each could compete against the other two. They walked with a measured tread, looking neither to right nor to left, and saying nothing to each other.

I was very much intrigued by this little group pacing as if it were on a march. I wanted to know as speedily as possible what they looked like from the front. Besides, I saw that the tallest girl had extremely pretty legs. It was the first time I had noticed the shape of a girl's legs. I wanted to see if she had the kind of face which I felt instinctively without instruction ought to go with the legs. So I quickened my pace, got ahead of them, and looked back. They were obviously three sisters, who were well looked after, for they were neat, well shod, trim, belonging to a careful mother who liked to see her children turned out well. The face of the eldest was what I had hoped and expected to see: that is to say, it was extremely pretty.

Much as I wanted to I could not talk to them. I had been brought up in the old fashioned way which forbade conversations, even between children, unless the parties had been introduced to each other. In any case I was too shy. So I walked on, looking back occasionally, pretending not to, no doubt looking rather foolish, and certainly squinting painfully. They finally entered a house, the number of which I fixed in my memory. I walked slowly home, bemused by the interest aroused in me by the eldest sister. It was a state of mind I had not encountered before. This was not because I had no experience in matters of the heart. At the age of twelve I had been charmed by women several times already, each time more deeply than the last. The last occasion had been only that summer up at Blackpool. In our childhood we made an annual pilgrimage to Llandudno in North Wales, or remained in Lancashire and went to Blackpool, stayed in a boarding house and played with spades and buckets on the sands. There was a red headed girl on the pier, whose name was Gertie, daughter of an acquaintance of my parents; she suddenly began to cry: 'I don't want to walk with Israel,' she exclaimed. 'You are pressing her too hard' I remember my father saying, with the air of a man of the world which even then I knew was quite spurious, and so perhaps I was ripe for my headlong plunge into love for Becky Marks.

The day after I first saw her I passed the same house with a boy from my school who told me that a family called Marks lived there. The father's name was Michael. He had a son and three daughters, and the name of the eldest was Rebecca. Becky.

The following Saturday I went to a children's party to which I had been invited weeks before. As I walked up the path to the front door I had strange mixed feelings, partly of how exciting it would be if Becky were there too, partly from speculating whether in fact she would be there. Becky was there. I edged my way over towards her and eventually found myself standing with her. In a characteristic way which remained with her all her life she turned round, looked at me, and without self-consciousness, began to talk to me. She was so open, relaxed and self-possessed I felt quite at my ease, and talked back to her with pleasure. We sat down on a sofa which was directly behind us. She asked me

1 Schooldays at Manchester Grammar School: Israel Sieff is second from the right in the back row, Simon Marks sits right front.

2 Dr Chaim Weizmann, his sister Gita and Lord Sieff in Palestine about 1918.

3 (*overleaf*) One of the original Marks & Spencer stalls in Manchester.

MARKS & S
ORIGINATORS OF

60 Brown's Studio

ADMISSION

TEETH

ST. PETER'S DENTAL SURGERY
ENGLISH &
AMERICAN
DENTISTRY.
FILLINGS

ENAMEL WARE
NEW REDUCTION

IN WOOL
ALL MENDINGS
NOW 1d EACH

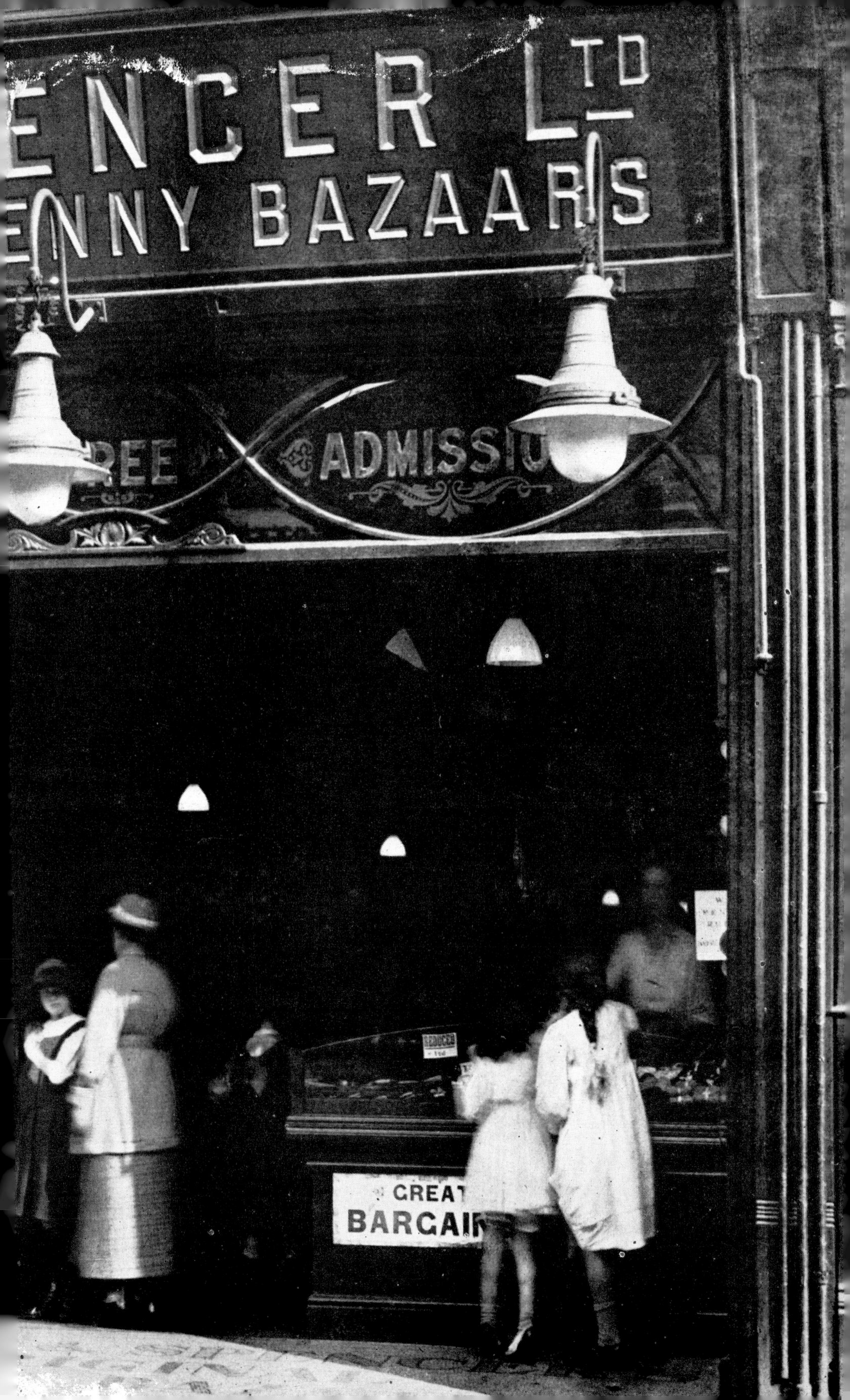
ENCER LTD
ENNY BAZAARS
REE
ADMISSIO
REDUCED
GREAT
BARGAI

4 Lord Sieff (*right*) and Lord Marks as young men.

questions, about who I was, and where I lived, and where I went to school. 'Do you know my brother Simon?' she asked in a curiously grown-up way. 'No,' I said. She said, 'Would you like to know him?' I said I would. 'Come and meet him now, then,' she said. I said, 'No, not at the moment.' I don't know whether he was at the party, or whether she was quite prepared to take me around to her house and deposit me with him. But I did not meet him on that occasion. Becky and I talked to each other for the whole of the party, except when we were coerced into playing games. I sat next to her whenever sitting was in order. We parted on friendly terms.

I'm not quite certain of how I came to go to Simon's house a few days later. I may have seen Becky at the gate, and she may have taken me in. Or perhaps I went there with another boy. But again, I remember the first meeting vividly. Simon, a little older than me, was just about to go out and play cricket in the field behind his father's house. He was virtually the captain of a team of Jewish boys. He owned the bat and ball and wickets, and without him, therefore, there was no game. But he was a natural captain too. His personality and appearance attracted me at once. He was smaller built than I was, dark, eager, vital, forceful, quicker altogether in his speech, gestures and movements. We were as animals very different, which was perhaps why we hit it off. 'What are you going to do?' I asked him. 'I'm going out to play cricket,' he said. He was perfectly pleasant, but he did not say 'Do you want to come too?' I said, 'Shall I come out and play with you?' 'Yes,' he said briskly. 'Come on.' And out we went.

I remember the first game well. It was like so many we played on the field behind his father's house. He was not dictatorial, and he did not abuse his power. But he did not conceal the fact that he was in control of the game and the players. If there was any doubt about whether a boy was stumped, leg before, or run out, Simon was the arbitrator. If a player refused to accept his judgement he ordered the offender off the field. The culprit inevitably had to go, otherwise he would not be invited to the game the following week. Our friendship began that Saturday afternoon. It lasted sixty-three years, up to his death in 1964. All through it he remained the one who possessed the bat, ball and wickets, and I was happy and fulfilled under his captaincy.

Even then Simon had shown signs of that paradoxical personality from which his genius – and I believe he was a genius – sprang. On the one hand he was self-assertive; not consciously, self-seekingly, with an eye to some advantage; if he dominated in a situation it was because he saw a challenge in it, threw down his own glove, fought and won. He *liked* to assert himself. It may have had something to do with being the eldest, and a boy, in a large family of girls. He kinged it over the girls. When once asked to mind the baby Elaine, I saw him put her on her tummy across his lap, spread the Guardian on her bottom, and nonchalantly read it. He liked to be in charge of a situation. He did not lack aggression. As a small boy he would often come home having been in trouble, fighting, with hair dishevelled and jacket torn, unabashed and not sorry for himself, whether he had won or lost – to be scolded heartily by his disapproving parents. On the other hand, he had an extraordinary wish to be like everybody else. Whether it was something racial or social or simply human which made him long to be like other people, or something of both, I do not know.

To illustrate the other side of him, there were the wooden clogs at Wigan. His first memory was of being aged four in Wigan, and hearing the patter of clogs on the cobbled stone street. 'I begged my father to buy me a pair, just like other children's,' he wrote many years later. 'At night, I would wrap them up in brown paper and put them under my pillow. I didn't want to be different from the other children.'

Soon after my first meeting with Simon and Becky, both families moved to Bury New Road. The Marks family had a new house built for them on the site of an older one, about six doors and a chapel down from us in the direction of the city, about fifty yards away. This was Knoll House. It was altogether more grand than ours – eight bedrooms, a summer house in the garden at the back, a large drawing room with, I remember, many stuffed birds under spherical glass covers. Again the Marks' furniture showed very little taste: again there was excellent china, and the inevitable piano.

It was about this time that Simon and I had our *Bar Mitzvah*. This ceremony, as I have mentioned before – the Hebrew words mean 'son of the commandment', or, more broadly, 'man of duty' – invests the young Jewish male with the obligation to follow the religious and ethical precepts of the Jewish people. It is not a Biblical ceremony: it dates only from the fourteenth century. Though it is frequently likened to the Anglican confirmation service, it is a ceremony, not a laying on of new power, but the boy does pledge himself to live up to the ideals of Judaism. It is a proud day for the parents. The boy has now become a full member of the Jewish community. The ceremony is held in the synagogue on the Saturday closest to the boy's thirteenth birthday. The boy is given presents and a *tallis*, prayer-shawl, from his father. Since the boys are usually required to deliver a prayer, read from the Torah and the Bible, they must learn Hebrew. I remember going to a Hebrew cheder four or five times a week conducted by Mr Kaiserman, interpreter at the Manchester County Court, whose son Joe was at the Grammar School with me. Simon's Bar Mitzvah cloak was red. The invitation for our Bar Mitzvah said, 'No presents', which was commented upon at the time.

Within a few months of us going to live near each other I had become not only the inseparable friend of Simon, but almost a member of his family. I seem to have been in Knoll House all the time. I went in and out at all times of the day as though I owned the place. As a result of this unabashed unthinking presumption at the age of thirteen I saw Simon's sister Elaine come into the world. Simon and I were going to catch a tram to the Zoo. He had not turned up at the tram stop, so I ran impatiently to his house, burst in through the front door as usual, and rushed through the house bellowing 'Simon! Where *are* you' in room after room. I dashed into one room, and there was a strange sight. Mrs Marks was in bed. A nurse was in the act of smacking a small pink object which she held in the hand. There was a yell. I gave a yell too – of mingled fright and embarrassment – and fled. But I had been the first to see and hear the new Marks baby.

It was with Simon that I made my first entry into the material world of business enterprise. This was one of the rare occasions on which the initiative was mine. We were about fourteen. I read in the paper one day that two substances, Casene and Lecethin, had been discovered and had excellent medical properties. They were available in powder form. Among the shops nearby was a small chemist's establishment, owned and run single-handed by a friendly and good-natured soul who always made us welcome. Simon and I went to him and asked him if he could make up Casene and Lecethin into pills. He said he could. 'Well, what are we waiting for?' I said. I borrowed a pound from my father, a large sum of money in those days, but my father could see I had a serious purpose in prospect, and the chemist, financed by me, made up a pound of pills, and put them into boxes, with printed labels executed at my direction 'Casene Lecethin – cure all your ailments'. We sold several dozen boxes, and we were showing a considerable percentage of profit, when Simon came to me one day, pale faced, and said, 'Israel! It's against the law! I've read it in the paper!' So we stopped. Not until years later did I begin to wonder what the chemist thought about it all. Either he was remarkably simple or he knew he was on to a good thing and was prepared to risk it.

Soon after our first meeting Simon and I became pupils of the Manchester Grammar School and because of our ages, in the same form. For the next three years we saw each other practically every day. Because he was nearer than I was – the school was a couple of miles down the road – I used to call for him every morning. I would walk up the short drive, open the front door, walk down the hall, and open the door into the dining room. After my first visit or two, I used to proceed somewhat gingerly. More often than not there would be a great deal of noise coming from it. Becky and Simon frequently had a row at breakfast. About the third or fourth time I went there Becky threw a plate at Simon. It missed and hit the wall a foot from my ear as I opened the dining room door. 'I'm sorry,' said Becky, who had not got used to me then. 'The plate slipped.' Another time she accidentally hit me with a Latin grammar. And so off to school.

A curious kind of sympathy developed between us of almost a telepathic nature. If Simon found a lesson difficult to assimilate, I too found it indigestible. If Simon found a problem easy, I sailed through it with equal ease. In the evenings we learned our prep and did our homework together. One day when we were in the Sixth Form, Simon arrived in the form without his homework – he had left his book behind. 'It doesn't matter,' said Mr Horsley, who was taking the lesson. 'I'll give you the same marks as Sieff.' I remember the day we took our first and final boxing lesson. Inevitably Marks and Sieff were put together to spar. Simon hit me on the nose and made it bleed. He was terrified. He looked so ill it was thought for a moment that it was I who had incapacitated him. He vowed never to don a boxing glove again, and never did. Neither of us was an outstanding pupil and neither of us was very academically inclined, but we enjoyed our schooldays, and soon began to take our reading seriously. Mathematics and the sciences did not appeal to us so much and neither of us was a natural athlete, but almost from the beginning we steeped ourselves in books. To begin with it was books of heroism and adventure: Jules Verne, Conan Doyle, Rudyard Kipling and the incomparable Henty. As our reading deepened – and we often congratulated each other on the encouragement we were given at the Manchester Grammar School – we turned from the Classics to Modern Literature. We were both fascinated by the great writers in French and German. In the French language we were enthusiasts of the Classical School: Molière, Racine, Boileau, and Corneille. The Romantics we did not care about so much, with the exception of Hugo and Gautier. It was Simon who set the pace on Gautier. He was enthralled by *Voyage en Espagne*. He loved the idea of travel, and Gautier's classic, with its remarkable range of colourful new words and phrases, many of them technical and quite unusual, used to describe a multitude of architecture, scenery and social structure stimulated Simon's prodigious curiosity and appetite for detail. Our German favourites were Goethe, Schiller, Lessing and Heine. The Goethe-Schiller correspondence deeply impressed us, and through their discussion on objectivity and subjectivity, begot a mutual interest in philosophy which we gratified in another way for the rest of our lives. The correspondence so engaged our feelings that when at seventeen we were parted for a year, Simon to sojourn in France and Germany, I to go to Manchester University, we wrote every week to each other modelling our correspondence on Goethe's with Schiller. I was sentimental enough to think the letters well worth keeping, and I persuaded Simon to surrender to me my share of the effusions. I was very sorry when the correspondence perished in the London Blitz. Simon professed to be relieved. He said he had shuddered on the rare occasions when he had remembered the Marks-Sieff *Briefwechsel* was still in existence.

Though the two families lived so near there was not a great deal of contact between them, in their early days, apart from Simon, Becky and myself. Our parents knew each other, there was mutual liking and respect, but the relationship was neighbourly rather than intimate. I shall write at greater length about Mr and Mrs Marks later on; suffice it to say here that Simon's father was not so much of a synagogue man as mine was in my boyhood, and in any case was to die young, only a year or two after we came to live near each other. So far as the children were concerned there was a gap of ages. Becky's younger sister Tilly was five years her junior. Miriam was two years younger still. Elaine was quite a tot. My younger brother, William, was nearly seven years younger than I was, and my second brother, Teddy, sixteen years younger than myself; my sister next to me in age, Pauline, was interested in music: she played the piano well, and lived her own life. My sister Miriam was several years Simon's junior; she was still a child when he was old enough to go and live abroad; there could be nothing between them in their teens of the kind that there was between me and Becky.

If I was not with Simon, in those boyhood days, I was with Becky. There was a curious triangular relationship between the three of us. I used to talk about Becky to Simon very often. Not as often as I wished because she was his sister and he took her for granted, and indeed somewhat disapproved of her because she resisted his tendency to boss his brood of sisters. When I was with Becky we talked a good deal of Simon. Her motives in questioning me about him were a mixture of curiosity and jealousy. 'What did you and Simon do this morning?' 'Why are you going for a walk with Simon this afternoon?' 'Why can't you come with me?' 'What do you two talk about?' If present at these catechisms, Simon would snort. Patiently I would try to explain. The only boy, with several younger sisters, he could not understand what I saw in Becky, why I often waited for her at the tram-stop when she alighted from the Dover Street High School, and walked back home with her carrying her satchel. Becky and I, on the other hand, precociously assumed that one day we would marry. When I was fifteen and we were out walking on Kersal Moor one day, she suddenly said as we strode along, 'Israel, what are we going to do about bringing up children?' She meant the question in general: I suppose the upbringing of children had been discussed at school the day before. I assumed that she was asking about her and my children, and answered, confidently: 'Don't worry: we'll bring them up as our parents brought us up.' Yet, Becky too always somewhat resented the triangular relationship, and in later life used to say that Simon and I arranged that I should marry *his* sister and he should marry mine so that the two men could spend the maximum of time together with the minimum of marital inconvenience.

Looking back on it, it was a happy childhood. Manchester was a good place to grow up in. The special virtues of the warm-hearted people of the northern cities are well known. Manchester, more than in these days of the great move of people, business and culture to the south, was a flourishing intellectual and cultural centre. The famous Hallé Orchestra was conducted first by Sir Charles Hallé, and, after his death, by Hans Richter. There was the *Manchester Guardian,* one of the great newspapers of the world, edited by one of the greatest journalists – and finest men – who ever lived, C. P. Scott. The University was adorned by many eminent men, including the scientists Rutherford and Perkin, philosopher Samuel Alexander, and historian T. F. Tout. It was the background of statesmen of the past, like Cobden, and the stamping ground of statesmen of our present, like Balfour and Winston Churchill. It had given its name to a historic school of politico-economic thought which had in its day flourished in national policy. We did not feel that we were living in the sticks.

The character of Jewish life in Manchester was most congenial. The Jewish community in some great British cities has not always been a happy one. In centres where a large proportion of Jews belonged to well-established long assimilated stock, mainly Sephardic, perhaps, and another large proportion was made up of recent immigrants, of Ashkenazim, the atmosphere could be uncomfortable and strained. The older settlers had frequently lost their Jewishness, become upper-class and even snobbish, regarding the immigrant, impoverished European newcomers as embarrassing refugees. Manchester was fortunate in this respect. Its thirty thousand Jews, a number large enough to provide that comparative lack of racial consciousness that comes from a sense of security, was composed mainly of Jews from Eastern Europe, some of them, so very recently arrived that Yiddish could be heard spoken in the streets around Strangeways. There was a much smaller number of German Jews in residence, but most of them had become assimilated, many being converted to Christianity. They hardly counted and did not wish to be associated with the Jewish community. The same was true of the Sephardi Jews. The centre of Jewish life was the synagogue; its self-expression was largely charity. Men like Nathan Laski, and Charles Dreyfus, successful and respected in the eyes of Jew and Gentile alike, were typical of the leaders of Manchester Jewry.

But when I look back on my boyhood days in Manchester my gaze is refracted as though prismatically by my life with Simon. We did everything together, and the sharing made every experience richer, every discovery more exciting, every moment sweeter. We never seemed to disagree, we certainly never quarrelled. Perhaps it was because we were so different. Simon was quick, outspoken, frequently explosive. In after life, if he had to reprimand a friend or colleague, he might hit out hard, though in a moment it was over, and his hand was out, and all was forgiven and forgotten. I was of a milder temperament, slower to react, more tolerant of the untoward, living at a lower temperature: so much so, that frequently Simon would persuade me to deal with his offenders: he knew I would be more diplomatic. He was an initiator, original in mind and bold in action. He dominated naturally. I was a natural follower, and was glad to follow him. There is a Yiddish saying: *'Der Rebbe meg'* – 'the Rabbi may.' Simon was the Rabbi. It was his privilege to have his way. There was the bond between us of good and loving parents, bringing us up in a common background of personal and social values; yet enough differences in character to make a partnership. He has often been described as a good man, but few realise just how essentially good he was. Simon was not naturally affectionate, forbearing, tolerant and full of the milk of human kindness: he had it in him to be aggressive, ambitious and even ruthless. But he tamed and controlled all this by a strict sense of duty. And therefore his moral achievement was altogether higher than that of the man who temperamentally has no problem of this kind.

In his old age, Simon penned some reflections on his struggle to retain control of Marks and Spencer for the Marks family during the first world war, an episode which I will describe in due course. He wrote:

During this bitter and difficult period, I was helped and encouraged by my brother-in-law, Israel Sieff, who, throughout my life, has been my alter ego. Without him, I do not believe that I could have succeeded. That David and Jonathan relationship was permeated throughout our lives. It will be seen as the story unfolds itself what that partnership in spirit and deed achieved.

Whatever Simon's judgement on what it achieved, the partnership was indeed one of spirit and deed. And its sun even now shines back through the shadows of old age to those golden schoolboy days in Manchester.

They were golden days to be sure. And how grateful I feel as I look back to the teachers of Manchester Grammar School. Perhaps the teacher who influenced us most was the High Master, Mr J. L. Paten, a man of great integrity and possessing a remarkable understanding of young men and women. He told us what to read and how to read the books which he recommended. By that I mean that he even went to the trouble of reading a chapter of a book in which he found delight so that we would get a feeling of single community with him. He was a great High Master. His influence on me was such that I sent my two sons for a long stay in St John's School in Newfoundland which he had taken over, so that they might also have a taste of his personality and his visionary approach to learning, art and the simple tenets of religion. I think most of his pupils adored him: Simon and I were certainly amongst them. My two sons also had a great affection for him. There is something else about our boyhood in which we were both blessed. Though Simon and I grew up in comparatively well-off families, we lived in districts in our impressionable days in which the parents of most of the children were working folk or in very small businesses. It was a working-class ambience, not a bourgeois one. We had, therefore, the best of two worlds: freedom from poverty and economic hardship of any kind; but also the warmth and contact of the working-class milieu. I am grateful for the good fortune of my Manchester background, and aware of what I have owed to it over sixty adult years.

Notwithstanding our joy in literature and music, if Simon or I had been asked at the age of seventeen about what we would like to do with our lives, we would have answered, 'Go into my father's business'. Such an attitude was typically Jewish. Into the bargain we revered our fathers and in a real though unspoken way we felt it a privilege to attempt to succeed in their footsteps. I assumed we would both start work when we left the Sixth. I was taken aback, therefore, one evening, a few months before I was expecting to leave school, when my father said to me, 'Israel, you must go to the University'. I said, 'The University? Me? The matric is in a week's time. I shall never pass. I have not done enough work. I thought I was going to leave school. Why do I have to go to the University? Simon is going straight into his father's business.' My father said: 'Today I was talking to our insurance agent. He is a very sensible man. He is sending John (his son) to the University; he is going to learn economics. He will learn all about supply and demand, money and goods. You must go too. You might win a degree.' I said, 'You have a successful business, but you have no degree'. He said, 'How do you know what kind of business I would have if I had *had* a degree?'

He was an exasperatingly difficult man to argue with at times. This was never because he was domineering or opinionated, but because sometimes a point seemed so obvious to him that he could not understand why I did not see it. In such cases instead of concentrating on persuading me why his point of view was right, he furrowed his brow in trying to fathom why his intelligent son could have an opinion so wrong.

I could see that he would be very unhappy if I did not go, not because I would have gone against his wishes, but because he would have thought that he had failed to persuade me to do something that was good for me, an omission which in later life I might have regretted when he was no longer there to temper the wind to me. So I got out my books, and buckled to. I filled in my application form with no more than hours to spare, and for several weeks sat up half the night swotting for my matriculation. When the results were announced I had just about scraped through.

I enjoyed my time at university. I would have missed a great deal if I had not complied with my father's wishes. Simon always envied me the experience. He regretted not having gone to a university all his life, and had more regard than I think was always justified for men who had had some academic training. He regarded my degree of Bachelor of Commerce with undeserved respect. When in 1939 he was given the Honorary Degree of Doctor of Science (Economics) by the University of London he was in transports of delight. Nobody was ever prouder of an honour.

I was at the University from 1906 to 1909, and read Economics and Commerce. The Business Economics department was headed by Sidney (later Sir Sidney) Chapman, later Professor of Economics. He was friendly and most stimulating. I must have done quite well because at the end of the second year Chapman proposed to me that I could be given my degree on my two years' work, on condition that I remained the third year and worked on a special project of his nomination. I agreed. The project he chose for me was a study of annual price movements by examination of weekly returns from 1840 on, so that the ups and downs of deflation and inflation could be plotted over the entire period. If I did the work satisfactorily, he said, it could be shaped into a treatise which would qualify me for the Master's Degree. The subject did not attract me from the outset. I began it with a pained impatience and the sense of its remoteness from what interested me most. After a few weeks I went back to him. I said, 'I cannot stick at this for a whole year. Can you possibly suggest another subject?' So Sir Sidney interested me in economic theory, saying that if I could do well enough at it he would like me to be able to instruct some of the men in their first year. So I abandoned my assault on the Master's Degree, and worked hard at economic theory for a year with the prospect – which I found attractive – of lecturing to younger students.

My second and third years at university were complicated by the pressure of Becky. Throughout my first year, in between violin playing – she had taken to the violin as soon as she had seen me do so – she quizzed me about what university life was like. The following year she entered the University herself. I was not altogether pleased. I anticipated what would happen, and I was right. She used to persuade me to go to *her* lectures with her, saying it would prevent me developing a one-track mind. I thus picked up quite a smattering of Anglo-Saxon philosophy, and T. F. Tout – you did not study mediaeval history at Manchester in those days: you studied the great Tout who was a subject in himself. Chapman was puzzled by my absences from the school of economics. 'I never see you,' he said to me once. 'You do your work; I've no complaint. But, tell me, how and where do you spend your time?'

From the University I went straight into business with my father. I had looked forward to it since I was thirteen years old, when one day, in the holidays, I went down with him to his warehouse. I wanted to see what he did. After I had been there for an hour or so, he said, 'Israel, would you like to earn some money?' I said I would. 'Very well,' he said. 'You shall do what I do. Here is a paper on which are printed descriptions of different kinds of qualities of cuttings. If you go by this, you will be able to select and grade the different types. You will learn how to tell the qualities of the materials, how the fibres of the materials differ from one another, which are strong, and which are weak. There are between thirty and forty here. If you grade according to this, you will master the whole secret of the business.' Then he gave me some cuttings to sort out. He came back an hour later to see how I had got on. 'Israel, you have done very well. You will make a good businessman, here is half a crown for you.' I have never been so proud of anything I have ever done as I was when my father gave me that half a crown. He filled with with confidence and pride. Nothing ever gave me as much satisfaction as obtaining the approval of my father; nothing ever hurt me so much as feeling that I had let him down.

I found that initial year learning my job in his business every bit as agreeable as I had expected. I got up at seven thirty am, having slept like a top, and sat down to breakfast with my father, mother and Teddy. My father and I would make a hearty meal, read the *Manchester Guardian* and *The Times*, and chat in broad terms about the day that lay ahead. 'You might like to go and see what Higginbotham in Batley thinks of what we are sending,' father might say. Or, 'Would you go to Blenkinsop in Bradford? There's something wrong with the deliveries.' We would then catch the tram to Dawson Street, a journey of about a mile, which took us about ten minutes, and cost a penny. If I was not going off to Batley or Huddersfield, I would go through the mail and see what orders were coming through. We always went home for lunch. My mother was always at the front door waiting for us. In the evening, we would get back for 'high tea'. Then, as I have said, theatre, committee meetings, or courting Becky. One of the things that strikes me when I look back is how my father and mother lapped me around with stable love and comfort: mother looked after me at home; father at work. I was spoiled.

At the time I entered my father's business, by then Sieff and Beaumont Limited, it was flourishing, his turnover being about £125,000 a year, rising steadily to what was to be its peak later on: more than £200,000 annually. It was, in essence, a very simple business. His main warehouse, fronting on New Bridge Street and Dawson's Croft, on the banks of the Irwell, about a mile from where we lived, contained several long rows of benches. Bags of mixed waste cuttings, woven and knitted woollen, cotton linen and silk rags and wastes, were emptied on to the benches. About one hundred women were employed in sorting and grading the cuttings, putting them into wooden chests standing behind them. The bags of material were hauled to the benches by men; men hauled the bales out into the yard for transportation to the buyers. The bulk of the material was sold in this country, but a great deal of it was exported. My father sold to firms in many parts of Europe, Canada and the United States. He made a speciality, for instance, of exporting waste from sheep skins. When sheep skins had been dressed, lumps of wool were left over, too small to use in the ordinary way. My father collected and graded these and re-sold them to Poland. He also supplied 'secondary raw materials' for the manufacture of Shoddy, Mungo for Woollen and Worsted Yarns, Cloth for the manufacture of high grade paper, including bank-notes, for Roofing, Felt and Linoleum, for Upholstery fillings and for breaking and re-spinning into Cotton Yarns for many different purposes. He had buyers in the

Scandinavian countries, in France, Germany, Belgium, Holland and Italy. He broke off his considerable trade with Germany, when it was certain that Hitler was persecuting the Jews.

As a youth I travelled frequently in these countries, calling on his buyers there. Often, I made five European trips in a year and picked up some useful impressions of European trading conditions. The one part of Europe to which my parents would not let me go was the part which they had come from. It had fearful associations for them. I wanted to go there, but they were adamant; I knew that to persist upset them greatly.

Once my father was convinced that I knew my materials well enough, he employed me mainly in expanding his sales in the textile manufacturing district of Yorkshire and Lancashire. He was obsessive about maintaining the standard of his goods, not only because of personal conscientiousness but because he knew his rise from rags to riches was due to keeping those standards high. Again I travelled a great deal and came to know much about the textile trades in general. I was inquisitive, and found people liked to talk. When later on I joined Simon in Marks and Spencer, I made good use of the knowledge which I had gained in this way. When Simon was staking a great deal on the production of hard-wearing garments at competitive prices, I was able to give him information about the qualities of materials in relation to cost. When Marks and Spencer went into textiles on a very large scale, my knowledge of raw material costs was useful in dealing directly – instead of through wholesalers – with manufacturers. My early peripatetics for my father also taught me something about people which I would not have learned in the office, and gave me the habit of going to see for myself. Again this proved useful later, particularly since Simon preferred by nature to be inside the firm, and was only too glad for his alter ego to do the leg-work in the world outside.

Some of what I came to know was not entirely reassuring, and I had to learn to be patient about it. One day my father said to me, 'Israel, I want you to make a special visit to Mr Sutcliffe in Huddersfield'. I said, 'What business does he do with us?' My father said, 'He does not do any business with us. That is why I want you to go and see him. He is enterprising, and I am sure we would be useful to him. I don't understand why he does not buy from us. I want you to go and find out why.' So the next day I went to Mr Sutcliffe's yard.

Across the yard, which was quite a large one, was a little office. The door was opened by a bright-eyed man with a little beard. He was direct, brisk, but not unfriendly in his manner. 'What do you want?' 'My father has sent me here to see if we could do business with you. We could provide you with first class cuttings. My father wants to know whether you would be interested.' Mr Sutcliffe looked at me appraisingly, asked me a few questions about the cuttings to see if I knew what I was talking about – I was not much more than twenty years of age. He seemed reasonably impressed with what he heard, and said, 'I am interested. How much?' My father's last word to me was that if Mr Sutcliffe looked like buying, I was to offer him cuttings at two shillings a ton below our normal rate. This price I quoted to him with alacrity. 'Good,' said Mr Sutcliffe. 'I will tell you what I will do, lad. I'll order a cwt. of each. What is your father's name?' 'Ephraim Sieff.' Mr Sutcliffe's face changed its expression. 'Jews,' he said. 'I never do business with Jews.' 'Why not?' 'I don't like them. You can't trust Jews. I keep clear of them.'

On the desk was a newspaper. That day it carried a story of how some local thugs had knocked a man down, and robbed him. I leaped up from my chair, as though in alarm. 'And I must keep clear of you,' I said, pointing to the newspaper. 'Look at this! You Yorkshire men are brutes. I am getting out of here before I get knocked down and robbed.' I made for the door.

Mr Sutcliffe looked startled. 'Wait a minute, lad,' he said. 'Sit down.' He looked at me hard. 'All right. The order stands. But I shall look at those cuttings carefully, and if there is anything wrong with them, you will have to take them all back. I won't pay carriage, either.'

I took my leave of Mr Sutcliffe. At my age then, had I been my own master, I am not sure that I would have tried to do business with him. However, when I described what had happened to my father, characteristically, he said: 'Only the quality of our goods can change his mind.' The cuttings were got ready for dispatch to Mr Sutcliffe. My father and I hovered over them like hawks for four days before they went. Two weeks after they had been sent off we had heard nothing from Mr Sutcliffe. My father said, 'Israel, you must go again, and find how things are.'

On the train I had a good look at the newspapers, but derived no inspiration from them. When I opened Mr Sutcliffe's office door, his first words were: 'I told you so. Never do business with a Jew.' I asked him what was the matter. 'Your stuff is not up to standard,' he said.

I said, 'Have you looked at them yourself?' It was a fortunate question. 'No,' he said. 'Jim Benson told me.' Jim Benson was his buyer. I said: 'Mr Sutcliffe, the cuttings we sent to you could not be bettered in the North of England. I would like to go and see the bales, and I would like you to come with me.'

We crossed the yard, went around the corner to a warehouse and there were my father's bales of cuttings, separate from the rest. They were unopened. Nobody had put a finger on them. I slit the first bale, pulled out a handful of cuttings and put them on the top of the bale for Mr Sutcliffe to inspect. He looked angry and ashamed. Without so much as a glance at the cuttings he said, 'Send me four tons a month from now on till I tell you to stop'.

When I got home my father was delighted. Apart from the vindication of our good faith it was a very useful order. For me it was a salutary experience. I realised that for Jews and Gentiles alike life is difficult enough when people generalise. When they generalise on the basis of mere hearsay life becomes even more difficult. The Sutcliffes of this world present us with problems. But it is the Jim Bensons who do the real damage, and when Jim Benson has spoken behind our backs we are not always lucky enough to be around to ask the Sutcliffes if they will come and look at our cuttings for themselves.

Here I should take up Simon's story. His father thought it would be better for Simon to go to Germany and France, where his father was building up a trade, for two or three years than to go to university, and, to be sure, a university education did not then have the attraction for young men like us – as I said, I was loath to go myself – that it had in later years. So Simon dutifully packed his bags and began a spell in Germany and France, which was to last for two and a half years.

He was to go first to Nuremberg, then the centre of the German toy industry, which was of particular interest to Marks and Spencer, and live with their contact there, a Theodore Guggenheimer. He set out, excited and nervous, with his father. He had never been out of England and his life, like mine, had been sheltered.

He was lonely at first; indeed miserable, and, though he liked the *gemütlich* Bavarian countryside, for weeks he pined for life in the Bury New Road. Soon, however, he became very fond of the Guggenheimer family, who came to treat him as a son. He was introduced to a small but very friendly Jewish community, and joined their *Tanz Kurs*, or dancing club – about twelve young men and twelve young ladies – and began to enjoy himself. He very much improved his German, which at the Grammar School had not been bad, and began to speak it really well. In the daytime he worked in a factory producing toys and games. He lived frugally; thirty shillings a month for his lodgings, including breakfast. His other meals he ate in restaurants, and for the most part alone.

About the Germans, Simon's feelings came out mixed. One of the tourist sights of Nuremberg was the museum of torture devices. I remember him telling me about his feelings on being shown them and his mention of the Iron Maiden, the iron case in the shape of a woman's body with spikes inside which cut the victim to pieces: he could not get over the fact that little models of the Iron Maiden were sold as souvenirs of Nuremberg, and that the Germans saw nothing odd in this. The city itself he grew to love – the walls, moats, towers and pinnacles of the mediaeval town kept so intact that he could walk, as he put it, from the twentieth into the sixteenth century. But he had misgivings about the Germans. He encountered a callousness and an arrogance for which Goethe and Schiller had not prepared him. On the whole, though it gave him a self-reliance and independence which he had not had before, I never thought that Simon's year in Germany was written down as his favourite experience, apart from the Guggenheimers. Years later when they were driven into exile he made a home for them in London.

Paris enraptured him. He did not find the intimate social life he found in Nuremberg. He was much more alone. Yet far less lonely. He was there for fifteen months, and his family had some difficulty in getting him back. The cosmopolitan in him came out in what was then the world capital of culture, art and fashion. French family life did not attract him much. It was, as it still is, far less easy to enter than the German; he felt the French did not mean to make you at home: their homes were not made for hospitality. But the boulevards enthralled him. 'Paris never seems to sleep,' he wrote. Reading his enthusiastic letters, there were moments for me when life in Salford seemed somewhat tedious.

Simon really did his Paris. He visited all the chateaux in the vicinity; art galleries, museums, theatres, music halls, cabarets, bistros and big stores. His curiosity was never satisfied. His business training was done in the Rue du Faubourg Poissonière in a firm of buyers called Alfred

Behrens and Company. They bought for Marks and Spencer as agents, had many European clients, and dealt directly with a number of French manufacturers. He struck lucky again with friendships. The head of the English department, whose job it was to supervise him, was an Austrian called Marschner who had settled in Paris, married a French woman, had never completely adjusted to France, and liked to speak German. This kept Simon's German up to scratch.

Simon learned more about the French in general and Paris in particular from a Nuremberg friend of his father called Obendorfer. Obendorfer came to Paris several times a year on business, though Simon told me that when in Paris Mr Obendorfer did not entirely neglect his pleasure. He sounded a most engaging mentor, and I wish I had met him. Notwithstanding his enjoyment of life he had studied the French people seriously and Simon and he often sat up late into the night discussing the scintillations of their mind and spirit. Any notion that Simon lived a life of luxury I must instantly dispel. He lived on 225 francs a month. He lived in a single room, paid a hundred francs for breakfast and supper, and sixty or fifty for lunch. This exhausted his allowance, and until he started to earn a hundred francs a month Chez Behrens he couldn't even buy clothes. In spite of his zest for life and good living he was and remained curiously puritan. I once said to him: 'Your father is generous: why didn't you ask him for a larger allowance?' 'Oh,' he said, as though struck with the idea, 'it never occurred to me to ask.'

After Simon had been away two years his family began to yearn for him. His father in particular began to press him to return. The remainder of this profound and poignant chapter in Simon's life, which begins a momentous one in both his and mine, I shall leave him to relate in his own words, taken from some personal notes he made in later life. I could not do it as well as he did it: and the account says something about Simon which I could not do at all:

On returning to Manchester, I immediately went into the business. By then my father had built a fine warehouse and offices in Derby Street. That was some few weeks or so before his death. He was obviously very happy and relieved at my return. I remember one Friday afternoon, I was sitting in his office checking invoices. He was sitting at the same table, smoking a cigar and watching me at work and not saying a word. The accountant, Mr G. R. Kenyon, came into the office and my father pointed proudly to me and said, 'Mr. Kenyon – my prince'. That was all.

We were nearing Christmas, which was the peak of the year's trading, and my father had had a particularly heavy week. All in that week, he had travelled to Glasgow where he had made arrangements for the purchase of chocolates from a firm called Reeves; he had travelled to Cork and back, where he had bought a considerable quantity of tinned milk in penny cans; he had travelled to London and back. He was convinced that we had to enter the food business. 'People must eat' – he was wont to say.

The day before Christmas at that time the best Christmas shopping day of the year, my father relaxed completely. He could do no more except visit some of the nearest shops. He invited Tom Spencer Junior, a business friend and myself to lunch at the Victoria Hotel, destroyed during the Second World War. After lunch, he and I walked together through Cateaton Street. I left my father to visit our Stretford Road branch, while he intended to go to his favourite shop in Oldham Street. Later that afternoon, I returned home to find my father ill in bed with a nurse in attendance. We were then living in our new house at 396 Bury New Road, Higher Broughton, Salford, also destroyed in World War II. I was not allowed to see him until three days later when he seemed much better. He then told me that as I was leaving him he collapsed in the street, shouting my name, which I didn't hear. On recovering, he was taken home in a cab and immediately put to bed. That day he was in a good humour and spoke at length about his early life. I am sorry to say that I have forgotten much of what he told me but he had had a happy, purposeful life. That night, the crisis came. He didn't recover consciousness, and on the last day of the year, in 1907, his spirit passed away.

I was left the head of the family of my mother, whose love embraced us all, and four sisters of varying ages, without experience, without any knowledge of the business, without guidance, I was left to steer the fortunes of my family. I felt indeed alone. But I was not entirely alone. There was always Israel who was our constant companion. There was the double attraction of my sister Rebecca and his affectionate friendship for me. He was a great comfort at the time. My mother could not adjust herself, could not forgive her fate which had torn my father from her at so early an age. She lived for a further ten years, but her health grew worse from year to year. She saw my sister Rebecca married to Israel and enjoyed her first grandchildren, Michael and Marcus Sieff. She witnessed the marriage of my sister Miriam to Harry Sacher. She was also present at my marriage to Miriam, but did not live long enough to see our first child, Hannah, who was named after her. My son, Michael, was named after my father. Each eldest son of the family bears his name.

In 1917, my mother died peacefully whilst Miriam and I were in London staying with Dr Weizmann. It was early on Saturday morning (20 April

1917) when Dr Weizmann woke me up to inform me that my mother had died. I was to have a similar feeling of tragedy when, in 1942 (11 February) I was to telephone Dr Weizmann, who was in Bristol waiting for a plane to the United States, to say that a telegram had been received stating that his son, Michael, an intrepid, valiant pilot of the Coastal Command of the RAF, was missing – alas never to be found. His mother, Vera Weizmann, did not give up hope for many years but that he would return. Four days before my mother's death, I took leave of her to come to London. She was lying in bed. She took me in her arms, kissed me passionately on my eyes, nose, mouth and drew me tightly to her. She was unusually demonstrative. This so surprised me and filled me with such emotion that I wept bitterly. She was saying good-bye. She had spent a happy Friday evening with my sisters, Israel and Harry; supped with them and went to bed as they left. By the time my sisters and their husbands arrived at their home in Didsbury, she had passed away, happy and without pain.

After a year or so working in my father's business I decided that there was no reason for delaying my marriage to Becky. One evening I said to my father, 'Father, I want to get married'. 'Married?' he said, incredulously. 'To whom?' 'Becky Marks, of course. Who else did you think I might want to marry?' My father said, 'Becky would make a good wife, Israel; but both of you are far too young'.

I had expected this kind of response and had thought out my tactics in advance. I was aware of the speed with which he had conducted his own matrimonial campaign. 'If you do not let me marry her, father,' I said, 'you are going to have trouble.' His face blenched. 'What kind of trouble?' he asked. 'If you will not let me marry her,' I said, 'you will make me elope with her.' He said, 'What will your mother say?' I said, 'Will you ask her or shall I?' He spoke to my mother at once, and she came to me with him and said it was nonsense; we were far too young and therefore would head for trouble. This was the only matter of any importance on which I remembered my mother being wrong; indeed I am not at all sure that she meant what she said at the time. 'If there is no announcement of the engagement in the *Manchester Guardian* before the end of the week,' I said, 'as soon as I see a chance I shall elope with her. You give me no alternative.'

A roughly similar contretemps took place five doors down the street in the Marks household. Again, it was a question of age. But within a few days we had got our way.

Once the decision had been taken both families were most co-operative. Until now my father had given me spending money and had paid my bills for clothes, university fees, holiday money and so on, but though I had been working for him in the business for nearly a year he had paid me no salary. A week before the wedding, he said to me with typical diffidence: 'Israel, have you any money for your honeymoon?' 'No.' 'Then what are you going to do?' I said, 'I hoped you would give me some'. 'How much do you want?' he asked. 'I don't know. I have never been on a honeymoon before.' 'Where will you go on your honeymoon?' 'I would like to go to London and Paris, and I would like to have a hundred pounds.' And my father said, 'There is only one honeymoon; I will give you two hundred pounds.'

Our marriage took place in the middle of the summer on the newly opened flat roof of the Midland Hotel. The *huppa*, the traditional wedding canopy made of white silk or satin, held aloft by four poles, symbolising the husband's domain for which the bride has left her father's house, was brought to the Midland from our local synagogue in Higher Broughton. It was an immensely jolly affair, apart from the contribution of my younger brother, Teddy, then five years old, who ate so many strawberries that he had suddenly to be taken home ill. Simon was the best man. My oldest son, Michael, was born nine months later to the day.

When I got back from our honeymoon, my father on my first morning back at work took me into his office. He pointed to a corner of it and said, 'There is the safe. Take your living out of that as and when you want it.' I did so. At the end of the year he said to me, 'Do you know how much you have taken out of the safe?' I said, 'No. You had not said anything about me counting it.' He said, 'Well, I have counted it, and this year you have taken out two thousand and three hundred pounds. I only want you to know.' At the end of the second year he came to me and said, 'Israel, you have spent a lot more this year – nearly three thousand pounds. From now on take three thousand pounds and no more.'

I did not feel as guilty as perhaps on the face of things I might have been expected to do. I had set up my own house. I had encountered all the expenses of the first year of marriage. Our first child had arrived. My mother quoted an old Yiddish saying: 'The child is born, and the roof is not yet on the house.'

From the beginning of our marriage I ceased to be spoiled. Becky was not the kind of woman to be waiting on the doorstep to welcome her husband home from work. If Becky had ever been waiting for me on the doorstep it would have been because she had mislaid her key. She could not have restricted herself to being a stay-at-home wife, like my own mother; she simply had to be out and about and doing things: a beautiful and most feminine woman, she had the mind of a dynamic man. As I, in writing these words, cast my mind back to the time of my marriage, I give thanks again for the privilege of having Simon Marks as my friend, and Becky Marks for my wife. Though I was an unimportant corner of it, I was certainly part of a remarkable human triangle.

4
The Beginnings of Marks and Spencer

When I first met Simon Marks, in 1902, his father had been in England for twenty years and Marks and Spencer had been going strong for eight of them. Michael Marks was born in 1863 in a village near Bialystok, a city within the Pale, in what was then Russian Poland. He came from very much the same kind of Jewish family as my father except, from what I gleaned, his parents had not been in such good circumstances as mine. As well as the tensions of the time shared by all Jews in Poland, Michael suffered from the deprivation of a mother's love: his mother died in giving him birth. The youngest of a very large brood he was brought up by an elder sister. His father lived, it was said, to be over a hundred years old. They were, on the whole, a long living family. Michael's brother, Maurice, was well over ninety when he died in California and Ephraim was eighty-five when he died in Manchester.

Michael Marks must have been one of the very first Polish Jews of the new diaspora precipitated by the assassination of Alexander II in 1882. What little we know indicates that he had left by 1882, when he was nineteen years old. He made straight for Britain because he understood that his elder brother Barnet had already gone there, but when Michael arrived he found that Barnet, after a short stay, had left again for the United States. Quite why Barnet had come and gone so quickly nobody seems to know. He was a man of great personality, living in independence and with wanderlust in his blood. There was a family story that in Britain he met a woman who was keen to marry him, and in order to avoid her permanent embraces without hurting her feelings – he was a sympathetic creature – he put the Atlantic between her and him. Whatever the reason, to America Barnet went. He arrived in time to participate in the Gold Rush to the Yukon. He did not discover unmined gold, but he opened a store in Dawson City, and made good profits by trade which later enabled him to establish himself in comfort much further south, with less snow and more sun, in Los Angeles.

Michael arrived in London, therefore, in circumstances that were not propitious. As well as having no English, unlike my father, he had no trade, and he had practically no education. His ability to read and write was no greater than that of any child who left school in those days at the age of thirteen, and it has been said that he could not read or write at all. He stayed in London only a very short time, perhaps just days, and then he went north to Leeds in Yorkshire, presumably because he learned that Leeds had a Jewish community of several thousand, and that a firm called Barran's had a reputation for giving work to immigrant Jews from Eastern Europe. What happened to him when he arrived in Leeds is best described in the words of Mr Alistair Dewhirst, the chairman of I. J. Dewhirst Ltd., a firm from which Marks and Spencer still buys goods. Alistair Dewhirst's grandfather, Isaac Dewhirst, was a wholesale merchant in Leeds. Among other things he sold goods to low-priced shops, market stalls and pedlars.

One day my grandfather was walking down Kirkgate when he was addressed by a stranger with the single word 'Barrans'. My grandfather spoke to the man and quickly realised that he did not speak or understand English. With my grandfather, however, was his manager, Charlie Backhouse, who spoke a little Yiddish, and was able to talk to the man in that language. He discovered that he was a Polish refugee, who had come to Leeds looking for the firm of Barran Clothiers, whose generosity in giving work to refugees was known as far afield as Poland.

My grandfather was fascinated by the stranger. He took him back to his warehouse, where he learned that he was looking for work and had no money. He offered to lend him £5, and Michael Marks asked if he might use it to buy goods from the warehouse. My grandfather agreed, and as Michael Marks paid off the debt in instalments, he was allowed to make further purchases to the same amount. This was my grandfather's first contact with Michael Marks; my grandfather's behaviour was very typical of him.

When Michael Marks gave up peddling he took a stall in Leeds market, which was not more than a hundred yards from the warehouse. He came in daily to make his purchases, and during his absence from his stall, Charlie Backhouse, whose son is a director of Dewhirst's today, used to go and take care of it for him.

Tom Spencer was then the firm's cashier, and he was greatly impressed by the business which Michael Marks was obviously doing, and by the way in which his account grew.

I can see Simon's father now, as clearly as if I had been walking at his side, plodding through the Yorkshire Dales and mining villages, knocking at doors, standing at the street corners, presenting his tray to the villagers on the green, or outside the village pub. If he had been a man of strong physique he might have gone on peddling for years. But he was frail. He was described at that time as 'a small made man, of a fair, almost ruddy complexion, physically not strong, sensitive in spirit, kindly and sympathetic'. The Yorkshire countryside in winter was hard on a young man who tramped day after day through the open air with his twenty pounds' worth or so of buttons, pins, needles, darning wool and stockings in a knapsack on his back. He made up his mind to get indoors as soon as he possibly could find a business which permitted it.

The wheel of chance was now to spin fast and fair for Michael Marks. Leeds, then, as now, one of the six leading cities of Great Britain, was in 1884 a rapidly expanding town of 310,000 people, an important railway centre, a centre of the clothing, manufacturing and mining industries and a market town which served the surrounding hinterland of Yorkshire, England's biggest county. It typified the characteristic phase of economic development through which Britain was passing in the 1880s, a period marked by one of the most impressive rises in real incomes that the working people of Britain had ever known. There was no better time for a man to start marketing simple, essential, domestic articles. The new customer was a mass customer; he was not interested in variety of choice and exclusive quality but in basic necessities supplied cheap. There was something else. The industrialisation of Britain had led to a great movement of low level wage earners from the countryside to the town – again, Leeds was an outstanding example of the process. The village craftsman was rapidly giving way to the retailer in stores and shops located in the towns, selling not articles he had made himself, but goods purchased from wholesalers. The pedlar was being superseded by the shopkeeper. Big stores for the middle classes had emerged some years before: the equivalent for the working classes was rapidly evolving to meet the needs of the working man and his wife. There was a great expansion of the Co-operative stores and multiple shops. The beginnings of the chain store, as we know it today almost all over the world, were taking place when Michael Marks went to Leeds. And the story of his success is the story of the particular contribution he made, by thought and circumstance and the turn of chance, to this general development.

To understand what that particular contribution was it is necessary to begin with something which has largely passed from the scene in Britain: the old-style market and fair. The fairs took place from time to time: the open market was a weekly, if not bi-weekly affair. The open market was held in the market place. Those who wished to sell their goods in it arrived on market day and laid out their wares in booths or on wooden tables erected for the purpose. These vendors did not usually sell at pre-fixed prices: they usually sold their goods at prices negotiated, 'haggled', between them and the customer. Michael Marks while still a pedlar, set up a stall in the open market in Leeds; it consisted of two trestle tables six feet by three. His experience as a pedlar had shown him exactly what people wanted to buy: his trade flourished from the start. Leeds had only two market days a week, and he soon found he was doing so well – how and why he did so well I shall deal with in a moment – that he was emboldened to seek additional outlets. So on the other days of the week he went to the markets in the neighbouring towns of Castleford and Wakefield. Turnover in Leeds was so good he soon needed help. He went back to Dewhirst's and asked if they could find him two young ladies who would serve at the stall with him. They were able to oblige. The two girls were competent and trustworthy, and good to look at. A day came when he learned that two markets would be open in the same day. He left Esther Brown in charge of Leeds and went to the other town himself. The decision was revolutionary for him: the idea of delegating sales to persons in whom you have confidence is the essence of the multiple shop.

At this time another development was taking place from which Michael benefited: the open market was in many towns being superseded by the closed, or covered, market, the roofed market hall. These permanent market halls were frequently known as 'bazaars', from the Persian word meaning market, the term being used particularly to describe lines or rows of stalls. It was out of the permanent stall in the covered market hall that the chain store as we know it today evolved.

This could not have happened had not the covered market halls been so popular. A Saturday night visit to the market was one of the main entertainments of the week for parents and children. There were all the stalls to look at. There were fascinating medicines which could cure all ailments. The patter of the 'cheapjacks' was a theatre in itself. There were acts: strong men lifted iron bars, 'fakirs' swallowed fire and provincial Houdinis escaped through ropes or shackles. Meat pies, mussels, eels and cockles were on sale for immediate consumption on the spot.

As soon as he felt he could make it pay, Michael took a permanent stall in the new market hall which was now open six days a week. His stalls were different from those of his competitors. He could hardly speak English at this time and he certainly could not write it. Far from being put down by his shortcomings, he instinctively exploited them, seeing that many of his customers were similarly situated. He could not haggle over prices, or vaunt the merits of his wares, so he put his goods in open baskets, and displayed their price in large and simple figures: his customer could take the article or leave it, seeing without asking what its price was. He had another idea. He divided his stall, even when it consisted of a single trestle table, into two halves, and drew a chalk line down the middle. On one side of the line were various baskets of goods, each category clearly and simply marked with the price. On the other side of the line were a great variety of goods, above which was prominently displayed the simple caption: 'Don't ask the price, it's a penny'. Michael Marks, my brother-in-law Harry Sacher once said, 'discovered the world of a penny'. He put his sign up on his market stall 'M. Marks: the original Penny Bazaar'. He did not invent the bazaar, and he did not invent the penny. But he brought them together. He invented the 'Penny Bazaar'.

Here entered Michael Marks's experience as a pedlar knocking at doors in the Yorkshire Dales. He knew what people wanted and he found that if he looked around for it, much of it could be supplied to them at a profit for a penny. The prospect of such a narrow profit margin would not have attracted an ambitious British businessman. But the perspective of a Polish immigrant was different. He was grateful to be alive in a free country, able to worship as he wished, go and come as he pleased. He was rich in the best things of life already. His personal and material horizons were relatively limited. The 'Don't-ask-the-price-it's-a-penny' approach to life, therefore, was quite congenial. Applying it he found that for a fixed price of a penny he could supply his customers with a very wide variety of goods: handkerchieves, tapes, needles, and hatpins: cups, saucers and plates; hammers and chisels; nails and screws and locks and bolts; soap, candles, dusters and mousetraps; toys, including children's books; and, stationery, of which writing paper, pencils, and notebooks were the best selling lines. All these were bought from the wholesaler who gave him his start in Leeds – Isaac Dewhirst.

Within two years he saw it would pay him to open new permanent stalls in covered market halls in different parts of the country. He opened up in Yorkshire and Lancashire and even as far afield as Cardiff in South Wales. A larger corps of assistants was required. It was the profits of the sale of articles at a penny which financed his expansion, and he concentrated on this end of the business. The main need was the selection of articles which could sell well at a penny, and at this he was an unrivalled expert. So he became the central buyer for his own business and delegated sales to his local managers. A chain of stores appeared in the big towns and cities of the country, all marked, 'M. MARKS – ORIGINATOR OF THE PENNY BAZAAR'. These were soon known for what apart from the penny, they had in common: people could come in, walk round, inspect all goods, buy or not buy as they pleased, knowing what the price was in advance, and be sure of getting value for money.

This method of retailing simplified business for Mr Marks, but more important it simplified it for his customers. And the simplification of buying for customers is a cardinal retailing principle. In shops at this time, which more often than not were small and dark and poky, it was still customary to keep goods in drawers under the counter or on shelves behind it. You had to ask for everything before you even saw if it was there. It was, and remains, a feature of people who acquire a purchasing power to which they are not used to be shy sometimes of going into shops and discussing purchasing: sometimes they avoid it, in case they show their ignorance, or for fear that sophisticated shopkeepers, or shop assistants, might look down on them or exploit them. This did not happen when people came to shop with Simon Marks. They could walk around Michael's penny bazaar, thirty to seventy feet in length, six to thirteen feet in width, without being pestered to buy. They were at ease. Out of the psychology of this approach to selling goods were to emerge two of the most important principles of mid-twentieth century retail distribution: self-selection and self-service for the customer, and the organisation of the emporium to that purpose. Woolworths were to develop them in the United States; Liptons and Maypole, among others, in Britain.

Michael's penny bazaars flourished. He knew the value of display: he painted all his stalls an unmistakable red. 'Admission Free' was posted in large letters so that everybody should feel welcome. The working man and his wife poured into them at such a rate that other tradesmen jockeyed to get their pitch as close as possible to Marks's. Eight years after he had started business in Leeds, he was operating five Penny Bazaars: Leeds, Castleford, Wakefield, Warrington and Birkenhead (the last two in Lancashire), all selling under the same slogan: 'Don't ask the price, it's a penny.'

In 1891 he moved to Wigan. This old Lancashire town, which had become a coal mining, cotton, engineering and chemical community with a population of 55,000, was and remains, a byword for poverty in bad times and low level working class purchasing power in good. Wigan was not much of an attraction for the average businessman of that time, but it was ideal for a merchant who could make a profit at a penny. He opened a stall in the market hall and made his home in Caroline Street.

By now he was married. Two years after he had arrived in Leeds in 1884, he had journeyed north on a trading reconnaissance to the industrial town of Stockton-on-Tees on the north eastern British coast. On the evening of his first day there, at the time people were going home from work, the heavens opened and rain poured down in torrents. Michael took shelter, in a doorway, in the main street. There were several other people sheltering from the rain, and he entered into conversation with the man standing next to him. Michael's English was still rudimentary; but the man standing next to him could talk Yiddish. His name was Cohen. Some years before he too had emigrated from the Pale of Settlement to Britain. When the rain had stopped, Cohen insisted on Michael coming home with him, to dry out and have a meal. His benefactor had a daughter, Hannah. Michael met her, and a few months later she became his wife. She was twenty-one, he was twenty-two. Hannah was a wonderful woman, quite unlike my own mother, but a rare creature, too, small, slight, delicate, devoted. She was, in spite of being small, immensely energetic, a dominating little body who ruled her husband and her family. She was a wonderful dressmaker, and had a head for figures. In the early days of their marriage she and Michael would work together at night to prepare for the next day's work in the market. At that time her English was better than his, and she was extremely useful to him.

The year 1894 – he was thirty-one – was a turning-point in Michael's life. He took three big decisions. First, he opened a shop in Manchester:

secondly, he began to buy direct from the manufacturers instead of buying through the wholesalers. Thirdly, he went into partnership with another man. The partner was a man called Spencer. Marks and Spencer came into being.

Michael wanted a partner because he wanted to expand and if he was to expand, somebody was needed to share the main responsibility of central buying. He did not need capital, and he did not need expertise, but he did need a deputy. He turned first to the man who had launched him, Isaac Dewhirst. Dewhirst said, No: his own business was flourishing and occupied all the attention he could give it. But what about his cashier, Tom Spencer? Tom was capable, experienced and a good organiser. He wanted to get out of book-keeping and chance his arm in a business of his own; he liked the life of the countryside not the life of the town, and his aim was to make enough money to live on a farm and raise chickens. Michael welcomed the suggestion. He had a lot to do with Tom, and they had become good friends.

It was one of those friendships only found between men of strikingly dissimilar personalities. Michael was intense, self-driving, dedicated to work, almost puritanically high minded and somewhat ascetic – his only appetite was for cigars; he rarely had one out of his mouth, and some say his smoking caused his early death. Tom Spencer was quite different. He was the novelist's picture of a Yorkshireman; big, broad, heavy chinned and jovial. He had a loud voice, a bluff manner and a breezy presence. Some people found him plain spoken, some of his employees said he was domineering, but essentially he was good natured and frequently showed himself very kind. Michael, who had known him for years, trusted him implicitly, and there was a bond of mutual affection between them. Both were religious in their way. Michael, though not a synagogue-goer, had a strong sense of the ethical claims of Judaism. Tom went to church every Sunday, and by his lights was a good Christian. He was very good with children. Cricket was almost a second creed with him, and Simon and I often went with him to Old Trafford. I well remember us standing up for Lancashire when they were playing Yorkshire, against whom Tom would never hear a word, and of whose players and details he had great knowledge.

For a bucolic extrovert he displayed a curious parsimony: he would, for instance, allow no expenditure on the purchase of string or nails: the staff were instructed to provide their own string from incoming parcels, and nails were to be salvaged from incoming crates and packing-cases and, if necessary, re-straightened for re-use. He was good on detail, an office man with no breadth of mind or imagination. Expansionism was not in his nature. He spent nearly all his time in the headquarters office carrying out administration responsibilities, and so far as he could preventing an extra penny being spent. Michael, on the other hand, travelled the country, buying, visiting stores, prospecting sites, observing trading trends and divining possibilities. The partnership was most successful.

We have a note of the day the partnership began. In August 1894 Isaac Dewhirst wrote in his diary: 'Mr Spencer tells me that he is about to go into partnership with Michael Marks. We agree that 22nd September will terminate the services at my shop.' On 22 September Dewhirst noted: 'Mr Spencer left my services to go into partnership with Michael Marks of twenty Cheetham Hill, Manchester.' The firm of Marks and Spencer was formally established on 28 September. For his half share in it Tom Spencer paid three hundred pounds. He considered his investment a bit of a gamble, but before he died must have concluded that his bet was one of the coups of his generation. Michael Marks's capital in the business was four hundred and fifty pounds. He was thirty-one years of age, ten years younger than Tom. It was ten years since he had first humped his pedlar's pack into the countryside around Leeds.

He decided now to move his home to Manchester. He had bought the premises of a shop at the Cheetham Hill Road end of Irk Street. There was living accommodation above it, and the idea of living there attracted him because he would see much more of his family. Manchester was a much bigger city than Leeds, and its rail communications with the South and the Midlands were better. Its amenities far exceeded those of Wigan. There was a large and flourishing and hospitable Jewish community there, a university, good schools, theatres, music, all the cultural life which Wigan lacked.

The next decade saw a remarkable expansion. Only six years after the partnership was formed, the six bazaars and a shop had multiplied into thirty-six establishments – twenty-four bazaars in market halls, two as far south as Cardiff and Bath; and twelve shops, including three in London. Instead of the dilapidated warehouse in Manchester, Marks and Spencer now owned a Head Office and central warehouse of their own which they had built in Derby Street, complete with a dining-room and cooking facilities for the staff.

THE BEGINNINGS OF MARKS AND SPENCER

In 1903 they formed a limited company. Since the articles of the company were to be a source of much controversy which among other things led to my joining Simon in the company, I should make a comment on them at this point which will make a later portion of my narrative more intelligible: Michael Marks and Thomas Spencer were personal friends; they regarded their interests as mutually complementary, indeed, inextricably involved, and it never occurred to them that friction would develop in or around their happy association. The articles reflected this mutual trust, and were consequently simple to the point of being amateurish. The two partners now became the two directors of the new limited company. Control was divided between them. These articles made very good sense when they were drawn up, but as the accidents of time and human nature were to show, they were deficient in one respect: they made no effective provision for what might happen when the founders had given up control. On that account, consequently, they were to cause considerable trouble.

Thomas Spencer retired the year that the company was formed. This was greatly due to Michael's persuasion; Tom was drinking his health and strength away, jovially and good-naturedly, but doing it all the same. It is pleasant to recall that like so many Yorkshiremen he was a countryman at heart. He achieved his ambition, a chicken farm in the country, near Lichfield, his wife's old home. He enjoyed his retirement; only too much, perhaps. He lived only four years more, dying at the age of fifty-three. He was a good fellow.

Michael was already working under great pressure. The company was rapidly expanding both its overall business and the number of its branches. The twenty-five establishments of 1900 now numbered sixty-one. The Marks and Spencer organisation was now a national chain of stores. Two-thirds of the branches were now shops. It was clear that this was the direction in which the future of the enterprise lay. But shops meant more capital, more supervision, more work, more responsibility.

The year Tom died Michael looked around for a new partner. To take on Spencer's son, Tom Spencer junior, was not a practical proposition. Tom was far too young, and far from gifted, but there was a man, very close to the Spencers, who looked as though he might fill the bill. William Chapman ran a thriving handkerchief manufacturing firm in Manchester. He was a family friend of the Spencers, and was one of the two executors of Thomas Spencer's estate. The Spencers pressed for his appointment: Chapman would represent their interests on the board. Michael took the same view. Chapman was known to be an able, energetic, thriving businessman. He joined the board. Had Michael lived for even another ten or fifteen years, the new arrangement might have proved successful. But Michael, only forty-four years old, died within a few months of Chapman's appointment.

On Michael's death William Chapman was left the sole director. Two weeks later Bernard Steel, a friend of Michael, and an executor of his estate, was appointed to the Board. He was to represent the interests of the Marks family in the way that Chapman was representing those of the Spencers. The interregnum had begun.

Steel and Chapman were both men of ability, and they contributed a great deal to the development of the business. Between 1908 and 1914, profits before tax went up almost fourfold, from £8,000 to £30,000. The number of branches more than doubled – to 140, ninety per cent of them shops. But the two new partners did not hit it off together. Chapman's position was the stronger; he was Chairman, he was a forceful fellow, and he could count almost automatically on the support of Thomas Spencer junior. The weakness in his position was that he could give only part of his attention to Marks and Spencer, the remainder being required by the affairs of his own firm. Steel, on the other hand, though free to concentrate on Marks and Spencer lacked Chapman's expertise and drive. Chapman did not find it difficult to keep him firmly in the second place. There was a keen sense of rivalry between them, and some personal conflict. It did not prevent them ganging up on one occasion to further their mutual interests. In 1909 they proposed to increase the firm's capital, then £30,000, to £100,000. The Marks and Spencer families could not possibly have raised the extra £70,000. Chapman and Steel were in a position to do so. This proposal to increase the firm's capital could give them control of the business. It was strongly resisted.

This attempt to make Marks and Spencer into, substantially, Chapman and Steel, very much alarmed the Marks family, and they concluded that the sooner the Marks family were on the Board, if not in control of it, the safer their interests would be. In December 1911, Simon, then twenty-one and young Tom Spencer were elected to the Board. In 1912 Steel, a sick man at this time, resigned, and died the following year. The Marks interest on the Board was consequently halved: the other interest, nominally Spencer, but virtually Chapman, was now two to one. Obviously, Chapman should have initiated the election of a fourth member to the Board to restore the balance. He did not do so. The situation left him, in effect, in control of the company, and kept Simon Marks in a permanent minority. Marks and Spencer was, in effect, now William Chapman.

There followed an open struggle for the control – indeed, for the existence – of the company which was to last for five extremely fraught years. Chapman, having no sentimental or family ties to Marks and Spencer, was always ready to sell out to a bigger organisation if the terms were right. Simon, on the other hand, was already passionately involved in the life of the business his father had founded, and regarded it as his filial duty to build it up. His mother and sisters felt the same. So did his relatives and friends, including myself. We did not look on Marks and Spencer merely as a business: it was a way of life; it was *us*. A fight for control was therefore inevitable.

At the Annual General Meeting in 1913, Simon opened his campaign by proposing that a new director be elected to replace Mr Steel, pointing out that the appointment of a fourth director would only restore the status quo. Chapman opposed this. The articles of the company, he said, had stipulated that in the event of a dispute between the directors the matter was to be referred to the shareholders. It was laid down in the articles that if the shareholders were required to elect a new director a majority of three quarters was necessary to effect the appointment. The Marks family and their supporters held a majority of the shares, but, as Chapman pointed out, it fell far short of seventy-five per cent.

There was only one course open to Simon: if he wanted to get control of the company, he would have to try and buy back enough shares from those who were willing to sell to give him the necessary seventy-five per cent. This was easier said than done; at this time Simon and his family were short of cash. They were wealthy only in terms of capital sunk in the family business. Of their situation at this critical moment Simon wrote in later life:

> My father had died on the last day of the year, which was also the end of the financial year of the business. The dividends which had accrued were regarded as capital on which Estate Duty had to be paid. There were no liquid funds. My father owned nearly half of the Equity of Marks and Spencer. He depended on his Dividends; he was generous to a fault to his family, his relatives and his friends. He was a supporter of many charities of all

denominations. He loathed money-lenders and many a victim came to him for help, and if he were a non-Jew, he went out of his way to rescue him. We had to borrow money from the bank to live and await the next year's Dividends. The future without the pilot looked grim . . .

A matter of 1,000 shares held by outsiders actually controlled the company with the partners not being in agreement. The price was high and exorbitant – £14,000 for 1,000. Israel was insistent that the money be found. My mother gave half her savings – £5,000; I possessed about £2,500 – with the help of my uncle Ephraim Marks, and my father-in-law and Israel, we managed to get the money.

Israel, who had a business of his own, borrowed up to the hilt from the bank. It took him some time and hard work to repay the loan. It says much for the confidence in me, as then wholly untried, that they were willing to support me in so costly a fashion. It was Israel again, whose faith in me has never dimmed throughout the years, who helped me to face the real financial trial of my life.

I remember going to the bank to ask for my first £2,500 to buy Marks and Spencer shares. It was the first time I had taken money out of my account in any quantity. The bank manager, a friend of my family, said, 'Does your father know?' 'No,' I said, 'and I don't want him to, he'd worry.' Our efforts secured the shares but did not bring immediate victory. Chapman refused point blank to register the transfer of the shares. His view was upheld by the company's lawyer, who, I am bound to note, was a personal friend of Chapman.

For the details of the protracted conflict in the board-room which now ensued, those interested could turn to the official history of Marks and Spencer.* I refer to them because it is at this point that I make my first official appearance in the annals of the Company. In November 1915 Simon proposed that I become a member of the Board. The consequence of this move was a chain of events in the struggle for power in the board-room which led, ultimately, to the decision of the Marks family to go to law, and challenge the methods by which Chapman was holding on to his control of the Company. We won hands down. Mr Justice Peterson, in the Court of Chancery, ruled against Chapman and for Simon Marks on all points.

This was the turning-point. We did our best in the next few months to re-establish good relations with Chapman, but we got nowhere with him. In June 1917, he and Thomas Spencer, Junior, retired from the business altogether.

* *St Michael* by Goronwy Rees, Weidenfeld and Nicolson, 1969.

Thomas Spencer died soon afterwards. His shares were transferred to the Spencer Trust. His step-mother, Mrs Agnes Spencer, survived him by over forty years. The unhappy events which followed her husband's death had affected neither her trust in the Company nor her friendship with Simon. Two years before she died, in 1957, she gave the bulk of her fortune to the Marks and Spencer Benevolent Trust. It was a moving gesture from a very fine woman. Somehow it brought a sense of release from the tensions of those five years, and re-created that personal harmony which marked the original partnership of Marks and Spencer.

5
Secretary to Chaim Weizmann

One evening in the summer of 1913, Becky and I went out to dinner with a relative of ours by marriage, one Sam Cohen. Sam was most likeable, with a beautiful wife. They were Sephardic Jews. When we entered the dining room we found that there were two other guests. My eye fell upon the woman first: she was of medium height, graceful and well poised, dressed with a distinctive taste, though not expensively. Her eyes were hazel, her hair between colours, her brow was open and serene, her mouth broad, generous, amused. She was a beautiful woman. But impressive as she was, the impact of her husband on me was of a different order. I was struck by his personality almost before I had taken in the details of his appearance. It was magical, overwhelming, irrevocable. He was not above middle height, had a dark, small pointed beard, and a rather unusually youthful pinkish face for one who was clearly a Central European Jew. His eyes were full of life, but they were sombre. As he rose to greet us his mien was that of a man who knew he carried a burden, yet it was vigorous and utterly unpretentious. I remember noticing that he was immaculately dressed. Obviously he knew my host quite well, but he did not seem on intimate terms with him. The introductions were made: Dr Chaim Weizmann, lecturer in chemistry at Manchester University; his wife Vera. I had been a Zionist for seven years. At the age of seventeen I had joined the Manchester Zionist Organisation, a branch of the Zionist Organisation of England. I had known a good deal, therefore, about Dr Weizmann, before I met him. But the moment I met him he became my master.

There have been many accounts of the charisma of Chaim Weizmann, and I do not aspire to add to them. All I wish to do is to record the effect of it on me that night. The expressions on his face changed quickly and easily, as his discourse moved along, like illustrations of his theme. His voice had light and shade, but never lost intensity. He talked quickly and confidently with a heavy accent, which somehow one hardly noticed while he was speaking. He was an intellectual; yet he was pre-eminently what the Jewish people call *folks-mensh*, a man of the people, of the masses not of the élite, a leader in whose breast beat the common heart of man. I listened to him rapt.

He spoke first of his own particular conception of the way to establish a Jewish national home in Palestine and swept me off my feet. It was not just because his notion of what Zionism should be was in perfect form and depth what I in cruder terms believed: he made it sound as practical as it was poetical. I was so overwhelmed by him; and so wanted him to form a good impression of me, I behaved very foolishly. I showed off. He was talking about the Keren Kayemet le-Yisrael, the 'Perpetual Fund for Israel', the Jewish National Fund, the raising of money, pennies at a time in humble collecting boxes left in Jewish homes, to buy land for Jewish settlers in Palestine and I interrupted him. 'Pennies?' I asked. 'Yes,' he said, 'pennies. You know, Mr Sieff, most of our funds come, penny by penny, from the homes of Jews in the poorer parts of Europe, where a penny is worth a great deal.' My egotism, my longing to be well thought of by him, my impulsive urge to be of service to him, could not be contained. At the time I was secretary of the fund-raising campaign for the Manchester Jewish Hospital. 'But I've just raised £28,000 in twelve months, here in Manchester, in *pounds*,' I said. Dr Weizmann regarded me a trifle coolly; his tone, when he spoke after a slight pause, was a little dry. 'I too, would like the pounds,' he said. 'But so far I have to think in pennies.' He resumed his fascinating exposition as though nothing had occurred to interrupt it.

The following morning I telephoned Sam Cohen. 'I want to go to work for Dr Weizmann,' I said. I described the impact which Weizmann's personality and policies had had upon me. I told Sam how grateful I was to him for having arranged for me to meet him. Sam listened to my gush in silence. When I had finished he said: 'I'm glad you thought so highly of Dr Weizmann. He very much enjoyed meeting you and Becky; but he told me that when you started to talk about raising pounds instead of pennies he thought you were, well, rather a foolish young man.'

I put down the telephone, mortified beyond description. I had a feeling of resentment at being described as 'foolish', but this was nothing to my feeling of rejection. Somebody whom I longed to help, somebody I longed to have as my friend, had closed an opening door brusquely in my face. Fortunately for me I could not accept this. Later that morning I telephoned to Sam again. I said, 'At any rate, Sam, even though I behaved like a fool last night, you know I wasn't exaggerating. I *did* raise that money. I *did* get those pounds. If Dr Weizmann thinks I am so foolish I want a chance to get him to change his mind. Would you telephone him and ask if he would let me come and see him?' Sam called me back later on that day. Dr Weizmann would see me at his laboratory at four o'clock. I went. Before I went I armed myself with facts and figures about the year's fund-raising work. When I sat down opposite Dr Weizmann in that laboratory, I tried to sell myself to him as I've never tried to sell myself before or since.

He was impressed. He relented, he smiled on me. He offered me a cup of tea. He discussed my techniques with interest and address. Finally, he said, 'The Zionist Actions Committee is going to inaugurate a great new drive for funds when it meets in Germany next year in August. Could you come to it with me, and tell them what you have told me? There is great need of a good *schnorrer*.'*

The Actions Committee was the name of the General Council of the World Zionist Organisation. I was very flattered at the prospect of being asked to speak to it. Besides, I looked forward to showing off my German, for which there was not much call in Didsbury. Alas for my vanities, and for the peace of the world. That meeting of the Zionist Actions Committee did not take place. The first guns in the first world war were fired on the day it should have opened. But Weizmann and I had become friends that afternoon in the laboratory at Manchester, and our friendship remained for the rest of his life. It influenced me second only to my friendship with Simon. The following week I introduced Simon to him. Simon, too, immediately fell under his spell.

I mentioned that I had joined the World Zionist Organisation when I was seventeen. I recall the circumstances in which I did so vividly. One summer evening, I was in the front room of our house and heard a strange commotion in the street: raised voices, guffaws, some sounds

* (The *schnorrer*, in Yiddish, is the professional beggar. The term is by no means uncomplimentary, since the classical *schnorrer* in Yiddish writers is a man of wit, ingenuity and often culture.)

between snarls and sneers. I went to the front door, opened it, walked to the front gate, and, looking down Bury New Road, saw two young men begin to run down the middle of it, away from a group of youths who stood jeering at them from the pavement: 'Jew . . . Jew' were the only words I could catch. It was all over in a second or two, and no harm done. I supposed that two Jewish lads, walking down the pavement, had happened to encounter some other lads who had jostled them on to the road. There had been words, gestures and threats, and the Jews had run to safety. Now the street was quiet. In another moment I was alone in it. But I felt peculiarly disturbed. I stood there five minutes or so, thinking about what I had seen, thinking about what might have been, and, still upset, went to the back room of the house where my father was sitting reading the evening paper. I told him what I had seen. He listened without comment or question, and after I had finished he said, 'Don't be anxious, Israel. These things will happen from time to time. We must live with them now. One day all this will be settled. Such things will not happen one day as every true Zionist knows. When the Jews have a country of their own to go to, they shall have nothing to fear.'

I knew my father had been a Zionist for years. He was very proud, I already knew, of being one of the original investors in what is now the Bank Leumi le-Israel, the Bank established in 1903 by the Jewish Colonial Trust as the Anglo-Palestine Company, which soon became the central bank of Palestine Jewry. He subscribed to many Zionist funds, supported many Zionist causes. But up until that summer evening in Bury New Road, I had regarded the Zionist Movement as somewhat academic, rather above my head, outside the limits of my personal life. That night changed this for me. The following day I became a member of the Zionist Organisation. I began to read books and pamphlets, went to meetings and took part in seminars. I even wrote an essay on Jewish emancipation which I read to Simon. So I was a zealous and an active Zionist before I met Chaim Weizmann. But when I did so, he gave me, as he gave so many others, a vision and awareness, a sense of urgency and dedication, which made it seem in retrospect as though for me Zionism and Weizmann began in my life together.

From the night I met Weizmann in Didsbury in 1913 until nine years later, when on 24 July 1922 the Council of the League of Nations, meeting in London, finally approved a mandate to Britain to administer

Palestine and be responsible for the implementation of the Balfour Declaration, giving 'recognition to the historical connection of the Jewish people with Palestine and to the grounds for reconstituting their national home in that country', I was extremely close to Dr Weizmann. For much of the time I was his personal assistant and unpaid private confidential secretary. I have done nothing in life on my own account, but I have had the luck to see a very great man do a very great deal on his. Serving Dr Weizmann I had an intimate view of the events which led to the Balfour Declaration, of 2 November 1917, and to the establishment of the Zionist Commission, the body of eminent Jews, headed by Weizmann, which, with myself as secretary to it, spent several months in Palestine in 1918, to survey the conditions in which the Jewish national home, envisaged by the Balfour Declaration, would be set up when the war had ended. I also assisted Dr Weizmann at the Peace Conference of 1919, at which the Zionist Organisation asked for a Jewish National Home, and protection from Britain as Mandatory Power. I would like to relate some of the experiences I had as a result of performing these duties. To convey them as intelligibly as possible, I should sketch briefly the background of the Zionist Movement as it was at the time when Weizmann and myself became friends.

The term, Zionism, was coined in 1893 by Nathan Birnbaum, a Viennese Jew born in 1864 who studied law but became a journalist, to describe the movement to secure the Jewish return to the land of Israel. The longing of the Jews to go back to Israel was historic: it dated from the Babylonian Exile of 586 BC. But until the latter part of the nineteenth century it was a religious and cultural movement rather than a political one. From 1882 on, however, the year of the wave of Russian pogroms, men like Birnbaum thought and wrote in terms of Jewish nationalism, and sought support for the idea of the physical transfer of masses of Jews from where they were scattered in Eastern and South Eastern Europe to a Jewish homeland in Palestine.

The founder of Zionism in this sense was Theodore Herzl (1860-1904), a Hungarian Jew, born in Budapest, who studied in Vienna, and then became a journalist, playwright, and Paris correspondent for the Vienna *Neue Freie Presse*. Herzl was very much the Western European intellectual Jew, not a Central European *folks-mensch* Jew like Weizmann.

He was born and bred in a bourgeois ambience like that of any well-to-do Western European gentleman. His family were perfectly assimilated. The crossroads in his life was the trial of Dreyfus in 1894. Until then, even after the Russian pogroms, Herzl had taken assimilation for granted. The flood of anti-Semitism released by the Dreyfus case washed all of that away. The following year he wrote *The Jewish State*, published in 1896, in which he now argued that it was impracticable to assimilate the Jews. To adopt this as a universal policy was in fact to leave masses of them to deteriorate and suffer: the solution must be the founding of a Jewish State by international agreement. Palestine was the obvious choice. He urged wealthy Jews to come to an arrangement with Turkey, the suzerain of Palestine, and purchase a charter which would provide for the establishment of an independent Jewish Palestine. He failed to win support from the rich Jews of Western Europe so he turned to the masses of the Jewish poor in Eastern Europe. In 1897, at Basle, he convened the First Zionist Congress. This founded the World Zionist Organisation, of which Herzl served as President until his early death in 1904, and adopted as the platform of World Zionism what came to be known as the Basle Program. It began: 'The aim of Zionism is to create for the Jewish people a home in Palestine secured by public law'. For diplomatic reasons the expression 'Jewish State' was left out. Anybody could join the Zionist Organisation who subscribed to the Basle Program and paid a small annual levy called a *shekel*, the name of the silver unit of weight, later a standard coin which became current in the time of the Maccabees in the second century BC.

An important feature of the first Zionist Congress, with considerable implications for the future, was a difference of opinion about what the basic strategy of achieving a Jewish State should be. Some thought nothing was possible until an international diplomatic agreement to found a homeland was signed by all the interested powers. Others thought that a homeland could, indeed should, gradually evolve from the settlements of individual and small groups of Jews, colonising Palestine on their own or Zionist funds. The first approach was called 'Political' or 'Diplomatic' Zionism, the second 'Organic' or 'Practical' Zionism. They were not mutually exclusive, of course; it was a question of emphasis. Herzl favoured 'political' Zionism. This did not mean that he discouraged individual Jews or groups of Jews from going to settle in Palestine. On the contrary, in 1899, the Jewish Colonial Trust was founded to support people who wished to do so, and in 1901 Herzl created the Jewish National Fund for the purchase of land in Palestine. But his guiding light was the idea of a refuge, guaranteed by international agreement, and this led him to concentrate his activities on lobbying the governments of the great powers. Herzl was so much more concerned with the idea of a Jewish refuge than with the reconstruction of Jewish nationalism that he was prepared to accept some territory other than Palestine as the site of the new Jewish home. Indeed, when Great Britain agreed to a Jewish settlement in Uganda, as suggested by Joseph Chamberlain in 1903, Herzl would have supported it. There was a tremendous and almost fatal split in the Zionist movement over the Uganda proposal, and the following year Herzl, having, after soul-searching and debate, felt compelled to reaffirm his exclusive support for Palestine as the site of the homeland, died worn out and disconsolate at the age of forty-four.

The Uganda project was formally rejected at the seventh Zionist Congress, which took place at Basle in 1905. Prominent in the opposition to it was a group of young men, mainly university students and lecturers, which called itself 'The Democratic Faction'. Prominent among them was a young lecturer in Organic Chemistry, son of a part-time timber merchant from Motol, Motelle as the Yiddish called it, near Pinsk, chief town of the Pripet Marshes in White Russia. Chaim Weizmann had gone to study in Germany, thence to Switzerland, and was now in Britain, teaching at Manchester University. Weizmann had become a critic of Herzl not only because of his opposition to Uganda but because he believed in 'practical' or 'organic' Zionism as opposed to 'diplomatic' or 'political' Zionism as advocated by Herzl. Weizmann believed there should be as much emphasis as possible on encouraging and financing the masses of the Jewish people to move physically to Palestine, and cultivate and colonise the land. The diplomatic activity which would one day establish the new state formally and legally should *not* be regarded as a preliminary condition: the first thing was to get the Jewish people there, on the ground, reclaiming the desert, replanting the crops, and building the houses.

The other important aspect of Weizmann's opposition to the establishment approach at this time was his refusal to regard Palestine as a refuge from anti-Semitism. This, he thought, was a wrong and dangerous conception, and he was very critical of those who entertained it. The motive for the return to the Jewish homeland was to be free to live again in the full florescence of the Jewish way of life – religious, cultural and political. The object of the return to Palestine was to translate into practical, social and political everyday life the historic longing to get back to its roots and grow a new life from them, a longing which had been part of Jewish consciousness in the Diaspora for 2,600 years.

In giving prior emphasis to 'practical' or 'organic' Zionism Weizmann did not turn his back on 'political' or 'diplomatic' Zionism. On the contrary, provided the proper emphasis was laid, he advocated both. To establish his belief in this dual approach he propounded what he called 'synthetic' Zionism at the Basle Congress of 1907. As it turned out, it was in fact by an act of the 'political' or 'diplomatic' Zionism preached by Herzl that the State of Israel was brought into being. Here it is worth noting what a clean break the opposition at Basle made with those Jews who still believed it was possible, even desirable, to assimilate into Western Europe yet remain a Jew. Weizmann expected a Zionist Jew, far from assimilating into Western European society, to wrench himself out from it and move to Palestine. This alone would have created a tension between his supporters and the largely middle and upper class Jews of Western Europe, the majority of whom were assimilated and believed it was the right and proper status. To this, however, was added another potential incompatibility: Weizmann believed that Zionism should be a mass democratic movement whose dynamism would be the Jewish proletariat of Eastern Europe. The assimilated middle and upper class Jews of London, Paris, Berlin, Rome and Moscow looked on this askance.

In 1904, Weizmann decided to come to England after the death of Herzl, when the European Zionist Movement was still foaming with controversy precipitated by the great debate about Uganda. He was thirty. Why he came to England is not altogether clear. He had paid a first visit the year before, according to his wife Vera's recollections, 'to rally British Zionists against Uganda and possibly to make some tentative arrangements for his residence in England'. Certainly he had a vivid prophetic revelation about the role Britain would play in the return of the Jews to the Promised Land. In his second letter to Vera from London he wrote: 'If help ever comes to us, it will come from England . . .' This was an extension of feelings he had expressed as an eleven-year-old schoolboy to his Hebrew teacher in Motol. Like some twentieth-century infant Samuel, he had spoken with a strange tongue about the present, past and future:

Let us carry our banner to Zion and return to the original mother upon whose knees we were reared. For why should we expect mercy from the Kings of Europe, except that they should, in pity, give us a resting place? In vain! All have decided that the Jew is doomed to death; but England nevertheless, will have mercy on us. . . .

But it was, according to Vera, in the following year that he made the great decision to settle in Britain. Was it to get away from the conflicts of Zionism in Europe? Was it because he felt that his love for Vera was domesticating him, distracting him, drawing him away from the road he had to travel? 'You can imagine how sad I am to be so far away from you. There are so many obstacles which still separate us from a life together . . . ,' he wrote *after* he had come to settle in England in 1904. Certainly he had to earn a living, and his academic progress in Geneva up to this time had not been dramatic. England, of course, was very attractive to all European Jews. He has said himself in his autobiography that he wanted to get away from the conflicts and tensions within the Zionist higher command. He was an impatient young man: he may have thought he was not being recognised sufficiently as a potential leader in European Zionist circles. He may have thought that with Herzl on the way down from the commanding heights of Zionism, Weizmann should have been regarded as his successor, as he certainly was not. England may, therefore, have been a retreat in which he might recharge his batteries; or a tent for Achilles to sulk in.

In later years he spoke himself as though he had intimations at this time that the Zionists' way to Jerusalem was via London; but it is doubtful if this was really strategically clear to him already. The role which British interests were to play in the creation of the State of Israel was the product of forces hardly in the making in 1904, let alone perceived and comprehended. We have his own *pronunciamento* on the subject: 'My flight to England in 1904 was a deliberate and desperate step. It was not, to be sure, real flight; it was in reality a case of *reculer pour mieux sauter.** I was in danger of being eaten up by Zionism. We had reached, it seemed to me, a dead point in the movement.' However, there was always the almost mystical orientation towards England described in the autobiography. As a little boy he used to listen to his

---

* To go back so as to be able to jump forward more easily.

grandfather tell of the works of great rabbis and Jewish leaders. He heard often of the visit to Russia of the almost legendary philanthropist Sir Moses Montefiore, the first Jew in Britain to be knighted, symbol of the freedom, wealth and honour which a Jew could have in Britain then as nowhere in the world. Montefiore made several visits to various parts of Europe to try and improve the lot of his fellow Jews. Weizmann's grandfather loved to describe how when Sir Moses came to Vilna the Jews came out to welcome him, unharnessed his horses, and dragged his carriage through the streets. Montefiore and England were fused in Weizmann's mind as an ideal culmination of man and milieu when he was still a child.

His first two years in Britain were distinctly wretched. He lodged for a few weeks with a Zionist tailor in the East End of London, inquired after jobs, found himself 'isolated, socially, intellectually and morally', and after several weeks of Zionist politics in London resolved to get out of the Metropolis, and play what seemed his only remaining card – an introduction to Professor William Henry Perkin of Manchester University. Perkin had studied at Munich, spoke excellent German, and knew some of Weizmann's former tutors. Weizmann set off for Manchester. He found the climate cold and depressing. His first lodgings happened to be with Jews who had assimilated the British way of life; they found Central European Zionists like him eccentric, disturbing. Soon, he went to live with the only Manchester person he knew, Joseph Massel, printer by trade, Hebrew poet by avocation, Zionist by faith, who was extremely generous to him. His beginnings with Perkin were not spectacular. He had gone to Manchester and Perkin because Manchester was a big centre of the chemical industry. The chemical faculty of its university had close links with local industry and a high reputation. Perkin's father had been the founder of the coal-tar dye industry. Perkin welcomed Weizmann, but offered him employment on the basis of research work which he would have partially to finance himself: he would, for instance, have to rent his own laboratory, a dingy derelict basement room in which, after scrubbing the tables and cleaning the taps, he had to erect apparatus which he paid for himself. This would have been beyond his resources if he had not been able to bring with him an income of about two pounds ten shillings a week, derived from a discovery which he had sold to a Baku oil man called Shrirow. He soon began to earn teaching fees; but he was helping to support two relatives in Europe and saving money for his wife-to-be's passage.

A miserable two years. He felt better when Vera arrived, but financially she added to his burdens until she qualified a few years later to practise her profession – she was a doctor – in Britain. He worked long into the night, after a long day's work in the laboratory was over, marking Oxford and Cambridge University School Certificate papers at half-a-crown a time, often with Benjy, his first baby, sleeping on his lap.

In these first few years he seemed to have little affinity with the Zionists in Manchester, who like the majority of Zionists in England were still thinking that 'Zion' would be best sited in Uganda. In England, at the time, he recorded, 'Only a few still adhered to those tenets which were the soul of the Movement. Zionism as such was in a state of stagnation, and Zionist activity was limited to the usual clichés and clap-trap performances of Jewish societies in English provincial towns. I felt no incentive to associate myself with this sort of thing.'

In August 1906 he went over to Europe and married Vera at Zoppot, near Danzig. They spent a couple of days at Zoppot, a seaside resort, and then went to Cologne for meetings of the Actions Committee. Their honeymoon was a few days third-class on a steamer up the Rhine. Then they headed for Manchester. At Manchester some of Chaim's new friends met them. They had spent their last penny on sandwiches to eat on the train, and had to borrow half-a-crown from my wife's brother-in-law, Harry Sacher, to get to their lodgings in Rusholme.

Vera's company changed his life. She was in many respects quite different from him. Though Weizmann came from a middle-class family, he was essentially from the people, and his background was Yiddish. Motol was a small Jewish half-town half-village with unpaved streets, a sea of mud in winter. It was in one of the most forsaken corners of the Pale of Settlement. As a boy he went to the *cheder*, the schoolroom where Hebrew is taught, in his case a squalid one-room wooden house, where the rabbi lived with his family, the washing hanging across the ceiling and the rabbi's babies playing around on the floor. He was in fact, a product of the *shtetl*.

Shtetl, a Yiddish word from the German *stadt*, meaning 'a little town', in the vocabulary of the Jews denotes not merely a place but a culture shared by millions of European Jews in the nineteenth century. It was the culture of the poor, faithful, fundamentalist folk, oppressed, defensive, inward-looking, ever fearful of the pogrom, dreaming of a return to their Holy Land which made the hardships of the world around them easier to bear. It was a culture of cobblers, tailors, labourers, shopkeepers, and pedlars. They wrote in Hebrew or Yiddish, the *shtetl* was the transmitter of the Ashkenazic German-Jewish common man culture as opposed to the more sophisticated upper-class cosmopolitan Spain-based culture of the Sephardic Jews of Western Europe and the Middle East.

Vera Weizmann's background was quite different. She came from an assimilated family and had been brought up in an assimilationist ambience. Her father, like millions of other Jews, when still a lad was conscripted into the Russian Army. Unlike most of them he adapted to it, served twenty-five years, fought in the Crimean War, rose to be a general and when he left the army used his special privileges to reside outside the Pale of Settlement and set himself up as a wholesale clothes merchant at Rostov-on-Don. Rostov-on-Don is in Cossack country – it has a character akin in some respects to the hard-riding flamboyant self-indulgent old South of the United States. Vera's home there was built in a neo-colonial style which later she compared to houses she saw in America. There were not many Jews in Rostov-on-Don. They numbered about one in ten, and the majority of them belonged to a liberal-minded Jewish intelligentsia which was not strictly orthodox. Vera was taught Hebrew, but her education came not from the *shtetl* but a fashionable French kindergarten, and when she was eighteen and decided she would like to study medicine she had the money to go to the place of her choice, Geneva. She took with her a bourgeois background, beauty, gaiety and a taste for the good life. She records at the time a 'lack of awareness of "the Jewish problem",' and, on the contrary, 'an innate feeling of being Russian'. It was at Geneva that she met Chaim. She was a student of nineteen, he a *Privat-Dozent* (an unpaid assistant lecturer) of twenty-six. They had in common strong magnetic passionate personalities. Their ideas were frequently in conflict: after all, Weizmann was a bitter critic of the Czars; Vera's father had fought for them and worn their honours. She charmed some of the self-devouring intensity out of his personality, and he educated her in the hopes and burdens of Zionism. Now, here they were living in two rooms in Manchester, on an income of 350 pounds a year, a hundred of which was currently going to Chaim's two sisters studying medicine in Zurich.

The liquidation of the Russian Revolution in 1906 led to bloody Jewish pogroms which in Manchester, as elsewhere in the country, begot a new spirit in Zionist circles. As he put it himself, 'The Manchester Zionist Society abandoned their "syllabus", as they called it (it was a hodge-podge of random speakers) in favour of a more serious programme of lectures in Zionism and Zionist aspirations'. Younger people joined. Through his printer friend Joseph Massel he got to know Charles Dreyfus, a director of the Clayton Aniline Works, and chairman of the Manchester Zionist Society.

The turning point for him in this early period in Britain was the arrival in Britain of Asher Ginsberg, famous in Zionist and modern Jewish literature for his essays published under his pseudonym of Ahad Ha-am, Hebrew for 'one of the people', one of the finest and bravest creative minds that ever affirmed without compromise that Zionism was a spirit, and that its only ultimate power was the will for redemption under God. The feeling of the nearness of his soul-mate – I think Ahad Ha-am was one of a handful of men whom Weizmann revered – fortified Weizmann in an hour of need.

It was at this time that Weizmann had his first meeting with Balfour, an encounter which was to bear great fruit in the future. In the General Election of 1906 Balfour was fighting the Clayton division of North Manchester. Charles Dreyfus, then chairman of the Conservative Party in Manchester, introduced Weizmann to him in a meeting at the Queen's Hotel, Dreyfus hoping that Balfour might convert Weizmann to the Uganda project. Charlie Dreyfus was to be disappointed. The boot was almost immediately put upon the other foot. While Balfour was in the middle of putting the Uganda argument Weizmann broke in:

'Mr Balfour, supposing I were to offer you Paris instead of London, would you take it?'

He sat up, looked at me, and answered: 'But Dr Weizmann, we have London.'

'That is true,' I said. 'But we had Jerusalem when London was a marsh.'

He leaned back, continued to stare at me, and said two things which I remember vividly. The first was: 'Are there many Jews who think like you?'

I answered: 'I believe I speak the mind of millions of Jews whom you will never see and who cannot speak for themselves, but with whom I could pave the streets of the country I come from.'

To this he said: 'If that is so, you will one day be a force.' Shortly before I withdrew, Balfour said: 'It is curious. The Jews I meet are quite different.'

I answered: 'Mr Balfour, you meet the wrong kind of Jews.'*

The conversation with Balfour taught Weizmann two lessons. First,

* *Trial and Error* by Chaim Weizmann, Hamish Hamilton, 1949.

5 Rebecca Sieff in the early days of her marriage.

6 An informal photograph in Palestine, early 1930s: (*from left to right*) Lord Sieff, Viscount Samuel, Viscountess Samuel, Lady Marks, Lord Marks and Lady Sieff.

7 Wedding-day picture of Israel and Rebecca Sieff; to the left of the bridegroom sit his m

...er and Mrs Marks. Simon Marks, who was best man, stands behind, to the right of the bride.

8 A recent picture of Lord Sieff at his country home.

that in spite of years of Zionist propaganda in England, even a perceptive highly informed and open-minded leading British Statesman like Balfour had only a hazy notion of what Zionism was about. Second, that if authentic Zionism could be clearly and cogently presented to men like Balfour, their sympathies, perhaps their active support, could be enlisted.

Weizmann threw himself again wholeheartedly into the Zionist Movement. He ceased to inveigh privately about the provincials, and went out lecturing on Zionism in Leeds, Halifax, Liverpool, Bradford, Glasgow and Edinburgh. He found, to his profound gratification, that a great many among his audiences were, as he modestly but enthusiastically put it, Jews like himself – poor but visionary immigrants from the communities he had known in Central and Eastern Europe, men and women who physically in England were spiritually in transit to the Promised Land. He deployed his discovery in his spectacular reappearance on the stage of European Zionism at the eighth Zionist Congress held at The Hague in the Summer of 1907. It was here he delivered his most eloquent, influential and seminal plea for the fusion of the 'political' with the 'practical' school of Zionism and expounded 'synthetic' Zionism. The same year, financed by a well-to-do Viennese industrialist called Kremenetzky, who was Chairman of the Jewish National Fund at the time, he made his first visit to Palestine. Its main effect was to confirm his view that 'practical' Zionism, colonisation, was basically the right approach. He came back to Manchester revivified, resolved to begin a new drive for funds for Jewish immigrants, but more than ever focusing on the importance of the spiritual life of Zion, determined above all to press for the establishment of a Hebrew University in Palestine, which would be the intellectual and moral power-house, and the living symbol, of the new Jewish homeland.

From this time on Weizmann was a happier man. There came changes in the leadership of the Zionist Congress which elevated men whose views on Zionism were much more in line with his own. But when I met him he was still unsettled. Money was still not plentiful; now, Vera's parents had fallen on difficult days. He continued to subsidise his relatives in Europe: he spent money freely on his Zionist activities. I often gave lunch to him, and to Vera – the municipal clinic she worked in was close to our store in Oldham Street and there was a restaurant nearby – not only for their company but because I thought it helped them out. I owned a car and employed a chauffeur; I insisted that Chaim should telephone and ask for it when he wanted to make journeys. He was not easy to help personally. He was proud. His pride was another source of discontent at this time. He felt he had been passed over academically at Manchester: he was still a lecturer when he felt that earlier on he should have been appointed to a vacant chair. A few months before I met him he had been on the point of leaving Manchester to take a job back in Berlin: Professor Perkin had retired; Chaim hoped and believed he would succeed to the chair. Instead it went to Perkin's brother-in-law. At the same time Chaim was offered a job in the Zionist bureaucracy at Berlin. He decided to take it. Vera, who could be stubborn, put her foot down. She had completed her medical examinations in Manchester and was not prepared to qualify again at Berlin. She told him so. Then she played her trump: 'You have already said that the road to Palestine is through London. Our road to Palestine will never go through Berlin.' Chaim did not speak to her for three weeks; but he stayed in Manchester: and, as a result, the world changed.

There was something else, I think, which stabilised Chaim in the six months' period of stress and strain before the first world war. In the latter part of 1913 the Zionist Congress officially committed itself to the idea of founding a Hebrew University in Palestine and Baron Edmond de Rothschild, the famous French philanthropist, agreed to help finance it. It is an interesting story, which tells much about Weizmann and the kind of man he was. He laboured patiently to obtain an introduction to the Baron, whose time was sought by every needy do-gooder in the West. The Baron eventually agreed to receive him at his house in Paris. He put the case for the foundation of the University to de Rothschild and begged him to put up enough money to finance it. A splendid site was available on Mount Scopus, just outside Jerusalem, looking over the city to the west and the Dead Sea valley to the east. The Baron said he would put up the money on one condition: that the famous biochemist, Professor Paul Ehrlich, noted for his diagnostic methods in haemotology and bacteriology, and famous for the cure for syphilis which had opened a new chapter in the history of medicine, could be persuaded to head the committee which would set it up.

Ehrlich, world famous, Nobel prize winner, devoted to his studies, was quite detached from Jewish affairs. Socially and professionally he was inaccessible. Weizmann cast about him for introductions. Eventually Ehrlich agreed to see him at his desk in the Speyer Institute in

Frankfurt. Weizmann talking passionately and cogently, Ehrlich, accustomed more to being listened to than listening, hearing him through in silence. Finally Ehrlich was persuaded. As he showed Weizmann out, he glanced at his watch and saw how long the meeting had lasted. Further down the corridor his waiting room was filled with important personages. Ehrlich could not resist pointing out to Weizmann that world statesmen queued up to get ten minutes of his time and Weizmann had occupied his attention for an hour. Weizmann replied, with his gift for getting to the hub of the matter with a candid, concise, sometimes epigrammatic phrase: 'Yes, Professor; but there's a difference between me and your other visitors; they come to receive an injection from you, and I came here to give you one.'

I must now resume my own story, and remain with it a little. The outbreak of the 1914-18 war, and the first few weeks that followed it, are forever associated in my mind with a comedy and a tragedy. The comedy was my joining the army. It is difficult for those who did not experience it to understand the gaiety with which the people of Britain almost danced and sang their way into what they were shortly to discover was going to be a slaughter-house for the flower of its manhood. I joined a local Lancashire regiment called the Derby Fusiliers: Lord Derby, though he took his title from another county, was the Lord Lieutenant of Lancashire, and had his seat at Knowsley. It was great fun. We marched, drilled, drank beer, got thoroughly fit and enjoyed ourselves, while our parents fumed at what at that stage of the war must have seemed to them a monstrous waste of time and energy. My father was particularly peevish about my military diversions. By now I had acquired enough experience to be of real use to him in the business, and he had realised that the war was going to make his business much more difficult to run. He put up with the situation for a month or two and then concluded he had had enough.

He was being asked to undertake extensive commitments in the provision of waste for the production of gun cotton, and felt he simply could not do the leg-work required to locate supplies himself, and superintend the processing as well. He applied for my discharge, and promptly got it. It was now my turn to be somewhat peevish, but at this stage the mud and blood of Flanders were still to come, so I returned to business fairly philosophically. Since, as a result of being a civilian, I was later able to play a more interesting part in the events of 1914-18 than I could ever have played in uniform, I have never regretted my father's initiative.

The tragic aspect of those early wartime days concerns my younger brother, William. Born in 1896, and seven years younger than myself, William was eighteen years old when the war broke out. He was a delightful lad, handsome, intelligent, sensitive and gay. He had just left the sixth form at Manchester Grammar School, and was intended for the University; but when the war broke out, without saying anything to his mother and father, who, he knew, would have done all they could to stop him, he joined up at the recruiting table and did not come home to Bury New Road until he had signed his name and taken the King's shilling. Before his parents could do anything about it he was gone again. Within a few days we had a letter: he was apparently at camp, Aldershot, in training, and enjoying it. There were a few more letters in the next couple of weeks; then silence. We became worried. We wrote. Days went by: weeks. Still no reply. I decided that I would go down to the camp and see how he was getting on. When I got there I had to make a number of enquiries because the information he had given us did not suffice for me to be able to locate him easily. He was now in billets somewhere in the vicinity; I found out where they were, and went to see the officer commanding. After some forceful enquiries, which took some hours, I found that my brother was being detained – I think that was the word used – in solitary confinement in an improvised cell, which was a windowless, airless cellar beneath the stairs of one of the houses in which the company was billeted. He had been lying there for ten days.

He was already ill. He was released, given treatment, made a slight recovery, but shortly afterwards his health broke down completely and irretrievably. He is still alive, in a nursing home in Zurich. He still recognises me, but for more than half a century he has never spoken a word. We were informed that he had misbehaved himself by saying something rude to his sergeant, though we never discovered what it was that he was alleged to have said. It was a scandalous case: the Minister of War finally intervened, wrote letters of regret, and offered compensation to my father. It nearly killed my mother, but eventually she got over it, though her last words on her deathbed were to implore me to look after William. I do not know what happened to the sergeant: we never even bothered to write down his name. I remember the party William had given the night he joined the army. The boy was in the seventh heaven because he was going out to fight for the country that had made his parents welcome and given them a new lease of life.

The outbreak of war in 1914 was the turning point in Zionism and in Weizmann's own life. It led to the combination of two factors which ultimately determined the whole future of Zionism and its expression in the State of Israel. The first was that European Zionism disintegrated, the German Zionists and the Russian Zionists being on opposite sides. The British Zionists, of whom Weizmann was now the acknowledged though not formal leader, were left in a dominating position. Secondly, the collision of British interests with those of her wartime enemy, Turkey, suzerain of Palestine, gave the British Government a life and death interest in the new power structure of that part of the Middle East which dominated its oil supplies and its communications with India via the Suez Canal. If Britain knocked Turkey out of Palestine, the British Government would have the power to set up an independent Jewish homeland there. It was Weizmann's historic role to mesh these factors through the personal standing he acquired with members of the British wartime Government, and to generate the drive which led to the Balfour Declaration and the establishment of the State of Israel. From the very outbreak of hostilities he was convinced of two things: first, that Britain would win the war and dominate the peace settlement; and that out of that settlement would emerge the opportunity for creating a Jewish State in Palestine.

Using Manchester as his base and Manchester Jews as his henchmen he sallied out and made the only Zionism that really counted in the early days of the war an all-British Zionism committed to British interests and the foundation of a Jewish State.

Two months after he returned to Manchester he had his first personal meeting with C. P. Scott, the editor of the then *Manchester Guardian*. The meeting was accidental: Vera Weizmann did a lot of work in a clinic called 'Schools for Mothers', taken up later by the municipality, who appointed her its medical officer. The chairman of the clinic, a Mrs Eckhard, gave a party to which both Scott and Weizmann were invited. They were introduced. Scott, whose interest in foreign affairs was limitless, began to talk to Weizmann about the Polish question. Weizmann, in characteristic style, dismissed the subject brusquely. 'Are you a Pole?' asked Scott. Weizmann replied: 'I'm not a Pole and

I know nothing about Poland, I'm a Jew, and if you want to talk to me about that, Mr Scott, I'm at your disposal.'

Scott and he began to talk about Zionism, which is to say that Weizmann poured his aspirations eloquently into Scott's wide open ears. Scott was most impressed. He was a personal friend of Lloyd George, and spoke to him about Weizmann. As a result Lloyd George arranged for Weizmann to meet Herbert Samuel in London the following month, December 1914. Until this moment Weizmann had assumed that Samuel, presumably typical of other leading families of Jews in British politics was the conventional kind of assimilationist, and therefore opposed to Zionism. When Samuel told him that he was at that moment preparing a memorandum on the foundation of a Jewish State in Palestine, Weizmann could hardly believe his ears. Lloyd George also advised a meeting between Weizmann and Balfour. Weizmann assumed that Balfour would have forgotten their previous meeting in 1906, and, wondering how best to effect reintroduction, he wrote to his colleague in Manchester, Professor Samuel Alexander, knowing that the two men were acquainted with each other through their philosophical pursuits. He asked Alexander if he would ask Balfour to let Weizmann call on him. Balfour sent back a postcard saying: 'Dear Sam: Weizmann needs no introduction, I still remember our conversation in 1906.' I was shown this postcard personally by Weizmann in rather interesting circumstances. One day, as we were walking home from a Zionist meeting he suddenly said to me: 'Israel, can you lend me five pounds?' Since he was not a borrower by nature, and if he were going to alter his habits, five pounds seemed a strangely small sum to alter them for, I was extremely curious. Since we were by then on intimate terms, also I thought he might be going to do something interesting with the money, and I did not want to be done out of doing it with him. So I said: 'Certainly. But what do you want it for?' A rare smile of self-satisfaction illuminated his countenance as he replied: 'Mr Balfour is willing to talk to me in London, and I would like to borrow the fare.' I said, 'I won't lend you five pounds. I will take you to London myself.' And we went together.

We spent the night at the Waldorf Hotel, as we were to do many times in the next year or so, and the next day I walked round with him to Balfour's house in Carlton Gardens. The meeting lasted several hours. In the course of it Weizmann felt that though Balfour was, in general, keen on the idea of a Jewish National Home, he believed that the funds for its foundation would have to come from the rich Jews of Europe, mainly in Germany and France. About these Balfour had many doubts and reservations. Weizmann was delighted that this consideration had been brought out into the open and that he could wholeheartedly range himself on Balfour's side. He pointed out that *his* concepts of the Jewish Home rested not on a handful of rich Jews but on the Jewish masses. He saw Balfour growing more and more interested. This important discussion in the history of Zionism ended with Balfour saying, 'Mind you come again to see me . . . it is not a dream. It is a great cause, and I understand it.'

Scott's next step was to arrange a meeting between Weizmann and Lloyd George for 15 January 1915. There was a second meeting a few months later. Lloyd George took a great fancy to Weizmann. It was partly the instinctive appreciation of one great man for another, partly the Welshman's love and understanding of the Old Testament story fortified by an imperialistic sense of what the foundation of a Jewish State on the Suez canal could do for British interests in that area. He warned Weizmann that there would be opposition to his schemes inside the Cabinet, notably from another Jew, Edwin Montague, later Secretary of State for India, who, unlike Samuel, did represent the rich assimilationist Jews who were out of sympathy with Zionist aims and aspirations, indeed regarded them as disturbing if not dangerous. How, they queried, could a Jew be loyal both to Britain and to the Jewish Homeland? There was, they said, no place for dual nationality.

Weizmann continued to make contacts with British politicians for the next two years, his main purpose being to penetrate the mind of Balfour. The next step which is easy to describe was taken towards the end of 1915, when he received a visit from Dr Rintoul, the chief research chemist of Nobel's, the big explosive manufacturers. At the beginning of the war, Weizmann, along with every other industrial scientist, had been invited by the War Office to report any discovery that might be of military importance. He had promptly offered the War Office details of his fermentation process. He heard nothing at that time, but in the spring of 1915 Lloyd George was organising the new Ministry of Munitions, and C. P. Scott mentioned Weizmann's fermentation process to him. As a result Dr Rintoul was now asking him if he would put the process at Nobel's disposal. Through Nobel's interest the process was brought to the attention of the Admiralty. In the summer of 1915 he was summoned by the First Lord of the Admiralty, a Mr Winston

Churchill, who greeted him almost immediately with: 'Well, Dr Weizmann, we need thirty thousand tons of acetone. Can you make it?' Winston Churchill explained that there was a serious shortage of acetone which was the solvent in making cordite for high explosives. Weizmann consequently, as he put it, 'took upon myself a task which was to tax all my energies for the next two years, and which was to have consequences which I did not then foresee. . . .'

'The centre of gravity of my life shifted once again towards my Zionist interests, and from this point on the tide of events moved rapidly towards one of the climactic points in the history of the Movement and, I believe, in the history of the Jewish People – the issue of the Balfour Declaration.' This was his great opportunity to penetrate the minds of men in the War Cabinet. He seized it. For several months he travelled up and down from London, but towards the end of the year he took a flat at 3 Justice Walk, Chelsea, which he shared for a time with Vladimir Jabotinsky, a fascinating Russian Jew who later formed the Jewish Legion to fight in Palestine and become one of the most colourful, if erratic, of the early leaders of Zionism in Palestine. Early in 1916 Weizmann moved his family to London, and set up house first in Campden Hill, and later at 57 Addison Crescent.

It was the dramatic series of events in late 1916 that gave Weizmann his chance to press his advantageous position home. The situation of Britain was grim. The German submarine blockade had reduced food supplies to a dangerously low level; manpower was fully stretched: her armies were bogged down in France. Would America come into the war? Could some kind of a 'second front' be opened in the Middle East – to take the pressure off the Western Front? Lloyd George very much favoured this. On 7 December the Prime Minister, Asquith, was ousted and Lloyd George succeeded him, Balfour becoming Foreign Secretary. The two chief men in the new Government, therefore, were friends of Weizmann, openly sympathetic to Zionist aspirations, and saw them in relation to Britain's strategic needs in the Middle East. Highly important at a time when the fortunes of the Allies were at their nadir, and the outcome of the war was in great doubt, both men also appreciated the influence which British Zionists working with American Zionists might exert to bring the United States into the war. This was Weizmann's great tactical chance: he allied himself wholeheartedly with 'The New Imperialists' and exploited the general situation. He nailed his colours to the British mast, staked all on a British victory, and strove to integrate the idea of a Jewish state in Palestine into British war aims.

There were two main obstacles in the way of Weizmann's hopes. First, as I mentioned earlier, there were influential British Jews, led in the Cabinet by Edwin Montague, who were opposed to Zionism. Secondly, the foundation of a Jewish State was in conflict with another line of British Foreign Policy which was currently being pursued. On behalf of the Foreign Office, Sir Mark Sykes, one of the two Assistant Secretaries to the War Cabinet (Leopold Amery was the other) had been conducting secret negotiations with our main ally, the French. The object of the negotiations was to mobilise the Arabs against their Turkish overlords, liberate the Middle Eastern peoples from the Turkish yoke and to replace the Ottoman Dominion with regimes favourable to French and British interests in that area. The pillar on which the new power structure in the Middle East was to rest was an Anglo-French condominium over Palestine. There was to be provision for a Jewish homeland within it. These objectives were already enshrined in a secret pact between Britain and France, the famous Sykes-Picot Agreement. The Agreement was inconsistent with the policy Weizmann was pursuing for the establishment of an independent Jewish State in Palestine, though Sykes favoured a Home for Jews in Palestine. C. P. Scott discovered the existence of this secret agreement and told us all about it. We were extremely disturbed.

If I ever played a role in Zionist affairs outside that of Weizmann's servant it was now. Simon Marks, Harry Sacher and myself were strongly opposed to anything but a Jewish Homeland under the sole aegis of the British Government. For us a purely British Palestine was the right and only solution. A joint administration of Palestine was totally unacceptable. Our feelings on the subject were formed and fortified by the outstanding journalist of his generation, Herbert Sidebotham. Sidebotham had been the senior leader writer on the *Guardian* for many years. He was a brilliant publicist and an incomparable strategic thinker. He was not a Jew; his whole interest in Zionism was a by-product, or extension, of his conception of British Imperial interests, and perhaps for that reason above all others the power and persuasiveness of his arguments were of the greatest possible support to the Zionist cause.

We were extremely disturbed by the news of the existence of the secret pact and the four of us began to get alarmed because we felt that

Weizmann was too ready to trust Mark Sykes and the Foreign Office. Something, we felt, should be done, before we were saddled with a categorical British commitment to an Anglo-French condominium over Palestine. We decided to conduct a public campaign to prevent this happening. When Weizmann had moved to London in 1916 Simon, Harry Sacher and I had opened an office in London, the general object being to have a bureau from which Weizmann could operate, an office for research, correspondence and official meetings with the Foreign Office men. It consisted of three rooms, at 170 Piccadilly, rented from my father's accountant at a rent of £150 a year. We also decided to establish a monthly journal called *Palestine*. The object was to publicise the Zionist cause, and to try and impress everybody with the importance and resources of British Zionism. We were a lobby. We called ourselves the British Palestine Committee, and the office, the Palestine Bureau. Simon and I put up the money, Harry Sacher edited the journal, and Herbert Sidebotham wrote most of it with occasional pieces from Harry and myself.

The first number of *Palestine* appeared on 26 January 1917. (See illustration on facing page.) It was quite clear to the reader where *Palestine* stood.

We were particularly pleased with the quotation from the *Spectator*.

The first issue of *Palestine* was a broadside against any plans for a condominium, or the partition of Palestine, and a counter-blast of proposals for the future boundaries of the Jewish State. We soon found we had at least one avid reader. Sykes was most upset. He told Weizmann that if *Palestine* pursued that line in public it would make it impossible for him to work constructively with the French. If, he claimed, the French came to think that Britain was manoeuvring to control Palestine single-handed, the Anglo-French *entente* in the Middle East would collapse, the allied cause would be gravely endangered, and the future of a Jewish national home would consequently be back in the melting-pot. He persuaded Weizmann to write to me, and ask me to promise that *Palestine* would keep its mouth shut on the subject. Sykes represented himself as a great friend of us Zionists and his arrangements with the French to be in the Zionists' best interests.

Sykes *was* a great friend to us Zionists as it turned out, but though I liked him personally, I did not at this time trust him diplomatically. Encouraged by Sidebotham, I persuaded my colleagues on the Palestine Committee to ignore Weizmann's plea that we should pull our punches.

PALESTINE.

THE ORGAN OF THE BRITISH PALESTINE COMMITTEE.

VOL. I., No. 1. PRICE, TWO PENCE. JANUARY 26TH, 1917.

THE BRITISH PALESTINE COMMITTEE SEEKS TO RESET THE ANCIENT GLORIES OF THE JEWISH NATION IN THE FREEDOM OF A NEW BRITISH DOMINION IN PALESTINE.

"*If he [Lord Beaconsfield] had freed the Holy Land, and restored the Jews, as he might have done, instead of pottering about with Roumelia and Afghanistan, he would have died Dictator.*"—"THE SPECTATOR."

ENGLAND AND PALESTINE.

THAT Jews should ardently desire to return to the old home of their race in Palestine, there to become a nation once more, has been at all times to Englishmen an ideal readily understood and deserving of respect. It is the more intelligible, and the more worthy of respect, in the middle of a war which has for its chief impulse the vindication of the rights of nationality.

We cannot truly respect and understand an ideal without taking active steps to promote it. Is this ideal of a return of the Jews to Palestine one that this country ought to make its own? Has Jewish nationality the same claim on the affectionate interest of Englishmen as the nationality of the Belgians, the Serbs, and the Poles? The British Palestine Committee, whose organ this publication is, answers "Yes" to both these questions. It is anxious to establish an alliance between Jewish aspirations towards Zion, and English strivings after international justice and righteousness. And, lest it should be thought that Jews are merely adding to the burdens on the war-weary shoulders of Atlas, the Committee indulges grateful thoughts of the return that a Jewish state in Palestine might make to England in the East, sees our common English and Jewish ideals firmly anchored on common interests, and asks that Jewish Zionists

We redoubled our attempts to sabotage the Sykes-Picot agreement. We got to work on a second broadside in *Palestine* and I wrote a letter to Weizmann taking him to task in blunt language for his attitude to the first issue. I told him he was in danger of betraying the true interests of the Zionist Movement. I urged him to make it clear to Sykes forthwith that the 'Palestine Committee' would not lose any opportunity of exposing, attacking and defeating the policy which we had heard he was pursuing. A few days later Weizmann had his first formal meeting with Sykes. At this meeting the English Zionist, Dr Gaster, suggested that France should be invited to act as the Protector of the Zionists in Palestine. Sykes, showing no signs of being influenced by the first issue of *Palestine*, said that this would be acceptable to the British Government; and again he asked Weizmann to persuade *Palestine* to pipe down. We responded by producing the issue of 15 February. I had by then made a study of the geo-political problem of Palestine, and guided in my thinking by Sidebotham, contributed a piece myself outlining an idea of the proper frontiers of the Jewish State and arguing strongly for the incorporation of the Sinai Peninsula in Palestine, both for the sake of the independence of the canal and the greater security of the Jews. (My proposal was made just fifty years before the War of 1967.) This time Sykes was really furious. He wrote a trenchant letter to Weizmann, and Weizmann penned a pungent protest to me. On behalf of the Committee I replied in the strongest possible terms. There should be no compromise with Sykes: 'After all, we do not come to him as beggars but with something to give. Without us Zionists his Palestine problem is going to be a very difficult one and he must be made cognizant of this.' Sykes seemed to be working for the Arabs, 'whose support is of much greater importance to him than that of the Zionists.' I added Sir Mark was, after all, 'carrying on the English tradition of foreign policy', which appeared to be opportunism.

I wrote this last letter with a heavy heart, and, though I felt I had no alternative but to do so, I was not at all happy as to what the outcome would be. It was already clear to me, after seeing a great deal of him for nearly three years, that Dr Weizmann did not take kindly to critics. One of the reasons why Harry, Simon and I had become so close to him was that we were much younger men than his generation of Zionist leaders and did not claim to have his experience and knowledge of Zionist affairs. Now that we young men appeared to be in revolt at a time when he was clearly anticipating a break-through in his efforts, he was obviously chagrined and I frankly wondered how he would react.

There now followed some weeks which occasioned him the greatest difficulty. The British Foreign Office made an important change in policy: Balfour began to manoeuvre to try and get the Americans to involve themselves in a Palestinian condominium. Once he heard of this Weizmann became desperately anxious. The American Zionists, as Weizmann knew well, were at that time prepared to support a separate peace with Turkey which would leave the Turks in authority in Palestine and allow the future of the country to be decided somewhere, sometime, by a putative peace conference. Such a prospect would put paid to Weizmann's aspirations. It was essential to him that the British, and the British only, controlled the destiny of Palestine. It was a curious situation, looking back on it: we were far more insistent on British suzerainty over Palestine than the British were themselves.

Weizmann's spirits began to sink. On the one hand the leading Zionists of his generation, including their American colleagues, were pressing him to go along with Balfour's line of policy and give the responsibility for a Jewish homeland to the Americans: on the other hand we young men, his group of personal adherents, his real strength, were urging him to insist on British responsibility or nothing. He was profoundly depressed. In August I was at Lytham St Annes – I had taken a house there for a family holiday. On the 17th I was handed a letter from Weizmann. It was short, bitter, fatigued, despondent. The Zionists were 'bankrupt'. He could not go on. He was resigning his presidency of the English Zionist Federation, an honorary post which had been created mainly to give him titular as well as actual status. He had come to the end of his tether.

I wrote to him at once. I begged him to change his mind. 'One of the first effects [of him stepping down] will be the resignation of the best elements in Zionism from the Movement', I pointed out. I challenged his assertion that Zionism in England was 'bankrupt'. I added, 'No real test has been made. Give the Zionists a lead.' As soon as I could, I hurried back to Manchester, where he was going to be. His son, Benjamin, had been spending his holidays with our children, and somehow, this made our meeting much easier. He was in a distinctly depressed mood, and lower than I ever saw him before or after. But the crisis passed. He remained our leader.

Less than two months later, on 2 November 1917, the Balfour

Declaration was announced. The story has been told in detail many times, and my friend Leonard Stein has said all there is to say. I will not dwell on it again here. The British Government publicly committed itself to 'The establishment in Palestine of a national home for the Jewish People', and promising that the British Government would 'Use their best endeavours to facilitate the achievement of this object . . .' The Declaration fell far short of what many Zionists had hoped for; Weizmann himself realised to the full every one of its shortcomings. His own description of his reaction to it is characteristic. Sir Mark Sykes brought the document out to him from the Cabinet room, exclaiming, 'Dr Weizmann, it's a boy!' Weizmann wrote in his autobiography: 'Well – I did not like the boy at first. He was not the one I had expected. But I knew this was a great event . . . [though] . . . a new chapter had opened for us, full of new difficulties. . . .'

The story of the acceptance and publication of the Balfour Declaration is, it must never be forgotten, the story of another generation, of an imperialism and an idealism foreign to the present political climate. But it could not be honestly told except in terms of the political realities of that day.

What is important, in the context of the conflicts of today, is to realise that it is not a story of a pro-Jewishness which was thereby anti-Arab. If the story of Britain and the Arab people during that time were told – as it often has been – there is precisely the same blend of imperialism and idealism. Both have the ring of truth belonging to the realities of the First World War.

The Balfour Declaration marked the opening of a British military campaign in Palestine which, four weeks later, led to the Turks being driven out of Judaea. On 11 December, the first day of Hanukkah, the feast which commemorates the victory of Judah the Maccabee over the Syrians in 164 BC and the consequent rededication of the Temple, Allenby entered Jerusalem. Three Jewish battalions of the Jewish Legion went in with him, Jabotinsky and Trumpeldor at their head. Weizmann's gamble had come off: the British had driven the Turks from Palestine: the British were in sole charge.

The following year, General Clayton, political officer to the Military Administration in Palestine, told me that if *Palestine* had not printed its broadsides based on knowledge of the Sykes-Picot Treaty the Balfour Declaration, the Jews' ticket to Palestine, might never have appeared.

In spite of its deficiencies and tragic ambiguities, the Balfour

Declaration was a milestone on the path to the State of Israel. Sir Isaiah Berlin has said of it: 'This cardinal act was universally regarded, though its architects were many, as a personal triumph for Weizma ... He had become clearly the greatest figure in the public life of the Jews since the death of Herzl.'

Whatever else the Balfour Declaration did, it gave Weizmann new strength to resume the uphill struggle. He spread again the wings which had hung down tired and broken ten weeks before in my house in Manchester.

6
The State of Israel is Born

For me, personally, the Balfour Declaration had some momentous consequences. When the Zionist Commission was appointed to go out to Palestine in 1918 to survey the situation and make recommendations as to how the policy implicit in the Declaration should be implemented, Weizmann, now President of the British Zionist Federation, was asked to lead it. I accompanied him as his personal assistant. It was my first visit to Palestine, and the beginning of a period of four years, climaxing in the handing over of Palestine as a mandated territory to Britain at the San Remo Conference of 1920, in which I was an amateur diplomat.

At first we discussed the possibility of Simon going, and of me remaining in London. Simon had gone into the army as a gunner in May 1917, a couple of months after we had won the struggle to make him Chairman of the Company. His first post was at Preston, not far from Manchester; we used to hold Board Meetings at the Bull and Royal Hotel. In July Weizmann moved from Manchester to London, and we set up the Piccadilly office for him: Simon was demobilised – Balfour personally arranged this – in order that he could become the official secretary of the Palestine Committee and run 170 Piccadilly. The translation in his status was dramatic; years after he could always make us laugh by describing the change of expression on the face of his sergeant-major when he read the official letter giving instructions for the immediate demobilisation of Gunner Marks so that he could deal on equal terms with leading generals and statesmen of the day. He hastily made it clear to Simon that the language he had been using to him when instructing him how to clean the lavatories and shine his boots had been a professional not a personal matter and that he had only been doing his duty. Simon shook hands with him and said that duty called us all in different ways.

After discussing the matter we decided that it was I who should go as Weizmann's aide de camp: Simon was not a natural leg-man and did not have the temperament of a personal assistant; and we thought I could get on better with our leader than he could. My father was not pleased about my leaving the business; my mother was apprehensive, because she thought our ship might be torpedoed. But their devotion to the Zionist cause, and their knowledge that I was going anyway, allayed their fears. Becky was rather put out, not so much because I was going to be away for a few months but because she wasn't allowed to go herself. She had developed into an intrepid independent-minded woman, believed in sex-equality, was a devoted Zionist, and saw no reason why she should not accompany me, rightly insisting she could do my job better than I could. It was announced that the Zionist Commission would leave from London on Monday, 8 March 1918.

Soon after the announcement of the Declaration there was a great gathering of Zionists at the London Opera House, Kingsway, to celebrate the occasion. Not all British Jews gave thanks, I might add. Those who had opposed Zionism treated it with reserve or dismay. The Board of Deputies of British Jews, the representative body of British Jewry, dating from 1760, thanked the Government for their 'sympathetic interest in the Jews' but pointedly refrained from endorsing the Declaration. None of the recognised lay leaders of Anglo-Jewry was present. Some of them had already responded to the Declaration by organising the League of British Jews, formed as a standing protest against the idea of British Jews accepting a nationality other than British. The audience that went to give thanks that night – the London Opera House, now known as the Stoll Theatre – came largely from the East End of London, and the largest component was of Russian Jews. Lord Rothschild presided. Balfour was present. Herbert Samuel, long regarded – as Chaim had regarded him – as an assimilationist non-Zionist Jew, made a speech in Hebrew and spoke the holy words, the traditional conclusion to the *Seder* service on the eve of the Passover: 'Next Year in Jerusalem.'

To my surprise and alarm I was suddenly instructed to play a part in the proceedings. I was sitting in the body of the hall, feeling very pleased with myself, when Sir Mark Sykes squeezed his way to me through the crowded seats. He wanted to speak to me at the back of the hall. I followed him there. He had a problem. A number of prominent Arabs were present. A message had been received from the Emperor Feisal and it had been read out in Arabic by an Arab. Only the handful of Arabs, naturally, had any idea of what it meant. It had been translated into English. Sykes wanted this read out, as it was important to make the Arab view public. But he wanted the impression to be given that it was being translated from Arabic on the spot. So I was smuggled out of the back of the hall, and at the right moment produced on the platform as an important person bearing a historic message. I was instructed to read it slowly as though I were translating it. This I did, pretending to a serviceable knowledge of Arabic, rendering a flawless translation to the receipt of thunderous applause, the like of which I have never received again. Incidentally, I discovered on that occasion how incredibly intoxicating applause can be. It does not matter if you know that you are merely reading – and badly – somebody else's words and do not deserve the applause. It does not matter if you know that the audience knows that too. You forget this. All you are aware of is the glorious music of clapping hands and the mesmerism of faces turned in your direction. Even when you think you do not deserve it, applause is like a drug. What it is like if you think you *do* deserve it I simply cannot imagine.

Three weeks later, Simon and I, Becky and Miriam, took the Weizmanns down to an hotel in Sussex for a few days' retreat. The weather was fine, we all enjoyed walking, we rested and breathed the fresh air. On the Sunday morning before lunch we were strolling in the garden of the hotel. Weizmann was silent. Suddenly, as though waking from a dream, he said, 'Boys! We shall need money. We must have a campaign. We must organise a campaign for at least £10,000' – at which Simon Marks and I, almost in perfect unison, expressed the view that we must establish a campaign for £100,000. The following day when we arrived in London we discovered that Joseph Cowen at the morning meeting of the Zionist Council had proposed that there be issued an appeal for half a million pounds. During the day a cable arrived from the Secretary of the American Zionist Organisation saying they had started a campaign to raise five million dollars. How men's ideas of what is possible escalate in congenial company!

Returning to London we found much to do. In Zionist circles there was much discussion in the weeks which preceded our going. Very few

Jews understood where the Balfour Declaration left them. Many Jews who should have known better, especially in America and in Europe, were under the illusion that the Declaration had solved the political problem of the Jewish State already. They spoke as though an independent state, complete with elections, governments and cabinets, would materialise in Zion within the next few weeks. On the other hand there were Jews who held the opposite point of view: Zionism had run into the sands; no sovereign state had been created; what home there would be for the Jews on Palestinian soil would not be their own. The Arabs' right to live in Palestine in unlimited numbers was internationally guaranteed. In face of all this Weizmann patiently expounded his doctrine that the Balfour Declaration was no more than a framework, which could only be filled by patient effort over many years. The Zionist Commission would be the first short tentative footstep along a path of which it could be said only that it led in the right direction. Had some of us been aware that the end of the war was in sight we might have been more sanguine; but there was still deadlock on the Western Front, the Germans showed no signs of cracking, their offensives were still terrible, and the submarines were at Britain's throat. I was young enough to view the mission with considerable elation; I myself plead guilty to having thought at the time that the Balfour Declaration had ushered in an independent Jewish State under the camouflage of a Jewish national home. Weizmann, however, fully divined what lay ahead.

If we had no inkling of the diplomatic difficulties we should encounter when we got back we should in any case have been forewarned by a last minute incident. A few days before we left, Sir Mark Sykes, who was organising our mission, thought it would be good for the prestige of the Commission if Weizmann on the eve of his departure were to be formally received by the King. Arrangements were hastily made, and, accordingly, on the Saturday morning before we left Weizmann bought and donned his first and last top hat, and went to the Foreign Office in order to be escorted to the Palace. Here he was met by an apologetic and somewhat flustered looking Sykes. Telegrams of a 'very disquieting' tone and content had been received from Cairo. The apprehensions of the Arabs, activated by the Balfour Declaration, worked up steadily for weeks by their more extremist leaders, had come to the boil at news of the Commission's imminent departure. They were protesting fiercely that the departure of the Commission was clear evidence that British promises of support for Arab Nationalism were worthless. The British military commanders out in Palestine, relying heavily on Arab Nationalist leaders to drive out the Turks, were urging that as little public attention as possible be given to the very existence of the Zionist Commission. Sykes felt the audience with the King should be cancelled.

Weizmann flatly refused to accept this. Having agreed entirely with the Government earlier on that publicity for the activities of the Commission should be discreetly limited, he had originally suggested that, much as he appreciated the honour, there should not be an audience with the King. Now while he and Sykes were debating the matter in 'heated and at times painful discussion', Balfour came into view up the Foreign Office stairs. Sykes took him into his room, and explained what had happened. Balfour, in one of his rare moments of decisiveness, decided that the audience should take place. He personally telephoned the Palace to say that the delay in Weizmann's arrival at the Palace was the result of his own late arrival at the Foreign Office. A second audience was arranged for the following Monday morning, the day of our departure. Weizmann told us on the boat that the King greeted him in the most friendly way with: 'You know, Dr Weizmann, Mr Balfour always *does* come late to the office, I quite understand.' The King talked with great interest and knowledge of the Commission's plans and prospects, and wished him every success.

The Commission, intended to be representative of the Jews of the principal allied countries, numbered seven, with several others attending in various capacities. Weizmann was the Chairman. Joseph Cowen, a manufacturer of women's wear – his factory was near Oxford Circus – was Chairman of the English Zionist Federation. David Eder was a doctor, the first man to practise Freudian psycho-analytical medicine in Britain; he was Joe Cowen's brother-in-law. Leon Simon, later Sir Leon Simon, was a civil servant, and a scholar. He was director of national savings in 1935, and translated several Greek classics into Hebrew. The French representative, Professor Sylvain Lévi, an oriental scholar of whom more later, was not a Zionist – indeed he was an avowed anti-Zionist. He had been put on to the Commission largely because of Baron Edmond de Rothschild who did not want the impression created that the French representative on the Commission was already sold on the idea of a Jewish State. Lévi was the President of the anti-Zionist French *Alliance Israelite*. The Italian representative was Commendatore (a former order of Italian knighthood) Bianchini.

He too was not a Zionist, and was more concerned to preserve Italian interests in Palestine than in a Jewish State. Officially designated secretary, I was the seventh member of the body. The Americans were notable absentees: since the United States was not at war with Turkey President Wilson did not feel able to appoint representatives to a body which was working under the auspices of Turkey's enemies. The Russian members, though the appointments were announced, were unable to join us as a result of the post-revolutionary situation in their country. It was made up, therefore, of representatives of Britain, Italy and France. The British Government was represented by Major W. Ormsby-Gore (later the fourth Lord Harlech), who was assisted by Captain James de Rothschild, and son of Edmond, and when we got to Palestine, also by Captain Arthur Waley and Lieutenant Edwin Samuel.

Our route was Paris, Rome, Taranto, in the heel of Italy; thence by ship to Alexandria, then to Cairo. On Monday morning 8 March 1918 I left the furnished house Becky and I had been renting in Gloucester Place, drove to Victoria Station, met my colleagues on the Commission and took the Boat Train to Paris. We stayed there three days, at the Hotel Meurice, in the Rue de Rivoli, overlooking the Gardens of the Tuilleries. On our last evening in Paris Weizmann and myself were entertained to dinner by Baron Edmond de Rothschild, James de Rothschild's father, at *his* house in the Rue St Honoré. It was a palace and an art gallery combined. The food and drink were beyond description. It was a great experience for a young and unsophisticated Manchester Zionist like myself to meet the elegant, cosmopolitan eclectic Baron in his own surroundings; this millionaire Jewish philanthropist who was not at all our kind of Zionist, but who had done so much to bring back Jews to Palestine. If he had not answered their prayers in the 1880s, the efforts of the first wave of Zionist pioneers, the *Chalutzim*, would almost certainly have collapsed.

The Baron was a strange man. In his heart, Weizmann told me, he felt the Baron ultimately wanted an independent Jewish homeland in Palestine; but the patrician in him recoiled from the democratic nationalism which, in his shrewder moments he saw, alone could bring that about. His fastidious individualism did not assimilate the thought of all the organisational machinery through which, he saw, Zionism would have to work. The Baron, however, was on the whole a great and good friend to us. Although he could become high-handed, in his cooler moments his residual wisdom and insight showed him things as they were. 'The Zionists could have done nothing without me,' he used to say in later life. 'But without the Zionists nothing I did would have lasted.' I see him now this March night in Paris, a man of seventy, incredibly youthful looking, with refined lean features, silken hair and luminous intelligent eyes, distinguished as only the great Edwardian figures have had the gift of seeming, with a wit to suit. 'What would you regard as a rich man?' Weizmann asked him. The Baron blew the smoke from his cigar in a perfectly directed cone. 'A rich man,' he said, 'is a man who lives on the income of his income.'

The next day we took the train for Rome. We stayed one night at the Excelsior Hotel. It was here, in the Excelsior, that the Zionist Commission held its first formal meeting. Weizmann outlined the major activities which the Commission ought to pursue in Palestine: and Ormsby-Gore outlined *his* instructions from the British Government. Quite a lot of useful work was done, but what stuck out in my mind was the portent of things to come as the result of a contretemps between the Italians and the French. Weizmann reported that Signor Angelo Sereni, the President of the Italian Jewish Community, felt the Commission might find it useful as well as courteous to pay an official visit to the Italian Foreign Office. The Frenchman, Professor Lévi, said No: the Commission had not visited the French Foreign Office when it was in Paris: if it visited the Italian Foreign Office, therefore, the Government of France would feel offended. So we didn't go! We had a few hours to spare, and Ormsby-Gore, who was very good with people, and did not discriminate between great men and servants, went out of his way to show me the city. He loved art and architecture, but did not bore one about it. 'Would you like to see the Vatican?' he asked me, in his kind, gentle way, as though he wanted to be sure that it met with my approval. And he took me through a great deal of it before we left.

So, on down to Taranto. The Gulf of Taranto being infested with German submarines had a boom slung across the harbour. We passed seven hot, not very useful days there, waiting for a warship to escort us through the waters of the Eastern Mediterranean. The mosquitoes were almost unbearable. I remember that when Becky and I passed through again in 1920, she woke up one morning with her face almost bitten to pieces. In spite of the heat we held a second Commission Meeting on March 18 on our boat, the *SS Canberra*. The rest of the time I spent walking on the beach, which gave a fine view of the harbour, and of the Italian fleet, which was not keen on vacating it, and talking with Weizmann to Leonard Stein, who was stuck there.

Eventually we steamed out for Alexandria, accompanied by a Japanese destroyer and an Italian one. The moment we got wind of a U-boat the Italian destroyer headed back for harbour, but the Japanese circled and circled around us all the way across. We zig-zagged across the Mediterranean for nine days, reaching Alexandria on the eve of the Passover. It was an interesting arrival. Many Jews met us, but few of them were Zionists. Those that were, assumed that we had come to lead them into a Jewish state in Palestine as strong and independent as the United States, and paraded before us enthusiastically with bands and flowers and flags. Here for the first time we met Arabs in the mass. Friendly Arabs were very worried about what we were going to do in Palestine. The British military and political authorities were not in any hurry to speed us on our way, since they seemed to have only vague ideas of why we had arrived there. Eventually we were allowed to get down to Cairo and I made my first real acquaintance with the Middle East.

My first impression of the Middle East was a rather weird one, and as a result of it I have never regarded 'The Mysterious East' as merely a romantic cliché. On my second day in Cairo I was told to take an official letter to a Major Tudor Pole, whose responsibility was the administration of conquered enemy territory. When I entered his office, he rose from his desk, and before I had had time to utter a word, said: 'You are bringing me a letter. It instructs me to . . .' And in a beautifully modulated voice he summarised the letter's contents. I did not know what was in the letter, so I handed him the envelope. He opened it and read the note. 'Quite so,' he said, and handed the letter back to me to read. He had got it pat. I did not quite know what to make of this: perhaps it was a common knack in the Middle East Command. We proceeded to our business. As I was leaving he said, 'Come down to the river sometime, and see my boat'.

A few weeks later I went down to the river, where he had the kind of small launch to be seen on the Thames in summer, decked and furnished, with a couple of berths. 'Delighted you have come,' he said, with his usual courtesy. 'I hope you won't mind if I have to break off for a spell around eight-thirty. I shall be in France. If I seem distrait, do not worry; just sit there quietly, I shall soon be back.' I hardly knew whether to take him seriously, but sat down, took a drink, and behaved as if I were accustomed to being welcomed with such information. We had a pleasant and interesting conversation for an hour or so, but at eight fifteen he turned down the lamp, an oil lamp, I remember, and lay back slowly against his cushions. His face became pale and his breathing deeper. He was obviously in, or pretending to be in, a trance. I sat there quietly and rather frightened. Fifteen minutes later he sat up, quite composed, and turned up the lamp. 'I've been to France,' he said, in a grave but otherwise normal voice. 'It's the Somme. The Germans have broken through; we're having a terrible time of it, there are frightful casualties.' His clairvoyance was beyond dispute. The Germans had blown a huge hole in the British lines and in a matter of days had pushed through many miles. We resumed our conversation and shortly after I left.

I saw Tudor Pole once or twice again before we left Cairo. After the war we kept up our acquaintance and we met from time to time in the post-war period. One day he said to me suddenly: 'Israel, I'm sorry to have to tell you, but shortly there is to be a tragedy in your life. Somebody you know and love is going to die. I wish I could tell you who it is; I can't.' Two weeks later there was a telephone call from Algeria. It was Tudor Pole. 'Israel,' he said, 'I must tell you that your sorrow is about to fall on you.' That was all, he said, he could say. The next morning, one of my sons died in an accident. I cannot explain either Tudor Pole or his extraordinary communications. I report them exactly as my memory records them.

Like Alexandria, Cairo had a big community of Sephardic Jews, and it was clear that few of these were in sympathy with the Zionism of the Ashkenazi. While many of them were friendly it was obvious that they were apprehensive about the possibility of hordes of Zionist immigrants streaming from Central Europe into the Middle East, and destroying the peace and prosperity of existing Jewish populations. A minority of them felt differently about it: they pumped us for information as to how they could cash in on the influx. We also met the leaders of the Arab communities who were polite, indeed charming, but whose subtle tissues of friendly remarks concealed concern and bewilderment; and we met General Wingate, the Sidar, as the Commander-in-Chief of the British Army in Egypt was then called.

From Cairo, where the Zionist Commission held two meetings at

Shepheard's Hotel, we went back up the Nile Delta to Alexandria, and entrained for Lydd, ten miles or so from Tel Aviv, a journey of about 350 miles. We crossed the Suez Canal at El Qantara, then puffed on east along the coastal plain, through El Arish and Khan Yunis, and entered the Shefelah, the southern coastal plain of Palestine, at Gaza, the city of the ancient Philistines. Then on up the plain until we arrived at Lydd. Here we got our first sense of the atmosphere we were to encounter from the Military Government of Palestine. There was a war going on around us, we knew, and the Turkish zones were only a few miles away. We did not expect a guard of honour or a band but we thought there would be somebody from the Military Administration to meet us. When we got down from the train on to the platform we formed up in a row. But there was only Ormsby-Gore, who had come on ahead from Cairo. He explained that there would be no reception. So, philosophically, we got into the motor cars and drove the ten miles or so to Tel Aviv on the coast, where we were to stay in the home of David Leventin, a Zionist friend and activist.

Next day I had my first real sight of the land of Israel. Today as you circle in a plane around Lydd (Lod) airport, Tel Aviv is a great expanse of grey-white cubes, broken up by skyscrapers and lofty towers. In 1918 it was a little town of three thousand inhabitants, most of them Russian Jews, many of them recent immigrants. Now nearly half a million people live there. Its story really begins in 1909. Of the eighty thousand or so Jews living in Palestine at that time, nearly a third lived in Jaffa, the chief port of Palestine, the old Joppa. It was from here that Jonah sailed, and where the Greek maiden Andromeda was chained to the rock in the sea before Perseus rescued her and slew the Gorgon. Not far from here (at Lod) St George, a Roman, later mysteriously imported by Merrie England, is supposed to have killed the Dragon. Jaffa's history goes back beyond recorded time. Tel Aviv is hardly born. In 1909 sixty Jaffa families, led by one, Meir Dizengoff, bought thirty-two acres of sand-dunes just outside Jaffa and built a city of their own. When Dizengoff predicted a city of twenty-five thousand some of his fellow builders were quite incredulous, but they got to work, drawing lots for the building lots along the one and only street, named after Herzl, going back to Jaffa every night to sleep. So began the first all-Jewish city of modern times. They called it Tel Aviv, the Hill of the Spring, after the Hebrew title of Herzl's book *Altneuland*, quoting Ezekiel: 'Then I came to them of the captivity at Tel-aviv . . .

and I sat where they sat, and remained there astonished among them seven days.'

There came the day when I first beheld Jerusalem. What man with the slightest sense of history, be he Jew, Christian or Moslem, could forget his first glimpse of the holy city? We drove a dozen miles south-east of Tel Aviv across undulating countryside rich with vines and fruits and came to Ramla – GHQ was at Bir Salem nearby – and saw the Great Mosque, originally a crusader church, and the White Tower from which Napoleon directed his army to attack Jaffa. Beyond Ramla, the highway from the coast meets the hills at Shaar Hagai (the gate to the valley) still known by its Arab name, Bab-el-Wad. The vineyards give way to the pine plantations. The road begins to wind. The bleak, stark, rocky mountains close you in. The 'aliyah', the going-up, to Jerusalem, is a hard ascent, despite the flowers in spring, the green grass which the sun will scorch in summer, the red-roofed cottages dotting the hillside, and at sunset the soft shade of pink and purple which soften the grim layers of the mountain side which never smiles. Ten miles outside the city we saw the Hill of Kiriat Ye'arim where the Ark of the Covenant lay for twenty years after it was recaptured from the Philistines, and before David set it up in Jerusalem. On through ancient Arab villages, crusader churches and monasteries, and past, on the horizon, the minaret that marks the Prophet Samuel's tomb, to the settlement of Mevaseret Yerushalayim, 'the Herald of Jerusalem', from which the first white roofs of the Holy City were visible that April evening on a ridge five miles ahead. I cannot remember any more of the physical detail I saw from there; only the strange deep peaceful sense of the soul coming for a time to rest.

It was now that we realised to the full what we were up against. We had never expected to be received with enthusiasm by the British military commanders. Ormsby-Gore had put us right about that. Even so it was impossible not to feel somewhat mortified by our treatment in the first few weeks. It varied from officer to officer – this colonel was obviously only barely aware of why we were there at all, this brigadier made no attempt to conceal the fact that he admired the Arabs and was dubious about the Jews. . . . The more responsible military men were inhibited by their knowledge that in view of the commitments given to Arab leaders, who were actively supporting them in battle against the Turks, for them to be more than barely civil towards us wandering Jews might have dangerous repercussions. The members of the Military Administration, it is only fair to say, were gravely preoccupied with the military situation. Many of their troops had been recently transferred from Palestine to the Western Front, in order to shore it up against the desperate counter-attacks which the Germans were launching. To turn aside from the critical military problem created in Palestine by the withdrawal of these forces to discuss what should happen to the Jews in a hypothetical post-war period understandably made great demands upon their patience. We soon discovered that the existence, let alone the contents, of the Balfour Declaration, our charter, our justification for being in that part of the world at all, were hardly known to even Allenby's senior officers. They were much more familiar with the infamous 'Protocols of the Elders of Zion', anti-Semite fabrications introduced to Western Europe by Russian émigrés at the end of the nineteenth century, alleging that the Jews had organised the Bolshevik Revolution in Russia as a prelude to establishing a Jewish State on the remains of the Arab Sheikdoms, from which they intended to destroy Christian society and dominate the world.

Weizmann recorded his first reaction to the situation he found in Palestine years later in his autobiography:

And this, though mercifully I did not know it at the time – was the beginning of the hard road which I have had to tread for practically the rest of my life. I was placed between the hammer and the anvil – conservative and often unfriendly British administration, military or civil, and the impatient, dynamic Jewish people, which saw in the Balfour Declaration the great promise of the return to them of their own country, and contrasted it resentfully with the administrative realities in Palestine.

In our first few days in Palestine we concentrated on establishing some kind of a working relationship with Allenby and General Deedes. We could only do this by getting them to trust us as human beings, and here Weizmann was eminently successful. Personal relations between him and General Allenby, the Commander-in-Chief in Palestine, and General Wyndham Deedes soon got on to a quite different basis. Once this had been achieved, within the limits of their directives and their understanding of the situation, Allenby and Deedes were splendid to us. It was, however, some days before we were deemed sufficiently 'safe' to be allowed free movement – a car, petrol and a private telephone – and to get on with our work.

It is, I think, worth noting that the work prescribed for us by the

British Government was of a considerable range. We had not come merely to look around and come to conclusions about how a Jewish State should be set up. On the contrary, we had come partly to establish it: though some of the Commissioners were to return in the near future, some were to remain to continue the Commission's work. The Commission, it should be understood, had come to stay indefinitely. Just as the Commission took over from and replaced the former Palestine Office, its duties were to be taken over by the Zionist Executive in 1921, and, when the Mandate was granted the following year, by the Jewish Agency for Palestine, until that body disappeared in 1948 when Israel became a state. In a very real sense, therefore, we seven members of the Zionist Commission were the first Government of Israel. On our arrival, therefore, we had to take over every problem of a governmental nature and more besides. We had to arrange for the provision of, and distribution of financial and medical relief; we were to reorganise the schools; we were to re-open the banks and reconstruct the banking system; we were to provide reading-rooms and social centres. We were to tackle the problems of repatriating Jews who had fled from the advancing Turkish armies or had been evacuated by the British. We were required to prevent land speculation and to re-plan for agricultural and commercial expansion. We were also to lay the foundation of the Hebrew University. Over and above this we were to establish contact with the Arab Leaders and representatives of other communities in Palestine. This list of our terms of reference explains how in the circumstances it was understandable that some people regarded us as somewhat theoretical and academic nosey-parkers, while others looked on us as an alien government.

I think it would help my reader if I gave a very short account of Jews in Palestine at the time we arrived there. They numbered about ninety thousand. Roughly speaking they belonged to one of three categories. The first, by far the smallest – indeed, a mere handful – were members of the Jewish Legion, young men, many of whom had recently arrived from different parts of Europe and the United States, many of them British Jews, to fight by the side of their British allies against the Turks. They were led by the brilliant, but somewhat volatile Jabotinsky.

Far more numerous was the second kind of Palestinian Jew: the *Challukkah* (pioneer) Jewry who were Jews and the descendants of Jews who, supported by charitable contributions from the pious and orthodox of many lands, had come at various stages in the nineteenth century to settle in Palestine for religious reasons, indeed, simply to live and die in the Holy Land. These Jews of the old *Yishuv* (meaning settlement) were usually advanced in years before they left their country of origin, arriving only to pass their remaining years in prayer and the performance of good works. They knew little of, and cared less about, the brand of Zionism which Weizmann had been preaching. They were hardly aware of the war, save that it had brought soldiers among them; all they knew was it had stopped the flow of alms to them from overseas, enforced the evacuation of some of their settlements, and had brought the terrifying sound of guns: what it was about and its scale in the outside world was another matter. Notwithstanding these interruptions and invasions, the *Challukkah* Jews continued to live in a different world; they had neither the capacity nor the inclination to enter ours. Yet we were to take responsibility for them: once we, the Zionist Commission, had come into being, all the affairs of all the Jews in Palestine were dumped into our lap. Even the funds which arrived for the *Challukkah* became our responsibility, as did the funds which failed to arrive. We were now responsible for their settlements, their scattered hospitals and synagogues, their schools, some of them in an almost mediaeval state of insanitariness. We found these peculiar and eccentric people admirable, frequently noble, but very difficult to deal with. They regarded us with dismay and anger and resentment. They looked on us as modern, graceless heathen, indifferent to the religious basis of their existence in the Holy Land. Our attempts to get this community into some kind of civic shape were most unwelcome. They appealed right, left and centre for protection to the Military Administration, some of whom, to our irritation, were inclined to humour them, partly, perhaps, to annoy us, and partly, perhaps, because as Weizmann said, the sacerdotal presence, the flowing robes of a rabbi of Hebron '. . . was the nearest approach provided by the Jewish Community to the Arab sheik!'

The bulk of the Jews in Palestine, however, were members of the third category: they were the products over the previous forty years or so of European Zionism. The idea of a return to Zion, of the traditional 'Next Year in Jerusalem' as a programme of practical activity, had its first fruit in 1870 when Charles Netter founded the original modern Jewish agricultural settlement near Tel Aviv. It was named *Mikveh Israel*, and is now the foremost agricultural institution in Israel, mikveh meaning 'a collection'. The pogroms of 1881 gave a tremendous impetus to settlement in Palestine: the immediate result of them was the rise of the *Hibbat Zion* ('love of Zion') Movement, which, with its slogan 'To Palestine', begot enthusiastic local societies in Russia, Poland, Rumania and Britain, whose object was to purchase land in Palestine for Jewish immigrants to colonise. In 1882, *Bilu* (the initials of *Bet Yaakov Lekhu Ve-Nelkhah*: 'Oh House of Jacob, come ye and let us go') was founded by Jewish students to send colonists to Palestine. More Jewish farming villages were established in the next few years, like *Petah Tikvah* ('Gate of Hope') and *Zichron Ya'acov* ('Memory of Jacob'). In 1883 Leon Pinsker founded the *Zerubbabel Society* at Odessa. In 1884 this and other colonising societies were federated as *Hovevei Zion* ('Lovers of Zion'). In 1897 nearly all of them joined the newly founded World Zionist Organisation and in it were prominent among those elements emphasising the 'practical' as opposed to 'political' Zionism. Up until now most of the funds for these ventures came from millionaire Jews like Baron Edmond de Rothschild and Baron Maurice de Hirsch, whose motives were a mixture of philanthropy on the one hand, and on the other, a somewhat less altruistic intimation that if Zionist-minded Jews, or, indeed, any Jews, were to pour out homeless and poor from Central Europe, it would be best for them to be encouraged to go East, rather than West. In 1898 the Jewish Colonial Trust, the first bank of the Zionist Organisation, was established. It was registered in Britain. My father, as I have mentioned before, was one of its first subscribers. Three years later the Jewish National Fund (*Keren Kayemet le-Yisrael*) was created. The purpose of both was to finance the purchase and development of land in Palestine, the latter by means of popular contributions. The death of Herzl in 1904 gave further influence to the 'practicals', the 'colonisers', the Weizmannites. From this time on the funds of Zionism began to play a major role in the financing of the settlements, and, correspondingly, the relative importance of the millionaire philanthropists began somewhat to diminish. In 1908 the World Zionist Organisation established the Palestine Office, the first institution it created to supervise practical work in Palestine. This established the first centre of administration for the Jewish community there: in 1918 its functions were taken over by the Zionist Commission. There came one more large infusion of Zionist enterprise before the Commission took over: in 1915 arrived the first crop of the new pioneering movements founded in the United States, this one inspired by a young man called David Ben Gurion. Many of its members came to Palestine primarily to join the Jewish Legion. These new pioneering groups soon federated under the name *Che-Chaltuz* – 'The Pioneer'. Their activities were to proliferate during the twenties and thirties.

Looking back on it, our encounter with the Jews of the Old Yishuv had its comic aspect. Our Commission was expected to take over responsibility for the recruitment of the Jewish battalions of the Legion. There were few youngsters among the old Challukkah Jews, and most of those were either not fit enough for military service or had conscientious objections. A hundred of them or so agreed to do agricultural work on the settlements to replace men who had voluntarily enlisted. They would do so, however, only if they could work strictly to religious rules. We had to arrange with the farmers to provide them with kosher food, and arrange transportation back to Jerusalem every Friday afternoon before the Sabbath began: war or no war they insisted on keeping the Sabbath in the Holy City.

Weizmann used to describe one incident which illustrates their attitude to life precisely. It occurred just as we were leaving for England at the end of September. Our train was to leave from Lydda: we were to be driven there by car. As we were getting into the car we were accosted by two very aged Jews, probably in their eighties. They looked most disconsolate. They said they were very surprised that we were leaving for they needed our assistance. *Succoth*, the Feast of the Tabernacle, was upon them and they had no myrtles. *Succoth* commemorates the gratitude of the Jews for the divine protection accorded the Israelites during their forty years wandering in the desert. During this period, according to the rabbis, the 'Nimbuses of glory' flanked them like a tent: *Succoth*, the Hebrew word for Tabernacle, is celebrated by the building of a booth, of which the roof covering must be of certain materials, leafy boughs of various prescribed kinds, and so on, and the religious Jews must 'dwell' or at least eat in it for seven days. Palm, citron, willow and myrtle are carried in procession in the synagogue. There was no myrtle, these two aged Jews complained. 'Surely,' said Weizmann, 'you can get myrtle from Egypt?' 'No,' they replied. 'For the Feast of Tabernacle, the myrtles must be of the very finest quality.' The nearest place from which these could be obtained was Trieste.

Weizmann explained, with great self-control, that there was a war on, and that Trieste was in enemy territory. He said that they would have to make do with myrtles from Egypt. No, said the aged Jews; that would in any case be impossible: the military authorities had imposed a quarantine on the importation of plants from Egypt. Weizmann said he would see what could be done. The two aged Jews departed, and he made a note of the matter for the permanent representatives of the Commission, who were remaining behind. We proceeded to Cairo where we were to spend several days tying up various loose ends. Just before our boat sailed Weizmann made a friendly visit to Allenby. As he was leaving, Allenby suddenly said, 'By the way, about those myrtles. You'll be glad to hear that we've lifted the quarantine and a consignment of myrtles will get to Palestine in good time for the Feast of the Tabernacle. You know it's an important business, it's all in the Bible: I read it up in the book of Nehemiah last night.'

The Zionist Commission accomplished three things. First, it came into existence, went out to Palestine, took over responsibilities, and continued to discharge them, under David Eder, and then Harry Friedenwald, President of the Federation of American Zionists 1904-18, until in 1921 its functions were transferred to the Zionist executive in Palestine. The second achievement was the meeting between Weizmann and King Feisal, son of Hussein, the Sherif of Mecca, and Commander-in-Chief of the Arab Army. The third achievement was the laying of the foundation stone of the Hebrew University.

Feisal was the eldest son of Hussein, and had put himself at the head of the Arab nationalist movement which had been formed to oust the Turks. Weizmann arranged to meet him at his GHQ in Trans-Jordan. He originally planned to take me with him, but for some reason the British Military Authorities thought he should go alone, accompanied only by Major Ormsby-Gore. I think this may have been due to the role I was known to have played on *Palestine* in causing trouble for Mark Sykes and his Sykes-Picot agreement. I always felt he had his eye on me. It was a tedious and hazardous journey. The Turks still held the Jordan valley, which meant that Weizmann had to make a huge detour, going by train down to Suez, thence by boat to Aqaba, sailing around the Sinai Peninsula into the Gulf of Aqaba, motoring up the Wadi Musa, completing the journey on camels. They met on 4 June at Wadi Waheida, the meeting lasting forty-five minutes. Ormsby-Gore fell ill and failed to complete the journey, so it was Colonel Joyce who accompanied Weizmann during his historic meeting with Feisal. Historic it was, for at that famous meeting Weizmann and Feisal arrived at a mutual understanding of, and agreement about, Arab and Jewish interests in Palestine that gave the lie to those who had been saying that they were in utter conflict and could never be reconciled. Weizmann promised Jewish support for the establishment of an Arab Kingdom in Syria with Feisal on its throne. Feisal said it was not merely possible but desirable for the Jews to come to Palestine. There was room for both. At his suggestion the two men were photographed standing together.

The third great achievement of our visit was the laying, on 24 July 1918, of the foundation stones of the Hebrew University on Mount Scopus, in the presence of General Allenby and his staff, and of Moslem Christian and Jewish dignitaries from Jerusalem. It was a poetically beautiful scene, the setting sun touching the hills of Judaea and Moab with gold. We could almost hear the sound of the guns on the northern front; Weizmann made a moving speech. We sang *Hatikvah*, and also 'God Save the King'. A scroll, to be buried in a casket on the spot, was signed by many present, including the Mufti of Jerusalem, who borrowed my gold pen but did not give it back. We had asked Allenby some weeks previously if we could have permission to lay the stones. 'But we may be rolled back any minute!' he said. 'What is the good of beginning something you may never be able to finish?' Weizmann said: 'This will be a great act of faith – faith in the victory which is bound to come, and faith in the future of Palestine.'

Weizmann spoke from the very depths of the convictions on which his whole Zionist policy was founded – the victory of his adopted country, Britain, against all the odds. On the way to the site of the University the Sudanese cavalry, riding in front of Allenby's carriage in which the General and Weizmann were sitting, raised quite a lot of dust. Allenby was at one stage almost choking. 'Dr Weizmann,' he said, 'you are a very intelligent man. Do you really believe that any damn Jew will come to this bloody country?' 'General,' said Weizmann, 'come here in ten years.' When in 1925 a dinner followed the opening of the University by Balfour, Vera Weizmann sat next to Allenby. She said to him: 'Did you think my husband completely hare-brained in 1918?' Allenby replied: 'When I think back to that day – as I often do – I come to the conclusion that the short ceremony inspired my army, and gave them confidence in the future.' Vera asked him if he would say that in the speech he was to make that night, and he did.

The laying of those stones meant much to Weizmann. From the beginning he had believed that if there were to be a Jewish Homeland in Palestine, whatever the charter, the international agreements, the treaties, the papers signed sealed and delivered in all solemnity and sincerity, the only thing that could really count would be the land that Jews cultivated there, the homes they built, and the institutions they would establish to generate home-grown Jewish life. As it turned out, on the face of it, it had seemed that the Herzl approach – international agreement between great powers – had brought about the beginnings of the Jewish State. But this, for Weizmann, was only an accidental means to the all-essential end. The founding of the University restated his priorities. And that afternoon on Mount Scopus refreshed his energies and elevated his vision when there was misgiving and confusion all around him.

We arrived back in London in October. We had hardly drawn our breath in the damp and chilly English autumn when the last gun had sounded on the Western Front, and the war was over.

The Peace Conference was to open in Paris on 1 January 1919. In December Feisal arrived in London on his way to it. By now Feisal had heard about the secret Sykes-Picot agreement. Everybody knew about it: it had been made public by Lenin. Shocked by discovering that his friends the British had come to arrangements – and in secret – with the French to exercise a condominium over Palestine, and to allow the French to dominate Syria, Feisal was even readier to formulate an Arab/Zionist agreement with Weizmann than he had been before. He then signed an agreement with Weizmann, by which they agreed to act in accord with one another at the Peace Conference and in particular to ensure that 'All necessary measures shall be taken to encourage and stimulate immigration of Jews into Palestine on a large scale and as quickly as possible to settle Jewish immigrants on the land through close settlement and intensive cultivation of the soil.' I have included in this book a copy of an early draft of this agreement, and a rough translation in T. E. Lawrence's hand, of the qualification which Feisal added at the time, a highly important proviso I deal with later on.

I now met Feisal myself. He was the gentlest man I have ever met; small, with features as refined as those of a woman, with a soft slow high-pitched voice, like a child's, with a melancholy air and self-deprecating manner and now and again a sweet ironic humour in his utterances. Lawrence, whom I saw several times in London, and later in Paris at the Conference, made little impression upon me. His physical appearance I found rather negative: his hair and eyes were light-coloured but had no glamour: he exuded nothing. I felt him competent but recollect nothing extraordinary. I saw no sign of an outstanding man or mind, certainly no emanation of charisma. I figured personally in Feisal's plans with Weizmann. They agreed that to promote their mutual interests co-operatively 'Arab and Jewish duly accredited agents shall be established in their respective territories.' Weizmann told me later that Feisal had asked if I could be the agent in Damascus.

This was a period of immense and delicate diplomatic activity in which Weizmann showed himself a genius, and, in my view, single-handed conjured a Jewish State out of the air. To understand the real nature of his achievement it is essential to understand the dilemma, indeed, the set of dilemmas he was in. First, his only real power was in what he could actually bring about – he had no authority other than his achievement. Unless he could dominate world Zionism, and in particular command American Zionist financial support, he could not bring a Jewish State into being. On the other hand he could only keep up his position as leader of World Zionism and mesmerise the American Jews into giving him the money by bringing the Jewish State into being. With only the Balfour Declaration behind him, and with the Sykes-Picot Agreement hanging over him, he had to convince Feisal on the one hand and the American Jews on the other that he, Weizmann, represented a strong and viable Jewish State. He had to behave towards the British Government as though World Jewry were at his back, giving him plenary powers. To leading militant Zionists on the other hand, he had to pretend that his power was very limited so that they would not try to push him further than the British Government could stand. Much bluff and counter-bluff was required. In 1919 Weizmann behaved as though he had a great Jewish State behind him. In fact all he had, if he had been asked to show, was his handful of Manchester friends, Scott, Sidebotham, Sacher, Simon Marks and me!

In February we submitted a memorandum to the Peace Conference. It asked that Palestine 'Shall be placed under such political administrative, and economic conditions as will ensure the establishment therein of the Jewish national home, and ultimately render possible the creation of an autonomous Jewish Commonwealth.' The following month Feisal wrote a famous letter to Felix Frankfurter, the American Zionist, and stated that he regarded the contents of the memorandum as 'Moderate and proper'. I cannot go into the events which led to the tragic breakdown of relations between Weizmann and Feisal – the diplomatic breakdown, I mean: their personal friendship and mutual respect never altered. All followed from the reservation, in rough translation by T. E. Lawrence, which Feisal made when coming to his original agreement with my leader.

When the British Government called off *their* deal with Feisal, Feisal was free to call off his deal with us.

At the Peace Conference of Versailles in Paris in the early weeks of 1919, we were first required to state our case to the Peace Conference's Council of Ten for the establishment of a Jewish national home in Palestine under British mandate to the League of Nations. A preliminary draft of our case and application was produced in London, and Simon was deputed to take it to Paris and show it to Ormsby-Gore. Simon returned, more than a little disheartened. Ormsby-Gore had told him we were asking too much. We must 'Come down to earth', he said. We made some modifications, toned down the language, but left it substantially as it had been before. A few days later Weizmann was summoned to Paris to appear before the Council of Ten.

We were admitted to the Conference Chamber at half past three, Thursday afternoon, 23 February 1919. Balfour and Lord Milner were on the Council for Great Britain; Tardieu and Pichon for France, Lansing and White for America. Clemenceau was there a part of the time. Our official case for a Jewish national home under a British mandate was put up by Nahum Sokolow, the Polish born Zionist who during the Paris Peace Conference was the President of the Committee of Jewish Delegations. It was a magnificent speech. Weizmann said of it afterwards: 'It was as if 2000 years of Jewish suffering rested on his shoulders.' Four other Zionists were allowed to speak; Weizmann made an excellent contribution, concentrating on the economic aspects of the Jewish case. The last speaker was Sylvain Lévi, who had been a member of the Zionist Commission. To our utter consternation he spoke *against* the creation of a Jewish national home in Palestine. We could hardly believe our ears. Palestine, he argued with complete

His Royal Highness the Emir FEISAL, representing and acting on behalf of the Arab Kingdom of Hedjaz, and Dr. CHAIM WEIZMANN, representing and acting on behalf of the Zionist Organisation,

mindful of the racial kinship and ancient bonds existing between the Arabs and the Jewish people, and realising that the surest means of working out the consummation of their national aspirations, is through the closest possible collaboration in the development of the Arab State and Palestine, and being desirous further of confirming the good understanding which exists between them,

have agreed upon the following Articles;-

ARTICLE I.

The Arab State and Palestine in all their relations and undertakings shall be controlled by the most cordial goodwill and understanding and to this end Arab and Jewish duly accredited agents shall be established and maintained in the respective territories.

ARTICLE II.

Immediately following the completion of the deliberations of the Peace Conference, the definite boundaries between the Arab State and Palestine shall be determined by a Commission to be agreed upon by the parties hereto.

ARTICLE III.

In the establishment of the Constitution and Administration of Palestine all such measures shall be adopted as will afford the fullest guarantees for carrying into effect the British Government's Declaration of the 2nd of November, 1917.

ARTICLE IV.

All necessary measures shall be taken to encourage and stimulate immigration of Jews into Palestine on a large scale, and as quickly as possible to settle Jewish immigrants upon the land through closer settlement and intensive cultivation of the soil. In taking such measures the Arab peasant and tenant farmers shall be protected in their rights, and shall be assisted in forwarding their economic development.

ARTICLE V.

No regulation nor law shall be made prohibiting or interfering in any way with the free exercise of religion; and further the free exercise and enjoyment of religious profession and worship without discrimination or preference shall forever be allowed. No religious test shall ever be required for the exercise of civil or political rights.

ARTICLE VI.

The Mohammedan Holy Places shall be under Mohammedan control.

ARTICLE VII.

The Zionist Organisation proposes to send to Palestine a Commission of experts to make a survey of the economic possibilities of the country, and to report upon the best means for its development. The Zionist Organisation will place the aforementioned Commission at the disposal of the Arab State for the purpose of a survey of the economic possibilities of the Arab State and to report upon the best means for its development. The Zionist Organisation will use its best efforts to assist the Arab State in providing the means for developing the natural resources and economic possibilities thereof.

ARTICLE VIII.

The parties hereto agree to act in complete accord and harmony on all matters embraced herein before the Peace Congress.

ARTICLE IX.

Any matters of dispute which may arise between the contracting parties shall be referred to the British Government for arbitration.

Given under our hand at LONDON, ENGLAND, the THIRD day of JANUARY, ONE THOUSAND NINE HUNDRED AND NINETEEN.

Chaim Weizmann

<u>Reservation by the Emir Feisal</u>

If the Arabs are established as I have asked in my manifesto of Jan 4 addressed to the British Secretary of State for Foreign Affairs, I will carry out what is written in this agreement. ~~If no demands or changed so~~.

If changes are made, I can not be answerable for failing to carry out this agreement.

Feisal ibn Hussein

conviction, and well-marshalled arguments, was already over-populated, with a population of 600,000 Arabs; if more Jews were introduced, with their higher standard of living, Arabs would be dispossessed on a major scale. The Jews who would go to Palestine would be mainly Russians – 'politically explosive'; the creation of a Jewish national home in Palestine would introduce the dangerous principle of Jewish dual rights, which France, as a principal Mediterranean power, would not find acceptable. He was dead against it!

Lévi was our last speaker and our case was closed. How was this damage to be undone? Weizmann wrote later that 'Something in the nature of a miracle came to resolve our dilemma. The American Secretary of State, Lansing, addressed Weizmann personally with a direct question: 'Dr Weizmann: what do you mean by a Jewish State?' It was Weizmann's finest hour, his most brilliant minute. He saw his opportunity in a flash. He exploited it with superhuman subtlety and self-control. First, he answered Lansing's question briefly and discreetly, and asked if he had made his definition clear. 'Absolutely!' said Mr Lansing. Weizmann immediately, before anybody thought of checking him, turned to what Lévi had said. Gently but firmly he undermined the Frenchman's arguments one by one. He crowned his case with an illustration of what should be done in Palestine, taking as an example an outstanding success which the French had made at that time in Tunisia. What the French could do in Tunisia, he said, he hoped and believed the Jews would be able to do in Palestine, with Jewish will, Jewish money, Jewish power and Jewish enthusiasm. 'I think Palestine', Weizmann summed up, 'should be as Jewish as England is English, France is French, and America is American.' Balfour afterwards described his speech as 'The swish of a sword'.

We withdrew from the chamber. Balfour sent out a secretary to congratulate us on our success. Lévi approached our group and held out his hand to Weizmann. 'You've sought to betray us,' said Weizmann, and turned his back upon him. Sokolow did the same. None of us saw Lévi again.

In December 1920, the Conference of San Remo, called to settle various matters arising out of the Peace of Versailles, including the Middle East Mandates, confirmed the Balfour Declaration and ratified the decision to give the mandate, in the preamble of which the Balfour Declaration was enshrined, to Great Britain. Even the Arab Delegations seemed happy. In the dining room of the Royal Hotel, San Remo, the evening of the day when the ratifications were agreed the Jewish and Arab Delegations sat at the same table congratulating each other, while the British Delegation looked benignly on from across the room. It was a milestone of achievement in Weizmann's life.

But tragic writing was already upon the wall. The first frightful pogrom in the Holy Land had already taken place. Incited by extremist leaders, including Amin el Husseini, the notorious Grand Mufti of later years, Arabs concentrated at the Mosque of Omar in Jerusalem and, forming a procession, they marched through the streets, catching the Jews unawares, and killing six and seriously injuring several dozen. Jabotinsky had sought to defend the Jewish population and had been thrown into gaol by the British authorities. At the height of his great success, Weizmann had momentarily lost his temper in the hotel and had bitterly congratulated Philip Kerr, later Lord Lothian, and then one of Lloyd George's private secretaries, on 'the first Jewish pogrom under the British flag'.

7
As Weizmann's Man in Israel

While these diplomatic developments were preoccupying us, there were others which were to have great significance for me in the future. They culminated in the establishment of the Women's International Zionist Organisation, WIZO. Becky was its founder. There had been an English Women's Zionist Organisation since 1917: in 1920 David Eder's wife, Edith, Vera Weizmann and Becky collaborated with three leaders of the English body; Mrs Romana Goodman, Mrs Henrietta Irwell and Miss Olga Ginsburg. These six enterprising women called an international conference of Women's Zionist groups in July 1920 which led to the establishment of WIZO.

These years were the beginning for Becky of a lifetime of devotion to this cause. I mentioned that she was disappointed because she could not accompany me on the Zionist Commission. She made up for it as soon as she could by going to Palestine for a few weeks in the autumn of 1919, with Vera and Edith Eder. Their visit was a miniature Zionist Commission in itself: they wanted to see what the funds they hoped they could collect should be spent upon. Their visit was arduous. Any expectation of the romance and glamour and promise of the new homeland being manifest was disappointed: there had been no rain for months, the countryside was parched and colourless and covered with dust. There were hardly any trees, therefore no birds. They heard the jackals howl at night. They travelled farther and faster than they should have, and were bumped and battered in their cars. In November it began to rain torrents; they sat around small oil-stoves at night to get dry and warm before going to bed. But they returned fired by the sight of the pioneer women of Israel struggling by the side of their men – practising equality, not talking about it – digging, breaking stones for roads, hauling loads of rocks like draught horses. Becky had always had the mind of a man. She saw no reason for women to be treated differently. She resented men who kept women down. She had a powerful sympathy for women vis-à-vis men; particularly for women who faced poverty and hardship as well as the inferiority which men too often imposed on them. She returned from her visit to Palestine, therefore, with every element in her personality emotionally mobilised. From that time on I believe that WIZO was the dominant emotion in her life, vying with, and sometimes subjugating, her relationship with me and the children and the rest of her family.

From 1920 to 1940, she was Joint Chairman with Vera. Vera resigned in 1940, but remained a member of the world executive committee. Vera then devoted herself to Youth Aliyah.* Though Becky lived for this work, it took its toll on her. She travelled, inspected, spoke, looked for money, reported, corresponded, over the years worked herself completely out. The first years were the most exciting for her, but the most exacting. The male Zionists were opposed to WIZO. They thought separate organisation for women would weaken the movement as a whole. It was some years before Becky and Vera could feel that WIZO was inviolate and welcome, and well equipped to hold its own. Unfortunately but so easy to understand, Vera and Becky were not at all suitable for work in joint harness. The tension between them was partly personal, but partly a question of policy. Vera really wanted WIZO to work on and through the male Zionist organisation. Becky, on the other hand, had a 'Let-the-men-get-on-with-it-and-we'll-do-the-real-work' attitude to things. WIZO should stand on its own feet, and aspire to everything, everywhere. Becky wanted to make WIZO a world-wide organisation. Vera thought this would dissipate its strength. This difference in views about policy corresponded to differences in personality; Vera's mind was a woman's mind; Becky's mind was a man's. Both were able, beautiful, active, and expected men to do what they required. They were basically lifelong friends who fought each other all the time. I do not think either suffered from this, but their friends certainly did from time to time. I would have loved Vera for herself even if she had not been my master's wife, and regarded her as almost as much my personal and valued friend. Becky did not like this, and

* *Aliyah* means rising, or lifting up, or going up: the rescue and rehabilitation of children and youth organisation.

the more she saw the naturalness of my relationship with the Weizmanns, the more irritable she could on occasion be. WIZO for me, therefore, was and is an object of admiration and devotion; but some of my memories of it give me palpitations. If Becky started a new project without consulting Vera, I would be taken on one side and asked about it. If Vera jumped some gun, Becky would indignantly buttonhole me. I imagine it is not easy for everybody to be the intimate confidante of any two Joint Chairmen. When the Joint Chairmen are women, it becomes more difficult still.

Becky's new passionate concern for the fate of the women and children she had seen with her own eyes struggling in Palestine was one of the two reasons which took me to Palestine for nearly two years in 1920. The other reason was Weizmann's suspicion about the direction British policy would take. His feeling, which had erupted in the Hotel Royal at San Remo, was that for all that had been said at the time of the Balfour Declaration and at the Peace Conference, for all Britain being given the Mandate, British support would now swing away from the Jews and towards the Arabs. The promises to the Arabs and the promises to the Jews could not both be honoured: there were far too many contradictions in them. The Jews could not have an independent state in Palestine, and the Arabs simultaneously be the government of Palestine as well. In these circumstances, Weizmann correctly anticipated, the British government would put the Arabs first: the Arabs were the huge majority in that part of the world, and their régimes had been there a very long time. The British felt they knew where they stood with them and how to manipulate them. They *liked* the Arabs. They did not feel so confident about dealing with this new and unfamiliar incursion of East European and Russian Jews. Weizmann could not be in Palestine all the time. He had immense problems in the world outside, international congresses, fund-raising, delicate relationships with wealthy American Zionists. He therefore asked me if I would go to Palestine as his eyes and ears, as a kind of unpaid unofficial chargé d'affaires, watching to see how the Zionist Commission was being allowed by the British Government to get on with its job, and reporting immediately any instance of backsliding.

As soon as Becky and I had decided that we should go to Jerusalem, my first problem was my father. When I returned from Paris, after our share in the peace-making was over, I realised that I had neglected my father's business. I had thought, as young men working for able and indulgent fathers often do, that a business can thrive even if one of the partners is not there perpetually, but makes frequent, and, he may think, all-seeing inspections from time to time. Many a good business has suffered from this myopia in one or another of the principals; some concerns have sustained damage from which they have never recovered. These were my feelings when I got back to my desk in Manchester after several weeks of lobbying and exchanging views at the bar of the Hotel Meurice, Paris. Now, here I was, proposing to go off to Palestine for two years. When I went to my father to ask him if he would release me for some such period he expressed his feelings kindly but with force. He made it clear that in his heart he wanted me to go because he believed my going was a charge the family should be glad to pay on its debts to the cause of Jewish emancipation and to the British Zionists who had given that cause its first great historic opportunity. But he made it equally clear that he did not like the idea at all. We agreed that I should go on the understanding, as he drily put it, that I would return to Manchester as soon as Weizmann thought this would not prejudice the fate of the Jewish Homeland. This I solemnly promised him I would arrange.

So out we went. It was a great adventure. Becky was going to help the women of Israel to live healthy, fruitful, unharassed lives. I was going to try and bring Arabs and Jews together, and keep His Majesty's Government on the straight and narrow path. Our house, which we rented from a couple called Fineberg, was near the Jaffa Gate. We had two servants, and were well looked after. My life was regular. I got up about seven, and went to the offices of the Zionist Commission, where I had a room and a desk. The routine work was simply to examine the applications of people who wanted to come to Israel, and to sift them in relation to the main problems of buying land and settling people on it through the Jewish National Fund (*Keren Kayemet*) and bringing immigrants to the land, training them and supplying them with equipment. Soon after we got there Colonel, later Brigadier, Frederick Kisch, who had had an outstanding career as a professional soldier in the first world war, came out as Chairman of the Zionist Executive. He was the Zionist boss, and an able man he was. He became a great friend of ours, as well as of my wife's sister, Miriam and her husband Harry Sacher. (Harry practised for nine years at the Palestine bar.)

It was not an easy life, but it was exciting and rewarding. We lived comfortably compared to most; life for the majority was tough. Becky saw more of it than I did. Her job was to get around, give talks on health and welfare in the outlying districts, see where funds were most urgently required, expedite relief, determine priorities in the planning and building of hospitals, inspect schools and social centres. Most of the women she met were working and at the same time bringing up children – putting in a ten to twelve hour day. Butter was a luxury. They could not afford meat and fish. Bread and cheese was the common diet. It was tough going.

I was not there merely to open the mail, sift applications, and report back to Weizmann on how the British Government were backing up the work of the Zionist Commission: I was there also to play a role in the development of Israel myself. It was hard work. The first High Commissioner to be appointed to Palestine was Sir Herbert Samuel, who occupied the post from 1920 to 1925. He was not, I fear, a successful choice. I happened to be with Weizmann when the idea of appointing Samuel occurred to him. We were returning by boat from Tel Aviv to Cairo on a short visit we made in 1919. Weizmann suddenly got up from his chair and started pacing his cabin excitedly. 'Why ever are you walking about like that?' I asked him. 'I can't keep still,' he said, 'because I've had a brilliant idea. I'm going to ask Lloyd George if he will appoint Herbert Samuel to be the first High Commissioner of Palestine.' 'But what if Samuel refuses?' 'No Jew could refuse,' said Weizmann. He was right about Samuel, but wrong about the appointment. Samuel, an extremely good and just man, was so conscientious about the possibility of not being neutral in his judgements because of his Zionist prejudices that he leaned over backwards to make sure he was not unfair to the Arabs. He very much overdid it, and his well-meant attitude exacerbated some problems and created others. It was Herbert Samuel who appointed Husseini Grand Mufti of Jerusalem; the same Husseini who in 1936 organised the Palestine disturbances for which he was exiled in 1937, who assisted Hitler in World War II and was largely responsible for the mass extermination of Jews in the Moslem areas of Bosnia.

My personal experience in those eighteen months led me to the conclusion that little or no progress was made in developing the Jewish Homeland because the British authorities, having reverted to the policy of favouring Arab interests (as Weizmann had anticipated), were

9 Dr Chaim Weizmann at the opening of the Daniel Sieff Research Institute, Rehovot, 1934.

10 A four-generation picture: Ephraim Sieff (*centre*), Israel Sieff, his eldest son Michael, and Jonathan, first grandchild.

11 Edward Sieff, present Chairman of Marks & Spencer.

12 The Board of Directors of Marks & Spencer when Lord Sieff was Chairman.

13 An informal picture taken while Granada were doing a tape-recording of Lord Sieff's life.

14 Lord and Lady Marks.

15 and 16 On the occasion of Lord Sieff's 80th birthday: (*left to right*) Lily Sieff (Marcus's wife), Elaine Blond (sister-in-law), Daphne Sieff (Michael's wife), Lord Sieff, Miriam Sacher (sister-in-law, and sister of Simon Marks) and Judith Shechterman (daughter). (*below*) Lord Sieff with his son Marcus and his wife Lily; David, Marcus's son and his wife Jeni are on the left and in front are Marcus's two daughters, Amanda and Daniela.

terrified of upsetting the Arabs. Samuel made the smallest possible attempts to claim for the Jews what they had in public law been promised. I could give many examples of this. For instance, when General Allenby departed, he left behind, as Chief Administrator, General L. J. Bols. Becky and I saw a lot of him, and liked him very much. It was necessary for me to discuss such matters as the purchase of land with him. One day he told me that I could have the use of 30,000 dunams (approximately 7,500 acres) for settlement at Besan, one of the most fertile places in Galilee. Would I go to Nazareth to discuss the implementation of the project with the military governor of Galilee, Colonel Cox?

I went. We could do nothing that day, the Colonel told me: he must have time to go through the whole of the correspondence and consider what action he should take in the matter. I thought this somewhat strange: I had assumed he had received his instructions from his superior officer, Bols, and would, on my arrival with the proper credentials, at once prepare to carry them out. However, I retired for the night, staying with a local friendly Arab.

The following day I reported back to Colonel Cox. He told me that he could not allow me to have the land. He dared not act on his instructions. The bazaars were already buzzing with news of my arrival. All kinds of wild rumours were flying around. Tempers were rising. It was essential not only that the local Arabs be told that there was no truth in the belief that such a transfer of land was being contemplated, but that the project be dropped, and that I leave the area forthwith. He was very sorry. I went back to General Bols with my tail between my legs. 'Why did you send me there in the first place?' I asked him. 'You must have known there would be trouble.' 'Yes,' he said. 'I knew you might not get anywhere. But on the other hand you might have.' I believe Bols honestly thought we might make some progress at Besan and get our land without the Arabs being too upset. He thought it was worth while sending me, therefore, on what might turn out to be a fool's errand. But I am equally sure that Cox was of a different frame of mind. I believe that in the twenty-four hour period in which he claimed to be thinking about his instructions they somehow leaked to the Arabs, deliberately fomenting their feelings of hostility to us.

On another occasion I went to see King Abdullah himself about the acquisition of a *giftlik*, as a parcel of land belonging to the Moslem church is called. We soon came to an amiable agreement, and to mark his satisfaction with the terms we arranged, he sent round two beautiful milk-white mares to me the same evening. But before I had risen for an early breakfast the next morning the mares had mysteriously disappeared. If Abdullah's men had been sent to take them back by stealth, why had he risked public obloquy by presenting them openly to me in the first place? It was more likely that the local British – not the top men – had removed the mares; they did not want the development of good Jewish-Arab relations in case these undermined the local Arab-British entente.

Though these eighteen months were hard, and frequently disappointing and depressing, they were a wonderful experience. Becky and I were taken out of the world we had lived in from birth to our early thirties, and began a totally new existence. We were sorry to come home. It was well that we did. Looking back on that period, we ought not, I think, to have left our children so long being looked after by grandparents, relatives and nurses. I have often thought since of busy and devoted parents, diplomats for example, who feel bound to leave young children for lengthy periods at a time. Becky and I meant very well; but I am not sure we did entirely the right thing. We came back in 1921. My father's letters had for several weeks been stressing more and more clearly that the business was presenting him with many problems. Eventually a letter arrived which asked me bluntly to come back home and help. We wound up our affairs, and returned to Manchester.

I cannot resist making my own assessment of that great man, Weizmann, formed as it must be on limited experience analysed by imperfect judgement, subject to the prejudice of friendship. Weizmann's genius reached its peak, I think, in the period of the Balfour Declaration and the Zionist Commission. The marks of it were his knowledge of men, his sense of history, and above all his understanding of how the British mind worked in the sphere of power politics. His colleagues on the Zionist Executive did not have his feeling and insight. Many of them came from Russia. A revolutionary approach was natural to them. If they had not become Zionists at a very early age they might have become Bolsheviks. Certainly they did not feel that precipitating a situation mattered if at the end of it you got some action. The revolution was the object: if it succeeded, all would be well. Weizmann was a born *anti*-Bolshevik. He was almost born British in his assumption that only gradual development and expansion could achieve the long term aim. He used to say it would be no use trying to treat the British as if they were babies. As a country, they were ancient and mature: their minds worked to a pattern which was nearly a thousand years old. You could not force them into a new attitude of mind: if you wanted them to adopt one, you had to build it up gradually, brick by brick until they seemed to have completed the building for themselves. I think this bears on what is sometimes – not unkindly – said of him: that he concealed from the British his intention to create not a home for the Jews in Palestine but an independent country. I do not think that he wished to deceive the British or ever did so. He wished to draw them on to agree with him step by step in the building of what he was convinced could not but turn out to be the Jewish State. He believed that the right road for him was the right one for the British people, and that they would come to understand this when they travelled far enough along that road, and see the justice of the demand for a Jewish National Home and eventually an independent Jewish State.

Looking back to this time I admire more and more the speed and finesse with which Weizmann sized up the situation he found in arriving in Egypt on our way to Palestine. He bumped into Jews who were hostile to Zionism, Jews who wished to exploit the movement, Jews who knew nothing of it and therefore might help to make or break it. Egypt was a strange country for him and he had to find his way, and quickly. Then on to Palestine, where there was every temptation to be precipitate. It was terribly hard for him to keep going slow. He correctly decided immediately that above all he must be very wary of antagonising those who were powerful enough to destroy what he had already accepted in the Balfour Declaration. In later years Ben Gurion attacked the line Chaim Weizmann took in 1919 because all that it led to, he claimed, was the British getting more of *their* way as far as a Jewish National Home was concerned, and the Zionists less of *theirs*. I disagree – and I was there. I saw how wrong it would have been for Weizmann in those early days to have forced the pace. Had he forced the pace we would have been rejected. We probably would not have been allowed to do any work of a political nature in Palestine. I believed then and believe now that the British military authorities had made up their mind if not to sabotage what the Zionist Commission wanted to do, at least to prevent it from advancing and progressing along the lines of its raison d'être. And I believe that the British Government's archives will show it.

Some of the military officials we had to deal with not merely disapproved of the Government's policy enshrined in the Balfour Declaration and the Zionist Commission: they were anti-Semitic. Of course they did not want to go too far. They wanted to nullify our existence, thwart our efforts, neutralise our advance. But they did not want us to resign. Weizmann's greatness, his judgement, self-control and touch, came out in choosing just that inch of certain ground on which he could dare to make an issue. If he could not find that ground he could risk no move forward. If he could find that inch, he could if pressed deliver an unnerving counter-attack.

A perfect example occurred in the early weeks of the Zionist Commission's sojourn in Palestine, in May 1918, over Petah Tikvah, a famous early settlement founded in 1883 by Hovevei pioneers and assisted by Baron de Rothschild. It had been agreed that if this colony had to be evacuated for military reasons, the Zionist Commission would be given plenty of notice to make the necessary arrangements – for instance, lay on billets in Tel Aviv. On the Eve of the Feast of Pentecost a message came to us that the British had broken the agreement and the colony was to be moved the following morning. Two Arab villages, nearer the enemy lines, were to be left unevacuated: Arabs could be trusted, presumably, Jews could not. Weizmann asked to see Allenby, the Commander-in-Chief. 'Commander-in-Chief,' he said, 'if you evacuate Petah Tikvah, the Zionist Commission will leave Palestine and return to Britain.' Allenby was very shaken and asked for ten minutes in which to consider the matter. He left the room. After ten minutes' discussion with Bols who was in the middle of his dinner, he returned to the room and said: 'Subject to certain guarantees which we are going to demand from you, we will not evacuate Petah Tikvah.' That night Weizmann dined with Allenby and they sat up all night talking. From that moment his relationship with the Commander-in-Chief became one of trust, liking and mutual respect. And at once the Commission got under way.

Those who criticise Weizmann's progress at this time unfavourably seem to forget sometimes that the Zionist Commission was a divided one. Sylvain Lévi for France, or Bianchini for Italy, knew nothing at all about Zionism. Both were there to find out all they could for their governments. Myself and Cowen were enthusiasts. Eder wasn't. Leon

Simon was a very good Zionist but the kind of intellectual who disliked action. Weizmann had to walk warily.

Added to Weizmann's difficulties were his differences with the American Zionists, with whose great leader, Louis Brandeis – Justice of the Supreme Court 1916-1939, President of the American Zionist Organisation 1918-1921 – he was unfortunately soon to clash. Brandeis was a fine man, a puritan, an intellectual, a man of probity and courage, but inclined to theory as opposed to practice, and disposed to generalise from sketchy knowledge. Brandeis's views on what was possible, indeed, necessary in Palestine in 1919 – after one visit of two weeks – were fantastic; good man that he was, his aspirations were hopelessly over-ambitious, impracticable, visionary, misleading, uninformed. It was immensely difficult for Weizmann to try and get this well-intentioned but myopic zealot, who at the time was the doyen of the American Zionists, to get his feet back on the ground. He was most anxious not to offend a man who, though he knew little of what was happening in Palestine, controlled vast funds of which the Zionist Commission was in need. He tried hard, but failed to keep Brandeis and himself in step. In 1921, Brandeis, then President of the World Zionist Organisation, resigned over differences with Chaim. This in turn led to a great division in the American Zionist Movement and an additional burden for Weizmann to shoulder.

Of the death of my son Daniel in 1933 it is hard to speak and I can do so only because he lives on, beloved boy, in this, the continued story of Chaim Weizmann. Daniel was a boy of great good looks with an easy manner which engaged and often charmed. He drew his breath from human beings, but his mind was absorbed in science; the idea of being a doctor combined these interests: he planned to devote himself to medical research when he had graduated from Cambridge. He looked forward to Cambridge with all his heart. But he died before he got there. Simon wrote of him:

> It was a joy to walk with him through the garden and listen to him, young as he was, describing the life of the denizens of the garden – the insects and the birds; or the life in the pond – the fish and the plants; or the planets and the stars; and even Einstein's theory of Relativity – and all expressed in a simple, though very picturesque way.

One summer afternoon Becky, Simon and I went for a walk in Hyde Park with Dr Weizmann. Weizmann had been a great support to us at the time of Daniel's death. He knew the boy very well; his son Michael and Daniel had grown up together. Weizmann began to talk of something which had always fascinated him all his life, his conviction that the problem of the monopolistic position of oil, such a crucial issue in the future history of the Middle East, could be obviated by the discovery of a method of producing oil synthetically. He believed that if abundant supplies of root starches, like manioc, tapioca and cane sugar could be grown in, say, West Africa, and if a fermentation industry could be introduced, there would be a large yield of ordinary alcohol, both for power and the production of butyl alcohol and acetone. These three materials, in large quantities and at a low price, could form the basis of two or three great industries, among them high-octane fuel, and would make the British Commonwealth independent of oil wells. From talking about this favourite subject of his we went on to discuss science generally, the application of the discoveries of pure science to technological development; how it is impossible to keep the two apart because of the peculiarities of human psychology; of how the great scientists have been humanists; and so back to our beloved Daniel who had been told that if he made the scientific grade, he would have a research laboratory of his own. Suddenly Weizmann said: 'If you want a memorial for Daniel, why don't you build a scientific institute named after him? That's the only thing he would have wanted. I will be its first director.'

Simon Marks and Harry and Miriam Sacher contributed to the financing of the project. They were very, very generous. The site chosen for the new Institute was Rehovoth. Weizmann chose it for a number of reasons. Rehovoth is about fifteen miles south-east of Tel Aviv, as the crow flies, on the road to Jerusalem. Nearby is Yavneh, whither the centre of Jewish learning was removed after the destruction of Jerusalem by the Romans in AD 70. When the Jewish scholar, Yochanan Ben Zakkai was asked by the Romans what he would like in compensation for the destruction of Jerusalem he replied: 'Yavneh and all its sages.' In modern times this area below is associated with Zionist settlement. Five miles away is Rishon le-Zion ('The First to Zion') founded as a farm village in 1882 by Russian Jews, now the centre of Israel's wine-growing. Rehovoth itself was founded by Polish Jews in 1890. It was the location of the Jewish Agency's Agricultural Experimental Station, which had been transferred from Tel Aviv in 1932 and now stood in the heart of its citrus groves. This seemed to Chaim to be the ideal place for the new Institute. He threw himself into the work of building it up with the energy of a young man with a lifetime before him. We had agreed that the Institute and its work must be of the highest standard in the world, sufficient to compel the notice and attract the support of the greatest scientists alive. Though we were helped by the outflow of German scientists under the first persecutions of the Nazi regime it was not easy to get the best people, or indeed the apparatus and raw materials.

The foundation stone of the Daniel Sieff Research Institute was laid on 12 April 1933. During the next year Weizmann planned, worked, projected. The sea of sand and the neat buildings began to boast lawns and trees, flowers, shrubs and creepers. Weizmann was obsessional about cleanliness. As he wrote in his autobiography, '... every chauffeur in Palestine knows that the Sieff Institute is one place in Palestine where one does not throw cigarette ends on the floor, but in the receptacle provided for that purpose'. The Institute was formally opened in April 1934 by Professor Richard Willstätter, the German Nobel Prize Winner in 1915, who resigned his post at Munich University in 1925 as a protest against the University's anti-Semitic policy. The High Commissioner for Palestine, Sir Arthur Wauchope was present. Willstätter made a splendid speech. He gave a penetrating analysis of what such an Institute should do and how it should do it – an olympian view, and yet somehow one felt that at the same time he was down in the foundations of the edifice, talking of the concrete realities of day-to-day work. I particularly recall what he said of the 'aim of synthesis – the improvement of nature'. He quoted Leibnitz: 'Thoughts do not come of themselves to my mind; only when I am shown things or when I am told of ideas, do new, even better thoughts readily come to me.' He ended his speech by quoting the words inscribed above the gate of the Institute:

> Work for this country.
> Work for Science.
> Work for Humanity.

Weizmann made a short speech – but how moving his reference to the days in 1918 when the Hebrew University was founded with the guns firing less than half a minute away! Simon spoke of Weizmann at last having 'this Research Institute of advanced learning, where you could find repose, and where, in an additional field, you could be of service to your people. It is a very great satisfaction, indeed, that we, your old comrades, have been able to realise this for you'. My brother-in-law, Harry Sacher, made it clear to whom the existence of the Institute was due: 'The idea of the Daniel Sieff Research Institute we owe to Dr Weizmann. It is he who had the vision of it, chose the men, selected the equipment and laid out the lines of development.'

I do not want to sing the praises of my son's monument: others have done it with an authority I do not have. But I must record the strides it made under Weizmann in its first ten years because they led to an important development. Its intellectual potential lagged behind its buildings and equipment. At the end of that period, 1934, Weizmann was sixty years old and a number of his friends asked him what he would like to commemorate the occasion. His reply was: 'I need nothing, I want nothing, and you can do nothing for me personally.' When they insisted, he said: 'All right. Enlarge the Sieff Institute.' Among his friends present was Meyer Weisgal, a most lively, energetic and amusing character, who in his youth emigrated from Poland to the US and was Secretary of the Zionist Organisation of America 1921-30. Meyer was very good at raising money. His friends turned to him when they had left Weizmann and said, 'It's a good idea. Will *you* arrange for the enlarging of the Sieff Institute?' Meyer replied: 'Then who do I go to for money?' He decided that a new and enlarged institute to include the Sieff Institute, should be called the Weizmann Institute of Science. He could then, as he put it, 'go for money to the Sieffs!' Some of his friends wondered how we would feel about the absorption of the Daniel Sieff Institute into the projected Weizmann establishment, but for us it was no problem. Meyer set a target of a million dollars. The Sachers and I urged him to make it five million. Such was the magic of the Weizmann name that the sum was reached in a few years.

I have already described what I thought was the finest hour of Weizmann's powers, but I must add that I deeply admired his work in Rehovoth in these pioneering years of the thirties. He was nearly sixty. He lived for several years in a small temporary bungalow nearby the famous Weizmann House, with its wonderful view of Jerusalem and the Judean hills. He left it at eight thirty in the morning for the Institute, and frequently worked there until seven at night. They had only two small bedrooms and a living-room, which served for Chaim's study and library. It was particularly hard on Vera. But he had asked for his Institute, and, characteristically, he worked like a demon on it until he was sure it rested on secure foundations.

Weizmann was to make other unsurpassed contributions to the founding of the state of Israel. This is not the place or time to embark on an indictment of the British Government's policy towards Palestine between the two world wars but I must say that by 1947 it had led to such a bloody chaos that the British had nothing more to offer by 2 April 1947 than to throw in their hand and asked for the future of Palestine to be placed on the agenda of the United Nations. Many members of the UN were opposed to the idea of discussing the future of Palestine when, unlike the Arabs, whose states were members of the UN, the Jews were not going to be allowed to take part in the proceedings on even relatively equal terms. The General Assembly consequently passed a special resolution granting a hearing to the Jewish Agency, the organ of Jewish self-government which under the authority of the mandatory power, Britain, had administered Jewish affairs in Palestine. A committee of seven Jewish leaders was immediately appointed to represent the Jewish Agency at the UN – David Ben Gurion, Dr Abba Hillel Silver, Moshe Sharett, Hayim Greenberg, Mrs Rose Halprin, Dr Nahum Goldmann and Dr Emmanuel Neumann. As a result of these hearings the General Assembly established a special committee on Palestine – the UNSCOP. The Jewish Agency representatives urged UNSCOP to make the establishment of an independent Jewish State the basis of Arab-Jewish friendship in the Middle East. The Arabs bitterly opposed this.

It happened that some of the members of UNSCOP were in the Palestinian part of Haifa when the ship *Exodus 1947* arrived packed with desperate refugee Jews from Europe. They were illegal immigrants, so the British authorities refused them entry and forcibly deported them to the Displaced Persons camps of Hamburg. Whatever this action decided it ensured the immediate end of the British Mandate. It was a frightful and squalid end to a quarter of a century of government which any British government would find it hard now to defend. The UNSCOP recommended the partition of Palestine. In place of the Mandate Palestine should be divided, part going to existing Arab states, the remainder becoming an independent Jewish State, which would include the Negev. For this it would be essential to get American and Russian support and a two-thirds majority in the General Assembly. The Arabs subjected the UN in general and the US in particular to a tremendous pressure of lobbying. US policy was dominated by the State Department's determination to keep on good terms with the Arab States to get their oil.

It is my belief, and there are certainly many historians who agree, that it was Weizmann alone and personally, who, rising from his sickbed to visit President Truman in the White House, broke through the barrier which stood in the way of the foundation of the State of Israel. The discussion of partition took place at the UN in November 1947. The State Department, having decided, very reluctantly, to accept partition, had decided that the Negev, with its all-important port of Aqaba, should go to the Arabs. Weizmann pointed out to President Truman that unless the Jews had Aqaba, their sea-lines would be completely cut off from the East by the Egyptians closing the Suez Canal or by the Iraqis blockading the Persian Gulf. 'I was extremely happy to find that the President read the map very quickly and very clearly,' wrote Weizmann in his memoirs. 'He promised me that he would communicate at once with the American delegation at Lake Success.' The President telephoned Mr Herschel Johnson at three o'clock that same afternoon. American policy on the Negev was dramatically reversed. This opened the way to a vote in the General Assembly. On 29 November the United Nations resolved that the British Mandate would end as soon as possible but 'not later than August First 1948. . . . Independent Arab and Jewish States . . . should come into existence. . . .'

Six months later Weizmann persuaded President Truman to recognise the State of Israel. The importance of this achievement cannot be understood without reference to what happened after the passing of the 29 November resolution. The main factor in the situation was the policy pursued by the British Government in relation to the maintenance of law and order in Palestine. In the event of Arab opposition to the creation of independent states *after* the establishment of partition, the Security Council of the United Nations was to deal with it. If there were opposition *before* that time, the Mandatory Power, Britain, was to deal with it. The British Government, however, took the view both that it would be 'implementation of partition' – and therefore premature, and improper – to protect the Jews from the Arabs, and at the same time that the Jews had no right to organise themselves into a fighting force for their own protection. Into the bargain they refused to allow the United Nations into Palestine before the Mandate came to an end. It was an impossible situation for the Jews. The Arabs made hay of it. So-called 'irregular' forces poured into Palestine at several points, and laid about them almost with impunity. The Jews were provoked to breaking point. It looked as though having come into existence on paper, the new State of Israel would be destroyed before it was born. Faith in the viability of the State of Israel fell day by day. The Arabs would drive them into the sea – even some of Israel's friends began to talk like this. Had it not been a mistake to try and promote Israeli independence? Was is not urgently necessary to get the United Nations decision to establish a State of Israel reversed before there was a terrible catastrophe? Thoughts like this became talk in the corridors of power at the United Nations and in Western capitals. The road to the establishment of a State of Israel was being barricaded again.

When the situation looked blackest, in January 1948, Weizmann, then in London, was asked by the Executive of the Jewish Agency to return to New York and help them face the crisis. Delayed by ill-health it was 18 March before he was able to see the President. Mr Truman made it clear he personally was still firmly in favour of partition, and an independent State of Israel, but the following day the American representative on the Security Council made a statement in the opposite sense, proposing that partition be suspended and that a UN trusteeship should replace the Mandate when it ended on 15 May. When it was clear that Trusteeship was not acceptable in the General Assembly a programme for a Truce – a kind of general standstill – was substituted. Weizmann opposed this too. He knew that unless independence was achieved forthwith it might be spirited away into some hypothetical future. Day by day, beseiged, bombarded, lobbied and beseeched, he stuck to his guns. On one occasion the whole of the American UN delegation visited him on his sick-bed, begging him to accept it as a fact that if the Jews got their independence the Arabs would batter them to death and hurl them into the sea. Weizmann refused to be moved. Israel could and would defend itself, he said, and smash its invaders. He would not budge. On 13 May he wrote a letter to President Truman imploring him to recognise the realities of the situation and begging him to take the only course which could bring order out of chaos – 'recognise the Provisional Government of the new Jewish State.' He begged the President to do so the moment the

Mandate came to an end the following day. The same day came a message from Ben Gurion in Palestine via Meyer Weisgal who had just arrived in New York: Ben Gurion wanted to know if Weizmann favoured the proclamation of Israeli Independence. 'What are they waiting for?' demanded Weizmann – he had sent a message some days ago saying 'Proclaim the Jewish State now or never!' but it had never got there.

Then came the moment of high drama, and the switch in American policy which changed the fate of the world. On 14 May 1948, Sir Alan Cunningham, the High Commissioner, left Palestine. The Mandate was finally at an end. I doubt whether any country cleared out from a foreign land in a more disorderly fashion. Cunningham – I do not denigrate him personally – had his orders: he was not to co-operate with the Jews in any way. So, the railways stopped running, the mail ceased to be delivered, the assets of State were transferred to the United Kingdom or knocked down at auction, and the British – just cleared out. They left a mess for the new Jewish Government to deal with.

At four p.m. that day, at the Museum of Tel Aviv, David Ben Gurion read Israel's Proclamation of Independence in the name of the thirty-nine members of the People's Council, Representatives of the Jewish Community of Eretz-Israel and of the Zionist Movement. At that moment President Truman sat in the White House with his Secretary of State discussing the letter from Weizmann which lay in front of him on his desk. At five fifteen p.m. the President astounded the world, and indeed his own representative in the United Nations, Ambassador Jessup, by announcing that the United States of America had recognised Israel as an independent country. The following day the leading five Israeli statesmen cabled to Weizmann, the message beginning:

> On the occasion of the establishment of the Jewish State we send our greetings to you, who have done more than any other living man towards its creation. Your stand and help have strengthened all of us. We look forward to the day when we shall see you at the head of the State established in peace.

The next day they cabled to say he had been elected President of the State of Israel.

To me it will always remain a great pity, and something of a shame, that in this hour of greatness Weizmann was not treated by his colleagues with that degree of imaginative consideration which his unique contribution – fully acknowledged by them – should have received. I can quite understand why the Presidency to which Weizmann was elected was a symbolic one, on the pre-de Gaulle French model, and not an executive one on the American model: Ben Gurion was too conscious of the difference in views between himself and Weizmann to permit a Presidency which would give Weizmann the right and opportunity to participate actively in the conduct of Israel's policy. Ben Gurion wanted a nationalist State which would carve its way to power and security with alignments with the West, through such relationships – though they did not exist at the time – as NATO and the Common Market, and so on, while Weizmann envisaged the future of Israel in terms of a 'Middle Eastern Switzerland'. I can understand why from the beginning Weizmann's occupancy of the Presidency was such as to justify from my friend Richard Crossman the description 'The Prisoner of Rehovoth'. I did not, and do not, approve of how he was treated.

There were other matters which, though of less moment, were more avoidable: and because they seemed much more significant than in fact they were intended to be they should not have been allowed to happen. I mentioned that thirty-seven men signed Israel's Declaration of Independence. The list did not include Weizmann's name. He was upset by this. He assumed that these men were invited to sign because they were regarded as of outstanding eminence. In fact they signed as members of the National Council which had been set up to satisfy the United Nations' requirement that there be a body in existence to which provisional government could be handed over when the Mandate ended. He was hurt that he was not asked to sign. True, he was not in Palestine at the time, but in New York. But when the Declaration was signed by thirty-four men in Palestine, space was left for the signatures of three men who were absent at that time. Whatever the rational explanation of the names upon that roll, the document, after all, is the Declaration of Israel's Independence, and for Weizmann's signature not to be on it seems peculiarly inept and inappropriate. If I were to hear it said that the putative slight was unintentional, I would refer to Dickens's definition of a gentleman, as a man who is never rude to another *un*intentionally.

However, it is not my purpose to defend a great man who needs no defence, and if he did, would find it in his own deeds. Nor to complain about how he was treated. History will take care of the men who are big enough to belong to her. The rest is silence. My only object here is to record my gratitude for what Weizmann did for me. He transformed my life, as he did Simon's, bringing to it as well as a daily duty the thrill of service to the vision of a great cause. He gave us a new dimension of the enjoyment of life. He gave us his wisdom, his sense of fun, his prophecy: he opened our eyes, he warmed our hearts; he made our senses sing. He was loyal, grateful, strong. He was a giant. It is good to look back on this friendship with a great man.

8
Simon Reshapes Marks and Spencer

The first great period of Marks and Spencer was the Penny Bazaar period. The first world war brought that to an end. The age of the penny was over. During the war we had to buy what goods we could, whatever the price. A second new period of expansion was now to begin. I suppose, for convenience's sake, it could be called the Five Shilling period, though that would give an imperfect, if not misleading idea of what were its real and meaningful features. Michael Marks envisioned, planned and led the first advance. Simon did the same for the second. In a few years he converted a chain of bazaars into a national network of super-stores.

When after the war, Simon took stock of the situation, what impressed him most was the enormous competition of the American chain store, Woolworths. Whereas Marks and Spencer were selling a confusing jumble of goods of all kinds varying in price from a penny to three pounds and presenting them in stores which somehow seemed to belong to an age that was past, Woolworths were selling a more compact range of goods at a neat sixpence and threepence in stores that were modern, large, well-lighted and attractively laid out. By 1923 Simon had concluded that unless Marks and Spencer went through an almost revolutionary phase which would give it a personality, price range and appeal as attractive in their way as those of Woolworths, it would either struggle along as a kind of poor relation or go under altogether. He described the situation as he saw it as follows:

Woolworths had been making extraordinary progress and were rapidly developing throughout the country. They had become a household word, a great commercial institution. We had marked time, and could report no change since the days of my father, other than a few more branches.

I was conscious of my own shortcomings and ignorance. I had never worked in a shop. I had no training in the business, other than that which I was to acquire by trial and error. I felt that somehow I had to expand my experience, learn from other people how to face up to the competition of this commercial giant whose red signs were beginning to dominate the main shopping streets of Great Britain.

A distant relative from New York, Herman Germain, happened to be in London on business. I told him of my anxieties – how did others in the United States counter this opposition? Could other businesses live side by side and still prosper? He encouraged me to make my first trip to the United States and promised to give me introductions to firms who were operating successfully in the same lines of business.

This was in 1924. Simon travelled extensively in the United States and thoroughly enjoyed it. He renewed many of his Zionist contacts and warmed up old friendships, but he was anxious to get back as soon as he could. He concentrated hard, therefore, on a study of the main American chain stores. As he had anticipated it was from Woolworths he learned most:

It was there that I learned many new things. It was about my first serious lesson in the chain store art. I learned the value of more imposing, commodious premises, modern methods of administration and the statistical control of stocks in relation to sales. I learned that new accounting machines could help to reduce the time to give the necessary information in hours instead of weeks. There was no doubt that these methods of control were to help us in the speedy development of our business. Hitherto, we had always been behindhand in our information, which was a formidable handicap. I learned the value of counter footage, that is, that each counter foot of space had to pay wages, rent, overhead expenses and earn a profit. There could be no blind spots on the counters in so far as goods were concerned. This meant a much more exhaustive study of the goods we were selling and the needs of the public. It meant that the staff, who were operating with me had to be re-educated and retrained. It meant new people, new forces.

When he returned he was tremendously excited. I think that in what he used to say later about the lessons he had learned he was unduly modest: what he had seen and heard only confirmed what he had thought out for himself. But the visit had been essential: it cemented his confidence in his own vision of what his policy should be. I can hear him now: 'You see, Israel, what they do is this –' and then he would describe an American chain store doing something which I had heard him say *we* might do at least two years before, but which, for some reason or another, we had been prevented from doing. More of that later. Meanwhile, his American tour, in his own words, had shown him the need to pursue the following policy:

> ... nothing over five shillings, an extensive programme of enlarging and improving our shops and the introduction of weekly stock checking lists which control the production and flow of goods from factory to shops.

The implications of these three simple precepts were vast and complicated, and gave rise to problems which I shall deal with later. But at this point I should record that Simon came back to Britain with more than trading principles in mind. His tour had done much to crystalise his business philosophy. He came back also more than ever imbued with a general sense of the moral basis on which modern business should be conducted, so that all participants, management, employee and public could benefit. His father had always done his very best for the welfare of his workers. In America Simon saw that daring investment in better working conditions made for more efficient, as well as happier, employees. Accounting procedures which put more trust in individual workers not only brought down costs but, by showing that management trusted employees, got better service in the store. Thirdly, and most important, he saw that with a public becoming better educated and more discriminating every year, the firms that supplied the highest quality goods as a matter of moral duty and out of a sense of public service would have the best chance of being commercially successful in an age of intensifying competition.

Thinking of this kind is so taken for granted in the present day that it may be worth while noting that many British businessmen in those early twenties would have thought Simon's views dubiously sentimental if not positively dangerous.

The immediate problem in the way of his implementing this philosophy was finance. The Company was doing well, and on its present basis was highly profitable, but a commercial policy of substituting 'super-stores' for erstwhile Penny Bazaars was going to be extremely costly. Our old stores rarely had a frontage of more than twenty feet, and were relatively shallow in depth; much greater space was required. Simon's first experiment with the store of the future was at Darlington. It had a frontage of 20 feet, but a depth of 94. Blackpool, the next, had a frontage of 58 feet. This kind of change required more capital outlay than the firm could stand. That same year, consequently, the Board decided that the Company must go 'public'. Proposals were made to the British Foreign and Colonial Corporation. The response was not encouraging. Simon and his Board were told the Corporation could not support them: Marks and Spencer were advised to continue on existing lines. Simon, that issuing house thought, was getting above himself, and trying to bite off more than he could chew. He had to plod away on his own resources for a year or two until, supported by the Prudential Company – the beginning of a happy relationship which continues to this day – he was able to form a public company in 1926.

The second leg of Simon's tripartite policy was the weekly checking list. Michael Marks, even in the open market at Leeds, worked on the principle that it did not pay to stock low-priced articles which hung about on the trestle top: where the profit margin was narrow, only the goods which sold well and quickly must be stocked. The same principle held good for the five-shilling article: even at that level the profit margin was small enough to require that the volume and pace of sales remained high. Michael Marks, standing behind his trestle table himself, could see for himself what was selling and what was sticking. But the Chairman of a national chain of stores was not in the same position. The idea of the weekly checking list was to equip him and his central buyers with a pair of eyes. Instead of having to rely on quarterly or bi-quarterly returns on sales for their knowledge of what was selling and what was not, Simon now set up a system by which weekly reports were submitted.

Of his new policy, however, the one which most affected the development of Marks and Spencer was the five shilling limit.

One of its effects was to make textiles, and particularly women's clothing, our most important and popular line. It drove out a vast range of goods – the 'jumble' as Simon referred to it – which did not fit the modern pattern – and brought the textiles in. To look forward, and backward a little, in 1926 before Simon's revolution in policy bore fruit, the range of goods for sale would have been what a pre-war Penny Bazaar shopper would have expected, with the exception of the addition of gramophone records. In 1932 over seventy per cent of those items had disappeared. Textiles, on the other hand, had vastly increased. And this was because we soon saw that, particularly by dealing direct with the manufacturer, we could achieve the continuous improvement in quality and value in textiles which Simon felt was now the fundamental principle according to which Marks and Spencer should operate. The growth of the sale of textiles is perhaps the greatest single feature in this great fifteen year period of growth from 1925 to 1940. By 1940 textiles had become by far the biggest single section of the Company's business, at least three times as large as any other.

This development was of special significance for me personally. My mission for several years was to lead the campaign for increased direct dealing with the manufacturer – having in the field of textiles the experience I had acquired in my father's business.

We were, of course, only following and adapting to the new trend in the market for textiles. The demand for clothing had not only increased: it had changed. When Michael Marks was running his Penny Bazaars in the early years of the century the labourer had one suit of clothes for both work and relaxation, and the mechanic in the town expected his 'best' suit to last several years, if not a lifetime. The chances were that in the evenings when a man took his working clothes off and put on something else it would be the one pair of trousers and jacket he had, apart from his 'best' suit, if, indeed, he was lucky enough to have that. He would wear a cap and muffler round his neck and wear heavy boots which after some wear for 'best' would be worn to go to work. Light shoes, collar and tie for leisure were luxuries beyond the masses even when worn at their work. The woman's dress would frequently be heavy serge; she might wear a tweed skirt with a blouse of velvet or sateen. During the week she would wear a shawl, on Sundays a short jacket or coat. Her underclothing was, according to the season, one to three petticoats, usually of flannel. Her stockings, woollen in winter, possibly cotton in summer. Her corsets were made of whalebone or steel. Her camisole, cotton or flannel. On her feet she almost certainly wore boots, laced or buttoned. Thousands of women would have no headgear but a man's cloth cap. Many working class housewives made their own crude clothes or bought them second-hand.

After the first world war there was a change. Girls who had worked in factories during the war had come to regard their clothing as unnecessarily ugly and had learned that it was unhygienic and, in some cases, dangerous. They saw how much more comfortable and sensible, as well as more attractive, were the clothes of better-off women. The great change was in weight. Slips and knickers of cotton, silk or art silk, replaced petticoats. The outer garment became a dress or a costume coat and skirt, often knitted of stockinet. Stockings became silk or artificial silk. Home-made clothes were on their way out. The sale of dress material dwindled. The market for ready-made clothing much increased. The vogue of bicycling increased the desire for freedom of movement. Short skirts became fashionable. The light clothing industries burgeoned and spread rapidly in the twenties in London, Manchester and Nottingham. Steel-boned corsets disappeared, and factories began to turn out garments of elastic webbing. As well as the change in taste and purchasing power there were the effects of technological innovation and communication. The popular press, the radio, the cinema and the motor car made people much more aware of each other, and consequently of what they wore. The mass market in textiles made its appearance. It made successful buying more profitable, misjudgement of taste less easy to correct. In earlier days gone a manufacturer of women's coats who misread taste and could not sell his goods in London might hope to sell them in the north of England in the following year. But after the war all the girls knew what was around, and even the poorest of them who could afford to buy would not be fobbed off with what other girls had rejected.

The motor-car, the bus, the lorry and the local train had a considerable effect upon people's shopping habits, and therefore on the shape of the retail industry. Cheaper and easier communication made it easy for shoppers to get into the centre of the town. Retailers, therefore, were able to serve much bigger areas of population. The small retailers, especially the ones who were also producers or craftsmen, decreased in number. The big retailing organisations, on the other hand, grew fast.

Another feature of the twenties was a rapid development in the application of technology to the production of goods, especially of textiles. The war gave this a great impetus. New techniques much increased the productivity of labour, and scientific discoveries made possible the creation of new types and ranges of cheap manufactured goods on a scale never known before. The combination of these factors would obviously have suited Marks and Spencer in any event but we were very much guided and inspired to take advantage of them by the influence which Dr Weizmann exercised upon us. It was not only that his highly specialised knowledge as an industrial chemist enabled him to advise us about new developments – he was, for instance, instructing us in the possibilities of synthetic fibres long before they were an actuality – but that he schooled us in general terms in the habit of applying a scientific attitude of mind to the problems of industrial production. Under his influence we did not see ourselves as mere shopkeepers. We came to regard ourselves as a kind of technical laboratory. We felt it was one of our functions to provide our suppliers with expert technical information about the new materials and processes which the advance of technology was making available. We saw ourselves as, in our limited way, production engineers, industrial chemists, laboratory technicians. We learned to exercise an active influence on production generally, and on the textile industry in particular.

But I have run on through the 1920s into the 1930s. I must return to the point at which I joined the Company as full-time Director – 1926. Simon had moved from Manchester to London permanently in 1920, to take up residence in the London offices of the Company. At this time I was continuing to work as a Director of my father's firm, and though I saw and talked a great deal with Simon my only formal involvement in the Marks and Spencer Company was official attendance at regular Board Meetings. When I came to London I used to stay with Simon at his home, and we would sit up into the night talking business.

One Friday night as soon as I arrived I felt that there was something wrong. I knew that Simon wasn't happy. I said nothing to him, that night, but on the Saturday afternoon I said to him, 'Simon, there's something wrong, and you must tell me'. 'Oh,' he said, 'there's nothing wrong. It's your imagination. There's nothing wrong at all.'

I had a sleepless night. I knew perfectly well that he was not himself. On the Sunday morning I said to him again, 'Simon, I must know the truth. Tell me: what is the matter?' He burst out with the words, 'The truth is I can't – I don't want to – carry on very much longer – I can't. I've nobody to talk to.' And he poured it all out to me. The great flood of hopes, ideas and plans which had been canalised by his experience in the United States and which he wanted to direct into a great river of expansion was being pent up by his feeling that some of the people closest to him in the business were not so much unsympathetic as not really cognizant of what he was talking about when he let himself go. It was two years since he had returned brimming with energy and initiative from America and he seemed to be making no progress whatsoever. It was not so much hostility that frustrated him as lack of comprehension, which for someone of his quick and active spirit was even worse than flat resistance. He longed to drive forward the way he instinctively knew he and the business had to go, and he had nobody to talk to.

Simon always needed somebody to talk to. It was not that he needed ideas, reassurance or additional self-confidence: but he needed a back wall against which he could play his shots. He liked to think aloud, and though he was resourceful and fearless in an open argument, he also needed, introvert that he was, a solid comfortable trusted friend to whom he could tell his dreams without feeling inhibited by a sense of vulnerability.

'Oh,' I said, 'you want somebody to talk to? Well, that's all right. Who is in the office next to you?' He told me who it was. I said, 'I shall come down a week tomorrow' – that was a Monday – 'I'll join you for a year and sit in the next room so that you'll have somebody to talk to for a year at any rate.' Simon said, 'But what would your mother say?' I said, 'I don't know what my mother's going to say, but I'm coming a week on Monday.' 'I can't pay you what you're earning,' he said. 'You won't have to pay me anything,' I said. 'I'm coming free. I've got enough money. I don't want to get paid from your firm: I can do quite well enough out of mine.'

I came down the following week. I remember it very well because it was the day the General Strike began and I had to come down by car. He met me on my arrival, as he met me so many hundreds of times in the next forty years, when I returned from visits up and down the country, or abroad, and took me back to Marks and Spencer. 'Now, where's my office?' I said when we arrived. He took me up to his. He had had another desk moved in. 'You are sitting there,' he said. 'But I wanted to go in the next room, because if I'm in the same room I'll only bother you with questions.' 'No,' he said, 'you must be in here because I *want* you to ask me questions. That's exactly what I want.' And that's how I began as a full-time member of the Board of Marks and Spencer.

Not that I knew it at the time. I thought I had come only for a year. When I decided to stay for good, it was not so much my mother but my father with whom I had to deal. In case it should be thought that I regarded myself, or was regarded by Simon, as somebody who was already equipped to play a dominant and effective role in the operations of this remarkable Company at that time, I hasten to quote from a letter written by Simon to our mutual brother-in-law, Harry Sacher:

Israel has now definitely decided to be a permanent worker in the Company. We had discussed this matter often in the last few months without believing it to be possible. After a few discussions with his father, Israel decided a few days ago to come into the firm whole time. He has already entered on his functions in the creation of an Organisation Personnel dept. He is tackling the question of organisation of individual branches and the economy of the store generally. We are hoping by concentration on unnecessary expense, on re-arrangement, on reorganisation, to save very many thousands of pounds. Our aim is at least £20,000 without in any way harming the business, on the contrary, the efficiency of the personnel will increase, we hope. We have now had a year or more experience in the larger stores and we now know where to make our economies and on what points to concentrate. Israel is an apt pupil, and with his usual energy and initiative should prove himself a great asset to the Company. Once he has established his organisation dept., I will initiate him into the merchandising dept. So that the weaknesses of our executive will be remedied and the business need not be so dependent on me in case of accidents. That we owe not only to ourselves but to the investing public. I am happy that we have been able to arrange for Israel to come up permanently, as I feel I have at last that intelligent co-operation which is essential if we are to get the uttermost out of our business.

When I had settled down my main role was to assist Simon in using what knowledge I had of textiles, and my readiness to go out and meet people, to try and develop that direct contact between us and the manufacturer, by-passing the wholesaler, which Simon thought essential if we were to be able to market garments of reliable quality within the five shillings range which he had set himself. At the beginning, certainly, I did not find my mission easy. Some manufacturers, with friends or interests in the textile wholesalers' association, were hostile. Others had prejudices of one sort or another against us. Though I encountered it somewhat later in my mission I think I should recount my experiences with one firm in particular, since what happened in that case not only gives the reader a good idea of what we tried to do but is an instance of an association which had a mutually happy and beneficent outcome, the fruits of which are still being enjoyed today.

This firm, which was to be the first with which we were able to establish a direct relationship, was an old-established firm with a high reputation, located in the Midlands. I first went to see their Chairman in 1926, to ask if they would supply us direct with the goods which we wanted to retail. The first time I went, I was asked to wait at the front door and was then told that nobody wished to discuss anything. I went a second time, and a third time and the same thing happened. I had learned patience from my experience with some of my father's customers, so I went back on a fourth occasion. This time I was told that the Chairman of the Company would see me. Quite why he decided to see me I do not know. Certainly trade was bad, this was the year of the General Strike still, and manufacturers like him needed all the trade that they could get. Yet, it was clear, he had made up his mind to refuse me from the beginning. Perhaps he intended to try and discourage me from ever coming again. I was not aware of this when I began to talk to him, and did my best to get his interest. I put to him the case I was to put so many times to so many people like him. I said that his firm had very many agents, travelling around the country, selling a little of this here, a little of that there, unable to make sound profits because so many varieties and types of hosiery were being offered. Then I went on to tell him that Marks and Spencer's was a large retailing organisation whose customers wanted sound quality at reasonable prices, rather than expensive variety of choice, and that we could give him bulk orders based on the demand of our mass-customers, and offering regular orders for fewer ranges, which would enable his firm to increase its profit. He listened to me, and when I had finished, said: 'I don't do business with bazaars.' I said, 'We may be what you call a bazaar today, but ten years from now we shall be a national chain of super-stores. We are the future. I wish you would come with us.' His manner became less curt, and his tone more explanatory. 'We can't take the risk of doing business with you,' he said. 'All our other customers would object, and we should lose their business. They don't like your competition. And if I sold to you, they'd say we were lowering our tone. They'd leave us. I'm afraid that's all there is to it.' He made it clear that the interview was over.

As I was walking down the corridor to the front door, a man came up to me. He was a Director and in charge of production. He must have been in the room next to the Chairman's office or outside in the corridor; he had certainly heard everything that I had said. 'Mr Sieff,' he said in a low voice, 'could I have a word with you?' Once we were standing outside the front door, he said, 'Do you mean to tell me that you can give me an order for a thousand dozen of men's half-hose a week?' I said, 'Yes. I've just told your Chairman. I could give an order for a thousand dozen a week.' 'And you say you would only need that order in three colours?' 'Yes,' I said, 'three colours would be sufficient.' I shall never forget his face and tone. 'My God,' he said, 'I wish I could get that business. I could cut my costs, I could make a bigger profit. I could keep more men on. Half my problem would be settled.' 'I know you could,' I said, 'I only wish your Chairman would let you.' 'Well,' he replied, 'you heard what he said. It's not that he doesn't want to. He's afraid of what the others will say.' I said I quite understood, and added, 'Some manufacturers who do business with us ask me to use the back entrance in case some of their customers see the bazaar man coming in, and take umbrage.' He said, 'Mr Sieff: I'm going to do business with you on my own responsibility. I'll take an order from you now for the first month.'

I shook hands with him. When I got out of the train at St Pancras, Simon was waiting for me on the platform. I read in his face that he saw something promising in mine. 'Simon,' I said, 'I think we've made a break-through.'

One of the first important orders we were able to effect was with this firm. They were honourable to their obligations, and we eventually absorbed large quantities of their products.

These first deals saw the beginning of something which developed into one of the most important of our operating principles: we decided not to take the additional shilling either for the profit of Marks and Spencer or for the pocket of the customer. Instead, we discussed how the shilling could be ploughed back into production, so to speak, so that the quality of the product could be improved. The reduction in cost *was* passed on to the customer, but in the form of higher value for the same amount of money paid. We benefited because our reputation for quality was increased. Our suppliers benefited because they were now producing a superior article with better methods of production which they had not had to finance themselves. The customer benefited. And, last but not least, the workers benefited because fresh capital had gone into giving them better plant and improved working conditions, and had in many cases provided work for men who had been on the dole. Later, when we were strong enough, we did not hesitate to put pressure on firms to follow in the path that this firm had blazed when it was found possible to supply goods at lower cost.

I may as well say at this point that a similar operating principle enabled us to work constructively not only with employers but for employees. There was the case of a cotton ribbed woman's pullover which at one stage we were buying – it was a popular line – to sell at two and elevenpence. I came to the conclusion that without any sacrifice of quality this woman's pullover could be manufactured at a cost which would enable it to sell at one and elevenpence. Simon and I discussed the matter into the small hours of a November night. In consequence we made a proposal which satisfied all interests. We said that Marks and Spencer would cut its profit margin by five per cent. The manufacturer agreed to reduce his price to us. The result was eminently satisfactory. Sales multiplied five times. The manufacturers and ourselves increased profits; the workers took home each Friday evening not only higher pay but a far better prospect of continued employment. Thousands of women got cheaper pullovers.

Taking the mind back to the twenties, I find it difficult to uncover the minutiae which went to help us discover the methods most suitable for our type of business. The principles which now govern our business have been so frequently tried by events that we have no hesitation as to the direction in which our business will develop. We experienced a highly developing retail business which, in the early stages, almost gave us the impression of an unavoidable spiral success. Our market was widening as we developed our stores. We encouraged manufacturers to come to us and discuss their problems. We could not have dreamed when we made reductions in the price of goods that demand would so greatly increase and would enable us to place larger orders on an ascending scale, while practically eliminating all risks to the manufacturers who supplied us with goods. We saw, not through visionary idealists' clouds but from practical results in days of high competition which proved to us that production and distribution could become a co-operative process making a positive palpable contribution to the common good. Our own profits, the satisfaction of customer, the remuneration of the worker and the technological improvement of the factory plant went hand in hand.

It is true that at the first discussion I had with the Chairman of that firm in the Midlands we did not understand each other very well. But we were able to obtain an ever-increasing number of articles in quantities which enabled our business to develop so that by the year's end we were well on the way to their participation in the growth of their business and ours. The manager of the factory helped us considerably to develop the hosiery and knitwear sections of the business to the extent that he became a growing factor in the attractive goods which were being created and manufactured to everyone's satisfaction. We had many discussions and I remember once saying to him, 'You will shortly be able to afford considerable expansion of your factory because of us and you will bring a further reduction in your cost of production and bring another blessed run of events for all concerned.'

It was hard going for several years. We did not have the same good fortune with all the manufacturers. Several of them used to come in at the back door of our offices in London for several years: if they had been seen coming in at the front door they might have been spotted by somebody in the Wholesalers' Association, in which case they would have been black-balled and expelled from that, then, august body. What changed the situation, fundamentally, was the difficult industrial period through which Britain passed between 1929 and 1932, that terrible period of slump, when business activity diminished so much that innumerable industrial enterprises faltered or failed altogether and unemployment rose to an unprecedented level of something more than three million men and women on the dole: this was the period in which Marks and Spencer continued to expand.

Simon left his own brief account of these developments:

I was again fortunate that Israel, who had his own successful business in partnership with his father, decided that he would join me more permanently, and for a period of years, would collaborate with me. He was then a Director of the company but only attended Board Meetings. From my reporting to the Board of my impressions gained in the United States and perceiving the overwhelming burden that rested on my frail shoulders, he, without hesitation, gave up his own business to join with me in what might have turned out to be a fruitless partnership. Again that unlimited confidence in me. Why I can't say to this day. But it determined me in a course of action which neither he nor I were ever to regret. Our discussions, day in and day out, week in and week out, our work together resulted in our evolving a policy and a philosophical outlook of business and life which are the foundations of our business.

It was a great accession of strength. Our organisation grew rapidly and it was our task to impart the philosophy of our evolving business to our executives. They must know the why and the wherefore; why we must be selective and discriminating; production must be responsive to consumer demand. This meant a close collaboration with our manufacturers who should be regarded as partners and whose good will should be obtained and worked for. Mutual trust, confidence and respect for each other, and the understanding of each other's problems; continuity of production, the levelling out of the peaks and the valleys, was one of the main anxieties of the manufacturers. How could we help them? That task, in the main, devolved upon Israel. . . .

The confidence of the manufacturers and the confidence of the public could only be gained by service and in time. Our name was associated with cheap goods at limited prices from 1d to 6d. Now it was to be associated with rather more expensive goods, textiles, fancy goods, toys, clothing up to 5s per article. But our connections with manufacturers in this field was sparse. We had to learn who were most promising and they usually had their business connections from many years and we were regarded almost as interlopers. The Wholesale Textile Association made it difficult and impossible for many manufacturers to trade with us. The story of our breakthrough, first with that firm in the Midlands, and then with others, is an exciting and important chapter in the development of our business.

The break-through was made possible only by our philosophic principles and understanding our friends, and our desire that both parties of the deal should be happy in their business relationship. Perhaps it was a new phenomenon in commercial life, where the buyer and the seller were aware of their mutual interests – efficient production and rational distribution – partners in the service of the community.

Why did we continue, not exactly to flourish, but certainly to grow, when all around us our competitors found themselves in difficulties? Because we answered the people's prayer. Their prayer for goods at prices which even in their days of impoverishment they could just about afford to buy. Not all of them could do that, God knows. But what we had to offer was within reach of most of them. To the others, beyond the pale of purchasing power, we held out what we could. I remember the day when a letter arrived at our head office written by the Minister of the Baptist Church in Mountain Ash, Glamorgan, South Wales. I have said that at this time there were three million men unemployed. That, however, is a figure for the country as a whole: in some parts of the country, the north-east coast of Scotland, around Whitehaven, for example, in Glasgow, in Northern Ireland, or in Lancashire, the proportion was much higher: one man in three was out of work. That was the situation around Mountain Ash. And worse. There were four thousand people living in that town, and, the Baptist Minister said, there was hardly a man who had a clean shirt, or a clean shirt that wasn't ragged. It wasn't enough, he said, for men to have a clean shirt if that shirt was ragged. He had some money at his disposal, and he had worked out what the men of Mountain Ash could afford to pay: they wanted no charity, all they wanted was a chance to pay for a clean unragged shirt. Could we do anything about this? He had read something about our general approach to business, and he wondered whether we might.

It was not a very difficult decision. I gave instructions at once that five hundred dozen shirts should be sent free to Mountain Ash immediately. A curious story. By mistake, the consignment was invoiced to him, as though they were buying them – quite a natural error – at the cost price which was two and elevenpence. Simon and I knew nothing about this until a few days later we received a letter from the Baptist Minister. He said that he would never have believed a shirt could be bought for two and elevenpence, a price which he thought was within the purchasing power of even the completely unemployed man in Mountain Ash, and he thanked God for it. And he went on, 'thank God for men who understand what self-respect means to an out-of-work miner.'

We were extremely embarrassed to find he had sent us a cheque for the shirts. We sent it back, apologised for our mistake, and made it clear that we had intended to send the shirts to help, free. Later in life Max Nicholson said to me, 'You know, Israel, you've done something of tremendous importance. You've taken away envy out of the poorer classes. They can buy an article from you which looks like what a duchess can buy, and it makes them feel as good as she is. That is the real revolution.'

As the scale of our operations increased, of course, we came to have more influence on the development of the textile industry. Our demands, and we were not backward in expressing them, were demands for quality combined with extremely large quantities, which meant continued pressure for modernisation, re-equipment, technical innovation, and improved labour relations. One of the consequences of this was that we bought fewer foreign goods and more British goods, because under the benevolent pressure which our orders were exerting British industry became more able to supply the quality we required at the price which we felt it was fair to ask the public to pay. It is an interesting little story in itself. In the days of the Penny Bazaar, Michael Marks bought more from foreign suppliers than he could afford to buy at home.

To keep his price limit within the range of his consumer he had to go to Germany, Austria, and, later, Czechoslovakia and France. It was the same immediately after the war, partly, of course, because many British domestic supplies had been re-directed into munitions. During the twenties we bought more and more from Britain. When Hitler came to power we ceased to buy from Germany. From the commercial point of view the decision was unpalatable: Germany had been our largest supplier of artificial silk stockings. We turned to Czechoslovakia for those, and when that went under to Hitler, we turned to France. But by the time the second world war began we had very largely switched to British manufacturers. It was not only because they were doing the job so much better than the Europeans, but that it was so much easier to have the co-operative relationship with fellow-countrymen than with people overseas. Simon was intensely patriotic. He loved his country. He had a special sense of obligation to the people of Lancashire and Yorkshire. He felt it was a moral duty to provide as much employment as possible for the men and women who bought in our stores. And, another instance of a rising spiral of complementary interests, as British manufacturers saw that we were putting more and more men at work and more profits in the manufacturers' pockets, they were readier to modify their practices and standards to suit the programmes which we recommended to them. By 1939 we were buying ninety-four per cent British.

In the thirties there were three developments which assisted us to increase the influence we could exert upon production. In 1935 we established our own textile laboratory. It was small at first, but it grew spectacularly. The object was to enlist the aid of science in that cause which had always been one of our first principles – quality control. We did not do our own research: our scientists looked hard at existing materials, and reported back on them so that improvements could be made on the factory floor. The more we did this, of course, the more manufacturers decided they had better do the same thing for themselves. The following year we established a Merchandise Development Department. Here we tested for colour fastness and shrinkage, the character of yarns and dyeing processes, and probed into the problems of the production of textiles by modern mass production methods. It was at this point that there developed a very close relationship between us and the great firm of Imperial Chemical Industries. An important element in this was the personal friendship, based on common outlook on business and human sympathies between Simon and myself and the Chairman of ICI Sir Harry (later Lord) McGowan. In 1936, too, we established our own Design Department. The motive was the same. The team of experts we established were paid to scrutinise the latest trends in fashion and design and to tell the manufacturers exactly what we thought about them. It was the same idea: mutual but constructive criticism within the interrelated fields of production and distribution. We did not expect to be regarded merely as shopkeepers who took what was offered, and tried to make a profit out of selling it. Nor did we assume that producers were making only what they thought shopkeepers could be persuaded to retail.

The twenties and thirties were exciting times for us, a tremendous period of expansion, and a vindication of Simon's vision of the future. Between March 1927, when the first major seeds of his American visit were planted, and March 1939, the number of the Company's stores increased from 126 to 234. Dozens of them had been rebuilt and extended, and their amenities improved on such a scale that we could honestly say that we had a chain, not of Penny Bazaars but of the best department stores in the country. But when I look back on those, and later years, it is not so much the development of Marks and Spencer as a trading organisation in which I rejoice, but in its growth and maturing as a function of society.

Our conception of the welfare of the people who worked for us was two-fold. Like many other employers we felt we had a duty to look after them as best we could, give them decent conditions to work in, and, so far as possible, help them when they were sick and in old age. It was not an accident that when Michael Marks built his first premises in Derby Street, Manchester, his first national headquarters, employing only a dozen or so people, he built them a dining room, and gave them a place where they could cook their food. But there is another aspect of the moral welfare of the worker which in some respects I think more important: and that is the sense of participation, which cannot be supplied by the best of wages or the most generous bonuses, but only by signs of personal *trust*. Of what we have done on this score, of what we have tried to do I am very proud.

Welfare is something, which, like love itself, is always changing its opportunities and demands. There is no end to what is required in a happy marriage and in good labour-relations, simply because human nature and general circumstances are always changing in relation to each other. One day I was in one of our stores and I asked a girl to pack something up for me – she had no idea who I was, and assumed I was an ordinary shopper. As I asked her to get the things ready, Simon who was with me, glanced at the clock and saw her lunch-time had already begun. 'Don't you start on that,' he said, 'or you'll be late for your lunch.' 'Oh,' she said, 'that's all right, it doesn't make any difference, I won't be having any lunch.' 'Not have any lunch?' I said. 'It's very bad for you going without food in the middle of the day. Why aren't you having any lunch?' 'I can't afford it,' she said.

We were very shocked. We were doing our best with our wage schemes – one of the first things Simon had done when in full control of the firm as Chairman was to start drawing up a wage structure for the business as a whole – and we knew that what we were paying was not to be ashamed of. That night I sat up late with Simon talking. We came around to the conclusion that even if we paid wages which in the majority of cases were as fair and generous as general trading conditions could stand, and even if in the typical case we could feel morally satisfied with what we were doing, there would still be cases in which individuals, possibly because they had extra demands being made upon them at home – brothers and sisters out of work, an invalid brother, or some problem of that kind – would so wish to scrape the last farthing to take home that they would go without their lunch or tea. There was only one thing that could cope with this, and that was to provide a hot meal at a cost so low that an employee would have to recognise it as uneconomical not to pay for it and eat it. Out of that chance encounter with a girl in the store developed an expansion of our whole welfare apparatus, which was started by Flora Solomon and her acolytes.

The best example I recollect of our efforts to promote another kind of welfare – the stimulation and broadening of the employee's mind by giving him and her a sense of personal initiative and contribution based on trust – was also based on personal encounter.

Simon, as I have explained, was much more of a desk man than me. I was his leg-man and did the lion's share of labour out of doors. But Simon too liked personal contact. He regularly made frequent visits to the branches which lay along his line of country, favouring, therefore, the Marble Arch branch in London, which was very near headquarters, and the branch in Slough, on the main road between his country house and London. Approaching the Slough branch one night in 1956, but realising he was too late to get inside before the hour of closing, he noticed lights still burning in the store. He stopped the car and found two girls still working, bringing stock-cards up-to-date. This set him thinking. He made several visits in the next few weeks and encountered several incidents which made him think there was too much paper-work. We began to talk about this, but took far greater interest when we discovered at the end of the year that the 1956 estimates of administrative expenditure showed a large increase over the previous years. Simon always had a great mistrust of bureaucracy; so did I, and still have now. Our fathers had it before us, perhaps it had something to do with what they learned in Russia. On this occasion I remember Simon saying: 'Israel; it's not a law of business growth that administrative costs continue to increase. Anyway if things go on like this,' he said, 'we shan't be able to sell women's blouses for less than ten pounds apiece.'

We decided that, come what may, we would abolish a great deal of paper. At first we thought that everybody would welcome it with open arms. On reflection, we decided that there would have to be universal consultation about it: unless we explained to all members of the staff why we were doing it, and what was required, they would wonder what was going on, feel insecure and instead of relieved of burdens of responsibility fret under a sense of added responsibility. When something of this magnitude is set in motion, when familiar procedures are going to be swept away, it is essential that people are prepared to respond.

So off we went. The summaries of sales that had been requested for many years were not altogether eliminated, but far shorter versions were now to be submitted. What, after all, was the value of detailed records if people simply did not have time to read them? We gave up the attempt to get pedantic detail and worked on the principle of common-sense approximation. On this basis we could encourage people to give up rummaging through dusty muddling files and to open the storeroom door and have a look what was there for themselves – look at the stock, not the figures. Further applying the principle of trust, we eliminated the stockroom specialist, the person whose job it was to go to the stockroom and bring out stock to replenish the counter when the saleswoman reported that she had, or nearly had, sold out. We said, 'let the salesgirl go and get the goods for herself' as and when she wanted them, without supervision. We threw out a variety of accountancy checks saving almost immeasurable time, effort and money.

We abolished the time-clock. It was already the responsibility of the supervisor to direct and control her staff: if she could not do it for herself, a time-clock would not help her. We discovered the abolition of the time-clock led to a great improvement in punctuality. We abolished a number of staff categories aiming to make everybody below the managerial and supervisory grades feel more 'general' and 'interchangeable', more human and less functional in their work. Not only did we trust our own employees more than we had before, but we trusted the employees of other firms. In the old days when a consignment of merchandise arrived at a store for us, that store received invoices for the merchandise from the firm that had supplied it, and somebody at the store would then have to open those goods, and check them against the invoice before putting them in to stock. Under the new system bulk invoices went direct from the supplier to the head office. This alone saved the use of a quarter of a million dockets each week. We gave up checking railway transport accounts as a routine; we discovered that the cost of making a routine check was altogether greater than that of repairing the few discrepancies that we discovered. The gains in productivity were immense. We threw out twenty-six million pieces of paper a year, as a result of what we came to call 'Operation Simplification'.

What excited me and Simon most was the effect all this had on the people who were working for us. Once they realised the implication of what was happening they rose to it. The atmosphere improved. People flowered. The air was lighter and brighter. People smiled more. It was wonderful. As I said in the House of Lords in describing that operation, 'Our salesgirls, the people in the office, all the employees, suddenly began to blossom out. I could see them blossoming out. They felt that we trusted them, because the systems we adopted gave them the freedom to do what they wanted insofar as goods were concerned.' I remember going to one store and the manager saying to me, 'I think we've done a most wonderful thing, the girls are as happy as the day is long.' Everywhere I went I found evidence that 'A hidden treasure of ability' had been unlocked.

I wish more of this could be done. Other businesses know their own business best but what I've seen of government operations makes me feel strongly that more trust and less form-filling would be an experiment well worth trying. I have discussed the matter with leading politicians and I still find them opposed to the general approach. A very eminent political leader said to me on one occasion: 'That kind of thing is all very well for a private concern, Lord Sieff, but for a public enterprise it is out of the question. If a Minister loses a pair of boots or a knife and fork in his department three or four years later he may be called upon to give an account in Parliament of why and how the loss occurred, on what basis the replacement was made, and how the deficiency was financially made good: *that* is why I keep so many pieces of paper.' I said to him: 'If, when you were asked about those boots in Parliament you said you were sorry but you could not give the record of that pair of boots because you no longer had the piece of paper which referred to them, and that because you no longer kept such bits of paper you had saved a hundred million pounds of the nation's money, you'd be cheered to the echo.' Ministers ought to live in fear not of what they lose from time to time but what the people would say about paying the taxes to pay for the paper permanently to record the loss.

9
The Thirties: PEP

The problem which dominated the minds of thoughtful people in the thirties before the rise of Hitler and the resurgent threat of war was unemployment. Marks and Spencer was among those who were making money and expanding, but the level of unemployment was a challenge to every entrepreneur with a jot of social responsibility, and a terrible problem for many businessmen whose markets were decimated or disappearing altogether. It was a period of questioning as well as of commiseration:

Why is it that in spite of all the gifts and promises of modern science and invention most of us are still going short of goods and services which, we are told, could easily be supplied in abundance? Why is it that millions who want to work must stand idle while millions who want more food, more clothing and more shelter cannot obtain them? How can we get over these shortcomings, and bring to every family the supplies of food and clothing, the shelter and the employment which are needed?

Those were the opening words of a short book I felt impelled to write in the early thirties. I never published that book although it was asked for by a respectable firm of publishers who offered me a sum of money to write it. The sum was not large, but as a mere shopkeeper I felt proud of being asked to use my pen to solve a problem for whose solution the world was anxiously waiting. However, by the time I had finished the book, and read it in page proof, my pride had disappeared. I did not feel that what I had written was of enough importance to occupy the space between two covers. I did not regard my efforts as in vain: they had, at any rate, clarified my mind.

I came to the conclusion that our problem was one of fear. The solution was the title of my first chapter – 'The Conquest of Fear in Industry'. It seemed to me that the whole structure of our industries, and the everyday work we did in them – or those of us who were fortunate enough to be in work – was too often dominated by fear: fear of bankruptcy, fear of competition, fear of leakages of information, fear of unemployment, fear of destitution through illness or old age. The economic situation of the coalmining industry is an example with its memories of many bitter conflicts arising out of the fears of mine owners, mine managers, the miners at the coal face and the miners on the dole. This poison in the coal industry was to be found in lesser degree in many other fields: cotton, for instance, and steel.

The first step towards a solution of the problem, I thought then, was to rid society of the accursed notion that fear was a good thing:

> The assumption is still widely made that progress is impossible except in a world where everyone is afraid of starving as the penalty for not being able successfully to compete. It might be truer to say that in modern conditions progress is impossible until we can get control of the excessive and morbid fears fostered by individual economic competition, and give human beings the opportunity to discuss in a calm atmosphere, and without hysteria, the possibilities of constructive co-operation. . . . We must aim to persuade everybody to recognise that the elimination of poverty and distress is possible along commonsense lines, without resort to magic remedies, and that there is no longer any need to obstruct changes through fear that anyone's security would be undermined. If we can achieve this gradual and progressive elimination of fear in its more acute forms, politics and economics would be transformed.

To illustrate in which respects the general behaviour of British industry was failing to meet the challenge of the times I looked at the British cotton industry, pointing out that its particular problem was to cope with the competition which had been set up by Japan:

> How is the test being met? A glance at the trade tendencies of the past few years does not suggest a very reassuring answer to this question. Three main reasons are apparent for our not having had more success. First, the price of Lancashire goods is too high; second, the patterns do not always meet consumer taste; third, the methods used in marketing Lancashire's goods are inadequate as compared with the methods used by the Japanese industries.

Looking through the page-proofs of my unpublished book it intrigues me to see how much of what I wrote nearly forty years ago could be written about British industry today. Much has been changed, much has been accomplished, much has been learned. Much, too, however, seems to have been ignored or forgotten. The unemployment problem is not what it was, thank God. Industry, on the whole, is more enlightened, the employers are more intelligent, the workers are less anxious and society is more compassionate. But externally Britain's problems are still unsolved, and internally there is still a very great deal to do.

This brings me to my association with that remarkable organisation, Political and Economic Planning, which I had the good fortune to be asked to join at about the time of its inception in 1931.

In the world of today the word 'planning' is almost on everybody's lips: planned production, planned distribution, planned finance, planned transport, planned power, are all the subjects of innumerable articles and speeches. It is a fundamental error in planning to begin by establishing the limits of one's objective. Industry should work out the steps which will be taken to secure the adoption of the most suitable methods in the production and sale of its manufactured goods. Not, as is often suggested, to measure and fix rigidly the quantity of demand, and plan production accordingly.

These words, which I think are topical, come from a speech I made to it at a dinner in March 1933. I would not want to try and write a history of PEP here if I could but I would like to say something about it, since I was one of the original Council of Management, and Kenneth Lindsay, the man who did more than anybody else to establish it and keep it going, is one of the oldest of my friends. The organisation has done great work, still does, and still too few people understand what its nature and objectives are: a pity, in that it is in such organisations that an important part of the British spirit and genius for politics manifests itself.

Political and Economic Planning is an independent non-party institution founded in 1931 whose primary purpose is to collate current knowledge in the economic, industrial and social field and make it available to policy-makers in Government, social services or industry, mainly by reports and surveys. Its funds come from private sources, industrialists, educational trusts, private individuals. How voluntary its nature and spontaneous its inception can be seen from its beginnings.

In the early days of 1930 a young man called Gerald Barry, later Sir Gerald Barry, one of the outstanding journalists of his generation, was the Editor of a very respected literary political weekly called the *Saturday Review*, owned by Lord Beaverbrook, the proprietor of the

Daily Express. Lord Beaverbrook, then as always an ardent British Commonwealth man, insisted that the *Saturday Review* support the *Express*'s Empire Free Trade campaign. Barry refused, and resigned, his whole staff resigning with him except the City Editor and the man who did the crossword puzzle. Soon after, in March 1930, Barry launched a new paper – the *Week End Review*. He was surrounded by a brilliant group of young men – J. B. Priestley, not then famous; Ivor Brown, who had still to write his best work as a dramatic and literary critic and become Editor of the *Observer*; Vernon Bartlett, later a celebrated broadcaster and an Independent MP; and Duff Cooper, who was to resign from the Chamberlain Cabinet over Munich in 1938 and later to become Ambassador to France. But the key man on the *Week End Review* was my old friend Max Nicholson. He was its Assistant Editor, leader writer and resident brain. At a time when the mood of the country was deeply despondent, its morale seriously disturbed, unemployment tragically high and the trading position disastrously low, the *Week End Review* took a critical and independent line on public affairs, the most important problem being, of course, the economic one, which involved coping with the existence of three million men unemployed. Challenged by a group of MPs to 'say *something constructive*', Gerald Barry delegated the task to Max Nicholson.

On 14 February 1931, the *Week End Review* came up with a 16-page supplement containing a policy manifesto headed: 'A National Plan for Britain'. Pointing out that much of what was proposed was acceptable to all parties, the plan called for the formation of representative councils for each industry, limitation of profits, planned imports and exports, imperial economic partnership on the basis of long-term bulk contracts, 'friendship with Russia and the United States' as the first condition of settled world peace and internationalism to rank before imperialism. It proposed a speeding up of parliamentary procedure and overhaul of the machinery of government with a Cabinet reduced to ten, including a single Minister for Defence and another for Economic Planning. (We got the first in the 1950s, from the Conservatives, and the second, from the Labour Party in 1964.) Max called for a National Planning Commission, and a Planning Council in each industry, which would arrange for *real* increases in *real* wages and secure a review of all trade-union rules. Unemployment was seen not as an unfortunate accident, like a sprained ankle, which in time could be cured, but as a functional disease – irremediable unless the system was altered: 'Unemployment in its present chronic excess is a symptom of economic illness which will disappear with the revival of economic health'. Local Government, Town Planning, Transport, Fuel and Light, Trade and other fields of national activity came in for treatment.

A tremendous amount of what was put forward in 1931 has been implemented by various governments since and is now taken for granted.

Before publication the draft of the plan had been circulated to a large number of people interested in public affairs, for comments and criticism, many of them active party politicians, but most of them outside politics: Beveridge, the architect of the Welfare State, for example; Professor G. D. H. Cole, the left-wing Oxford don; Walter Elliott and Duff Cooper, Tory MPs; and John Strachey and Sir Oswald Mosley, then a Socialist MP, on the Labour side; Ernest Bevin and Walter Citrine among the trade-union leaders; Lord Melchett and Andrew McColl among the industrialists. Among those who had helped with the drafting of the Nicholson plan there grew the idea of a permanent organisation. These people met at two or three dinners at each other's houses and decided such a body should be established. On 1 March 1931, a dinner was held at the Ivy Restaurant, chosen because Gerald Barry liked going to this restaurant which was much patronised by literary and theatrical friends of his. It was quite a party – Gerald Barry and Max Nicholson, Julian and Aldous Huxley, Clough Williams-Ellis and Vernon Bartlett sitting among financiers like Sir Basil Blackett and industrialists like Laurence Neal brought along by Kenneth Lindsay. Sir Basil Blackett was appointed Chairman. A second dinner was held at the Ivy two weeks later. This time Kenneth Lindsay was appointed as organising secretary of the new body, and 'Political and Economic Planning' was adopted as its name. Clough Williams-Ellis passed round an advertisement he had sketched with a caption: 'PEP – try it in your bath'. The next organising meeting was held at University College the following week: Aldous Huxley drew a series of caricatures of those present. He withdrew from PEP soon after and the following year produced *Brave New World*. I hope he didn't get the idea from us. The organisation was established at the meeting at Dartington Hall in April, when Mrs Leonard Elmhirst agreed to guarantee the salary of the Secretary for three years. A limited membership of the group was visualised, reaching perhaps 250–300. There was to be no seeking after publicity – the basic idea was a study group of men who were open-minded, working together, drawing up information and feeding this to men of action in politics and industry who might put it into effect.

I personally came into the organisation through Lindsay. He came to me soon after the original meeting and told me all about it. The motive force, he said, was the feeling of frustration that many intelligent and conscientious men in various walks of life had had since the first days of the 1929 slump. There *was* knowledge, there *was* energy, there *were* solutions. 'Men like you in Marks and Spencer are actually applying them', he said. 'I want to see such great men get together and prove their knowledge and experience for the benefit of society as a whole.' Lindsay made a great impression on me. Though he was an idealist, a Socialist do-gooder who had worked at institutions in the East End of London like Toynbee Hall, he was not a starry-eyed theoretician. His feet were on the ground. I liked his unbounded confidence in Britain's capacity to adapt and recover in the new competitive world. There was a tremendous sense of 'get Britain going again' in his message; it was not only compassion and common sense of which he spoke, but of the excitement of getting an out-of-condition vehicle repaired, retuned and going fast again. I was impressed by what he said; not because it was new – Marks and Spencer had been at it in their own way for six years or so – but because it was so encouraging to hear that so many others were seeing things as we were and wanted to try and make the example the norm. I asked Kenneth who his colleagues were. 'You'd better come and meet them,' he said. And he gave a dinner for me, with the Chairman, Sir Basil Blackett, Leonard Elmhirst and a few others present. I was delighted. I knew it was my money they wanted in the first place, but I also felt they meant it when they said I could make a practical contribution. So I put up two thousand pounds and found myself a member of the Council. Indeed, I am an original member of the Council, and next to my service to Weizmann I am prouder of being an original member of the Council of PEP than of anything in my life.

There was now a development which had a great deal of bearing on the history of PEP and, incidentally, on my part in it. A division of opinion appeared between those who wanted to produce an overall Plan as the first great step forward, and those who wanted to concentrate on various individual fields. I was Chairman of the Industry Group. My group pushed on without waiting for the others to get cracking, and in November 1932 it produced a report on Industry. This report, which became known as A1, was well received in PEP and became the model report, setting the pace for many years' work on Iron and Steel (report in 1933), Cotton (1934) and Housing (1934). I was thought to have had some influence on these reports in encouraging their drafters to keep on a practical level. Whether this was so or not – theoretical and abstract approaches have always been above me – in December 1932, when PEP had a membership of one hundred, I was asked to succeed Sir Basil Blackett as Chairman. Disraeli's wife, several years older than he was, used to say in her old age that while she believed Disraeli had married her for her money, if he had the chance over again she believed he would have married her for herself. I think PEP came to me in the first place for my money: but I think they found me quite useful for myself. Anyway, I flung myself into the work with a faith and enthusiasm I have never regretted, and made close friends of some of the finest and cleverest men it has ever been my privilege to meet.

The same year, 1931, we moved to our premises in Queen Anne's Gate.* Between then and the outbreak of the second world war we produced one hundred and fifty broadsheets (as we called our normal publication or pamphlet), and fourteen special reports. It is amusing to look back on the generalisations made up about us when I recall how disparate a collection of characters we were and how conflicting were our views. I remember that when Becky and I entertained the members at our home at Cookham in June 1933, there was a clash between Sir Basil Blackett and Sir Arthur Salter about our approach to International Affairs: Blackett was for restricting the field to British and Imperial Interests; Salter wanted a global view which postulated international planning as the only guarantee against cyclical collapse. There was a division of opinion too on the question of Publicity: some wanted PEP to play like a high-pressure hose on the influential few with power; others wanted a flood of pamphlets and reports to flow into the media of communication. There were fundamental arguments about the role of planning itself; Noel Hall, Professor of Economics at University College, London, believed in capitalist planning and said so in a paper he read called 'Capitalist versus Communist Planning'. Hugh Gaitskell, later to be a socialist Chancellor of the Exchequer, but then a lecturer in Noel Hall's department, thought capitalist planning would not work.

* PEP is now at 12 Upper Belgrave Street, SW1.

If some of the people who wrote about us had studied us a little more, and seen what a wide range of political affiliations we had and how different the views of various members were, they would not have written such ridiculous stuff about us. Some thought we were Red; others that we were fascists. For some we were hatching up a Labour Party plot; for others we were the last hope of right-wing Conservatism on the defensive. In 1935 a Captain Bernard Acworth wrote an article in the *English Review* entitled 'Letting the Socialists in' as though he scented a communist conspiracy of which Israel Sieff was the secret manipulator. There was criticism from *The Economist* and the *Daily Herald*, the latter describing some of our proposals as fascist. However, we were nevertheless appreciated, and during the war, in a leading article on 19 January 1943, on the occasion of the publication of our two hundredth report or 'broadsheet', *The Times* wrote:

> The body familiarly known as 'PEP' (Political and Economic Planning) has now published number 200 in its series of reports or 'broadsheets'. In the twelve years that they have been at work PEP have scored a success and earned a reputation of no small significance. They have taken for their field of study, and by their efforts have done much to enlarge, that territory of the social sciences in which wide collaboration is practicable among men and women of different political views. The foundation of their method is derived from the natural and experimental sciences; it consists in a scrupulous attention to fact. There is nothing new in the contention that policy should be the outcome of research and knowledge. But to PEP belongs the credit of founding itself expressly upon this belief and of proving it true that an impartial approach is possible to many large questions in the realm of politics. Both the degree in which consent is attainable among those who are prepared to accept the discipline of inquiry and to follow the argument where it leads and the extent to which the method is applicable in current matters of public concern have had a highly encouraging demonstration in the experience of PEP.

It was, I think, not so much the intelligence, not even the good will, the desire to serve one's fellow men, and do so anonymously, that was the mainspring of PEP, though without these two qualities it could not have done what it did. The peculiar stamp, I think, of PEP, was its practical approach, only possible because so many men of practical experience voluntarily contributed their time and energy. In the middle thirties Lloyd George, who had been in opposition for nearly fifteen years, was preparing a programme for his Council of Action, drawing up projects and proposals for all aspects of the country's problems. He consulted PEP and, impressed with the results, asked Kenneth Lindsay how it was able to attract such a capable body of consultants and what it cost. He was surprised to learn that there was only a handful of paid workers – only two paid personnel, for instance, in the whole of the Civic Division, and that the bulk of the research came from voluntary members who drew from long experience with such bodies as the Board of Guardians, or gained it in Local Government, or in various voluntary organisations, or who had been Civil Servants, Town Clerks, Medical Officers of Health, or were, as Kenneth put it, 'pioneering professors ahead of their time'.

It was through PEP that I made the brief but memorable acquaintance of Sir Oswald Mosley, an episode I still find somewhat mystifying in some respects. Mosley, I think, was impressed by PEP in much the same way as Lloyd George, and needed a body of practical knowledge of industry with which to ballast his political theories. Having begun his political career as a Conservative MP and moved to the Labour Party, he had left the Labour Party in 1930 because the Government would not accept his views on what should be done about unemployment. There was a lot to be said for those views as they were at that stage. In 1931 he founded the New Party. He and his new party had no success at all in the general election that year, and in 1932 he visited Mussolini in Rome, was impressed by Mussolini's corporate state, came home and established the British Union of Fascists, outlining his general programme in September of that year, in his book *The Greater Britain*. It is only fair to say that at that time anti-Semitism was not a part of that programme. Some historians have noted that Mosley's anti-Semitism appeared only after the death of his first wife, Lady Cynthia, a daughter of Curzon, in 1933. If that is so, it would certainly explain part of what I propose to relate.

One day early in 1932 Lady Ravensdale, Sir Oswald's sister-in-law, another daughter of Lord Curzon, rang me up and asked me if I could spend some time in a discussion with Sir Oswald. I was very fond of Lady Ravensdale and said I would. Soon after I went to her house at Richmond. I spent almost the whole of the day there, talking, or rather listening, to Sir Oswald. He was, and is, a remarkable talker, with an acute and well-stocked mind, often extremely amusing, expressing himself effortlessly and musically in a well-modulated, faintly husky voice. It was quite clear what he wanted: if possible he wanted PEP to become the brainbox of his new party, wanted PEP to put itself at the disposal of his new party and become its technical committee. If that was not possible he wanted to be able to draw on its information and ideas as much as possible. I explained that the first was out of the question: we were non-party political, and proposed to remain so. As to his second request: we were already available to anybody who cared to make use of us. But there could be no assimilation.

Sir Oswald was still of a mind to get closer, if not to PEP, at least to members of it whom he hoped would support his plans for the future. He asked me if I would arrange for him to meet some of the kind of businessmen who made up my industrial group. I asked a dozen or so to dine with him at my home in Regent's Park. Our wives went too, but since we all knew we were in for an evening of political discussion, Becky gave the women dinner separately in the library. After we had eaten, I asked Sir Oswald if he would like to tell us about his plans for the New Party. Characteristically Sir Oswald got to his feet to do so. He had been speaking, and very interestingly, for about twenty minutes, when he made the point that a political party in his view must ultimately be based on emotion. Only feeling could win power and carry plans into effect. He said that a new movement must find somebody or something to hate. In this case it should be the Jews. He did not seem to think he had said anything particularly unacceptable, but the effect on the company was instant. I said, 'I must ask you to leave, Sir Oswald'. He strode out, calling to his wife, 'Cynthia, we are going'. His wife joined him, and I never saw him again. As far as I know that was the end of Mosley and PEP and certainly of Mosley and me. Until that moment I did not know what he felt about the Jews. The great Nazi persecutions had not begun, and I do not think he had met Hitler. I was most upset by this incident. Sir Oswald had impressed me until then as an egregiously able and dynamic figure, of that rare charismatic type which when suitably motivated can work wonders in the service of their fellow men. I was upset not only by my own reaction to his revelations but by those of my friends and colleagues whom I had urged to come and meet him. However, it was, perhaps, just as well that we all found out where we stood so soon.

A much more pleasant recollection, though also not without its mystery, looking back on it, was my contact with Edward VIII, then Prince of Wales. Lord Portal, who was the chairman and managing director of a firm which manufactured, among other things, paper for bank notes, and whom I had got to know through my father's business, decided to arrange fortnightly dinners at which fourteen or sixteen industrialists would discuss industrial questions in the presence of His Royal Highness. These seminars, as I suppose they might be described, were held at St James's Palace. Three or four of them were held, I think, and seemed to go down rather well. The next one was called off – that is to say, the Prince said he would be unable to attend – at only three or four days' notice. The series was thereafter discontinued. I often wondered what had happened. At one time it occurred to me that the series was broken off just about the time the Prince was being said to be too 'political'. Sometimes I wondered whether Mr Baldwin's concern about the active interest the Prince was taking in poverty and unemployment might have been responsible. I have often ruminated since on what might have happened if the Prince had maintained his interest in industrial affairs. He would certainly have been able to capture the imagination of the masses. What he could have done with it is not so certain.

In 1934 I was asked by the *Morning Post*, later absorbed in the *Daily Telegraph*, to do a series of five articles. I was described in the editorial introduction to the series as 'A recognised authority on the subject of Planning in Industry', an attribution which amazed me almost as much as it amazed my friends, and which, I suppose, was based on my role in PEP. Notwithstanding my misgivings about my qualifications for doing so, I made no bones, in my first article, about saying what I thought should be done in general to solve the country's problems:

Each industry should establish a corporation with certain statutory powers, enabling it to effect the reorganisation of its structure where necessary, and to come to the assistance of its constituent units when needed . . . on these corporations capital, labour, and management should all be represented. The State, which would grant the enabling powers, would have to protect the interests of individual consumers and of consuming industries.

I pointed out in this article that Mr Harold Macmillan MP, then somewhat at odds with official Conservative Party thinking, and not thought of as a future leader of it, or a Prime Minister of his country, had outlined a scheme on much the same lines in his recent book, *Reconstruction*, and I suggested that something of this kind would drive out the fears and suspicions that obsessed British Industry, and bring back into the Twentieth Century business concerns 'a new and better example of the friendly team spirit that has been crushed by *laissez-*

faire'. I went on to advocate three new industrial mechanisms: marketing boards; producers' associations; and developed the idea of industrial councils representative of management, capital and labour, which I have already mentioned. 'Eventually, when industry had built up an organic structure of the type briefly outlined, it should be possible to realise the ideal of a Parliament of Industry or National Industrial Council, representative of British Industry as a whole and enjoying full powers of self-government devolved upon it by Parliament.'

In my third article I dealt with the 'Population Bulge' caused by the soaring of the birth-rate immediately after the war, and I suggested raising the school leaving age to fifteen, and the establishment of day continuation schools at which half-time attendance would be compulsory between the ages of fifteen and eighteen. I also suggested regional industrial councils to direct and supervise the recruitment of young people into industry. In the fourth article I recommended the establishment of central marketing organisations, some instrument for bulk purchase, and another instrument for effective foreign investment as essential prerequisites for the improvement of our foreign trade. And in the fifth article I discussed the working out of a sound emigration policy.

I have not mentioned these articles because I think that they were of much importance. Indeed, the slightest suggestion that they contained original observations, thoughts or constructive proposals would be to insult the dozens of really well-informed men and women for whom I acted merely as one other convenient mouth-piece. I find the articles interesting because they throw light on what has been done, and what has been left undone in nearly forty years of intense human and industrial experience.

The articles evoked a considerable correspondence which continued for several days. The first letter, though far from pejorative in tone summed me up as 'an idealist and, in some aspects, almost a fanatic'. The second letter described me as 'projecting a scheme which could only work in a Socialist State with a Lenin, a Hitler or a Mussolini at its head'. On the whole, however, the response was favourable.

During the war years, in spite of the number of its members, and potential members, on active service overseas, and the preoccupation with the war effort, PEP was immensely active. But in the post-war period its activities increased greatly. The Council met only twice during the war, but in the four years between 1945 and 1949 it met ten times. In 1946, urged on by myself and Sir George, later Lord Schuster, it then evolved a PEP group to study human relations in industry. In June 1948, we developed a Press Group. The Government had decided to set up a Royal Commission on the Press: we decided that some research of our own would not come amiss. Members of the Committee asked for copies of our Report. During the debates in the House of Commons on the subject, Kenneth Lindsay wrote, 'copies of the familiar green PEP Report were as thick in the House as copies of the pink Order Paper and were brandished just as freely'. In July 1948 PEP published one of the biggest and best and most influential of all its Reports: *Britain and World Trade*. There followed in the next ten years or so some outstanding Reports: *Fuel and Power* was a little earlier –1947. *Government and Industry* was another good one, and I particularly enjoyed the review of it in *The Statist*, which referred to '. . . the special value of PEP publications, where views and theories of individual experts have had to run the gauntlet of detailed check and cross-check before being accepted as valid contributions to a composite picture'. Well, whatever else we failed to do at PEP, and however badly we fell short of our ideals, we certainly checked and cross-checked.

The Film Industry (1952) was a report which was the first to reflect PEP's post-war concern with the quality of society. In the thirties, as Max Nicholson put it, PEP was concerned with the basic organisational structure of society: now, in the fifties, much of the necessary reorganisation having taken place, we were concerned with the quality of that society, not so much now with its structure, but with the kind of life that could and should be lived within it. Housing, Health, Youth Clubs, democratic activities in national and local government, were among the fields in which new schemes and conceptions seemed necessary. We even tackled the Arts, and Football and Cricket. Yes, the fifties were great days. I remember a Council meeting in 1956. Leonard Elmhirst and I were formally thanked for the financial assistance we had given PEP; but I value much more the presence there of so many men whom I had come to know when PEP had begun twenty-five years previously. Twenty-five years is a long time in the life of a man. It is no inconsiderable span in the life of a country.

One of the great advantages of PEP was that it was able to exploit a feature of British political life not always understood in other countries, even those enjoying a democratic government; namely that all three parties, Conservative, Liberal and Labour have made great contributions to the social and economic well-being of the community, and that not all state intervention into the hitherto private sector has been the work of a Socialist Government. To take a few variegated examples, the Forestry Commission, the Central Electricity Board and the grouping of the main-line railways date from the first world war and were the work of a coalition government. The two great Education Acts of this century were the work of a Liberal, H. A. L. Fisher, in the Coalition of World War I; and of R. A. Butler, a Conservative, in the Coalition of World War II. While it was a Labour Government which instituted public control of the distribution of electricity, it was a Conservative Government which initiated public control of its generation. Unemployment and Health Insurance was the child of the Liberals in power; it was the Conservative-dominated National Government (with the Labour Party in Opposition) which set up a public authority to control London Transport marketing and which established marketing boards. It was the Labour Government which nationalised the coal mines: the Conservatives nationalised broadcasting. And so on.

It seems to me that PEP was a very British institution in many different respects. First, in the spontaneous manner in which it was brought about – born in a spirit of protest, but a constructive one. Indeed, it gave a creative outlet to many able and original men who, unable to fit in, might otherwise have retired from politics and civil service: PEP, said Max Nicholson, was at first a sort of transit camp for refugees from Conservative, trade-union, Labour and other quarters. Many civil servants were frustrated in the thirties: PEP gave them an outlet for their energies. On the other hand, publicists and journalists, seeking relief from the daily grind of reportage at popular levels, turned to PEP for more measured and argued avenues of thought. There was a very British sense of one's own specialism, a very British sense of proportion, and a very British sense of duty. 'The core membership', Kenneth Lindsay wrote, 'consisted of men of affairs who (a) were endowed with the gift of speculating about their own subject (b) had the capacity to regard their own function in a wider setting (c) cared greatly about "the relief of man's estate if not the glory of God" '. But through every virtue that PEP could boast there ran like a thread through crystals, the empirical, the practical, the refusal to get away from facts. I shall never forget one weekend at my home at Cookham when there was an argument about whether a plan that was being discussed could be put into legislative effect, and if so to what extent.

Sir Henry Bunbury, one of the most distinguished civil servants of his time, retired to the garden and reappeared an hour later producing a pencilled specimen bill detailing what a Minister could and could not do.

What effect PEP had on the history of Britain I do not know. It is certainly possible to trace close causal connections between our early papers and the policies of governments in later days. There were 250 members over a period of several years. Many others helped one or another of its twenty-five working groups. Even more outside, in the press, in voluntary organisations, in politics, made use of our findings. For instance, in the early thirties we had come to conclusions about the location of British Industry which resembled the basis of government policy fifteen years later; our series on the Cotton Industry, in which I naturally took a special interest, arrived at conclusions in the mid-thirties which were useful to governments twenty years later. A paper I wrote in 1938 called 'Experiments in the Marketing of Agricultural Products,' offered suggestions which ten years later were regarded as commonplace features of the existing systems. When the architects of the Welfare State, the Beveridge Committee, were sitting in the early years of the war, we sent a fat PEP report along ('. . . one of the best the organisation has ever produced,' wrote Lord Keynes) advocating a Ministry of Social Security. These are at least examples of the relations of PEP with the government of the day, if not of PEP directly influencing the government of the day, or a future government. But it will always be difficult to set a limit on what was contributed to the history of British society and institutions by us, PEP – the ginger-group of gradualness.

10
War and Post-War

In March 1940, the Board of Trade asked me if I would go to the United States and, in effect, try and sell as many British goods as possible to earn the maximum American dollars to help finance the war effort. Three other British businessmen were going. One of them was my old friend Leonard Elmhirst of PEP. I discussed the matter with Simon. He thought I should go – the idea had been put to us as a matter of national service: it would be unpatriotic to refuse. I felt so, too. Neither of us had any idea of how long I would be away. That was how it was in the second world war: *nobody*, nor his wife, realised how long he would be away.

So, in May 1940 I travelled up to Liverpool to board my ship. Most of the passengers were young servicemen, going across to the American continent for training. The Officer in Command of Troops at Liverpool happened to be a former manager of the Marks and Spencer store in Swansea. He was very glad to see me and told me I could have a choice of ships: I could have a berth to myself on a ship I shall call the *City of Los Angeles* or share a double berth on a liner, which I shall call the *Empress of the Isles*. The *City of Los Angeles* was a better sailer and more comfortable, but I plumped for the *Empress*: I could share with Leonard Elmhirst. Also, the *Empress* was going first to Canada, which meant I could see that country again, which I liked so much, and visit some of the members of my family who were in the Armed Forces training there.

We went aboard by night. While we lay in port there was a heavy air raid. In the dark before the dawn of a cold May morning we put to sea. Off the south-west coast of Ireland our convoy was surrounded by German submarines. It was difficult to sleep: we dressed and went on deck. There was a moon behind the clouds, and now and again when she peeped through we caught a glimpse of the other vessels. Suddenly there was a ghastly crash of light, which flooded the sea to the limits of the horizon, followed, as though accompanied, by an explosion which almost clubbed me to my knees. The ship immediately behind was blown out of the water. There were a hundred and twenty children on her, but we did not stop to rescue them: we were carrying a thousand servicemen trainees, and their lives were too precious to risk. My ship, under orders, steamed on as if nothing had happened. So did the others. The shattered ruin and its survivors were left to sink. I lost some dear friends that night. The ship that was torpedoed was the *City of Los Angeles*. It was a very long crossing. The shadow of the tragedy hung over us.

When we arrived at Halifax several days later I saw the destroyers which Roosevelt later made available to Britain. I spent a few days there, saw some relatives, and then went down by train to New York. Friends of mine had arranged an apartment for me. I reported to the Board of Trade representatives, and was soon in business.

My task was to sell suitings, cotton shirtings, cardigans, pullovers, fine cotton yarns and a few other lines including supplies of Nottingham lace. After I had been there a few days I had dinner with an American friend. I showed him the samples I had brought: 'How much do you think you might gross in the next few years?' he asked. 'Well,' I said, 'if I can get the thing going, over the next few years I'd hope to gross five million dollars.' 'Gosh! you're an optimist,' he said. As it turned out we sold six million dollars' worth in the first year. It is always well to heed advice, but if you know what you are talking about it never does to be depressed by what well-meaning friends might say. As we expected, the American manufacturers gave us no mercy – why should they have done? They had their order-books to fill, their wages to pay, and their overheads to meet. American cotton and woollen manufacturers realised that we would have difficulty not so much in taking first orders but in delivering; before our merchandise could appear on the counter and take its chances there it had to cross the Atlantic, and succeed where the *City of Los Angeles*, through no fault of its own, had failed. They thought this would permit them to put up the prices of their own goods, and they did that. We rather surprised them by confidently putting up the price of *ours*! Our quality was sufficiently competitive to take hold-ups in delivery and the price-rise in its stride. There was a certain sentiment in our favour on the part of many

American customers. Things went well. We earned those badly needed dollars.

I was there at the time the Japanese bombed Pearl Harbour, and brought the Americans into the war. I was in the middle of a speech on Zionism at a meeting presided over by Jack Strauss, the present President of Macy's stores. The meeting was interrupted in order that the audience should be informed of what had happened. The change in the atmosphere of that room was dramatic. Many men left that meeting changed. They knew that the United States would now have to fight the Germans, and many of them had been born in Germany, or had come from German stock. I felt terribly sad for them.

I had been some months in the United States and now the Americans were in the war. There was now a new work to do in Washington. This time it would not be selling goods but doing some kind of liaison work with American business circles. It sounded vague, but convincing. I was asked to go and see the Ambassador, the Earl of Halifax. Lord Halifax told me that Leon Henderson, one of the President's economic advisers, had asked for me to be loaned to the Office of Price Administration (OPA). Henderson was putting the American economy on a war footing. Henderson was a distinguished American economist in government whom I had come to know and like through PEP. He thought one or two British businessmen could help. Feeling out of my depth and rather startled I had no option but to accept.

My assignment was to travel around the United States talking to groups of American businessmen about the problems of rationing and retail distribution in time of war. Mostly I visited towns and cities on the Eastern seaboard and in the Mid-West, but occasionally I got to the West Coast. My audience consisted largely of Chambers of Commerce. I was well received, except in one or two places where there were American citizens of German antecedents in the audience. In one town I was subjected to a little boo-ing. The Chairman admonished the boo-ers. I asked the Chairman's permission to address the boo-ers, got it, and said I quite understood the mixed feelings on any matter related to the allied war effort which some of us, because of our antecedent loyalties, were bound to entertain. I said that, though I was born, bred and educated to admire the contribution of the German people to the civilisation of the world, I was nevertheless as a Jew emotionally involved in the subject of how *some* Germans, led and exploited by Hitler, had ill-treated a great number of their fellow countrymen, among whom Jews happened to be in a large majority. I appealed to those present who would like to discuss these problems with me to remain behind after the formal part of the meeting had been brought to a close. Several did so. We had a brief, wholly pleasant few minutes together, devoted not to the speaking of words but mainly to warm silent hand-shaking. I was never booed again, anywhere.

Now I take up the story of post-war Marks and Spencer, the second great phase of development in the history of the company.

That it was so is a remarkable tribute to Simon's genius, for certainly in the immediate post-war period trading conditions were almost the opposite of those for which the Marks and Spencer approach had been devised. Our first principle had been to try and give the customer what he really wanted, not what manufacturers or wholesalers decided to supply, and for its successful operation a free market in which the customer's demands could express themselves freely was essential. This was just what we did not have in the first ten years after the war. Rationing continued for many years, and economic circumstances and the policy of the Labour Government 1945-51 added further restrictions to the commercial life of a people whose energies had been drained by six years of exhausting war. There was an acute shortage of consumer goods of all kinds, especially garments. Much of what was produced was diverted into the export trade. Choice was restricted: most clothing was produced and marketed under the rigid 'Utility' scheme. Labour was scarce. Clothes rationing was not abolished until 1949. There were controls on buildings until 1954. They were ten frustrating years. In this period, however, Simon showed tremendous patience and vision, tenacity of purpose and imagination. It was in some respects his finest hour. When in the fifties the system of controls was dismantled, and Austerity gave way to an Affluent Society, Marks and Spencer's fortunes entered a golden decade of profitability and expansion.

As there had been after the first world war, there was another marked phase of sociological change, which Simon spotted at once. He saw – and there were many who did not – that though much of the austerity and enforced egalitarianism of the wartime and post-war period would disappear as soon as people could get rid of them, some of the new aspects of society would remain. The relatively well-defined class divisions would certainly become more blurred; some of the homogeneity in fashions and taste would not disappear when people took off their uniforms, and, on the other hand, people, especially women, accustomed by the war to a higher standard of living and a more independent poise, would translate this into a demand for good clothes of a classless character. After the war, Simon deduced, women would want light, comfortable clothes, the cheapest of which would not be greatly different to look at from the most expensive. Shop girls were going to expect to look like duchesses – as they had in the Wrens or the ATS – and feel just as comfortable.

It would not have been possible to give women the clothes for which they were going to ask at the prices which they could afford to pay without the arrival of the new man-made fibres resulting from the application of modern scientific discoveries in the textile industry. Here, I think, Marks and Spencer was fortunate in having had a long-standing interest in the relation of science to industry, and, indeed, made the assumption that scientific development in industry was its most important creative factor. Our original predisposition in this direction had been stimulated by Weizmann, who had been filling our heads with fascinating ideas of what kind of clothes could one day be manufactured a quarter of a century before the first new fibres had been produced. Other merchants were not as sanguine as we were in the forties: some were sceptical about man-made fibres ever being able to replace silk and cotton and wool. We got off to a fast start, and it made all the difference.

We already had a Design Department; Simon had set it up in 1938. After the war we also set up a Print Design Department which advised both our own buying departments and their suppliers on types, patterns and colours of prints, and created original designs for scarves, dresses and other garments supplied to us. Later, after we had established the kind of thing we were interested in marketing, we left it to the manufacturers. We kept in very close touch with fashion houses on the Continent, in order to know the latest trends. The result was that as well as stepping up the quality and design of the garments for what I would loosely call 'working-class' women, we found we were selling large quantities of goods to what I might even more loosely call 'middle-class' women. In this we were both reflecting, and at the same time, helping to bring about, that democratisation of demand which was a feature of post-war Britain, and which invariably goes with, and, again, helps bring about, a more egalitarian society. By democratising demand

I mean not persuading or forcing everybody to buy the same design, but giving a wide range of choice at high quality and low price. To do this at a high profit requires men of outstanding ability at the head of the affairs. Vigorous and viable democracy requires a handful of aristocrats in the Aristotelian sense who have great gifts and love their fellow men.

During these post-war years, especially the period of expansion during the fifties, we became aware of a change in the attitude of customers towards us. We had always felt appreciated; we had always felt that people came to us, and came again and again, because they felt they got good service in decent conditions and value for money in an accessible range of goods. But in the fifties we began to feel, and continue to do so, that people began to look at us not so much as a shop as a national institution, into their relationship with which entered traces of the feelings which normally exist between people and people, not people and things: traces of affection, trust and friendship. I think too that people came to feel that the goods they bought in our stores at the prices we charged for them represented something healthy and progressive about British society – our goods were meant to be for all purses, their design and colour suggested that *all* people had good taste, and *our* success suggested that there was a future for efficiency and imagination and faith in the mass market – in its democratic approach to merchandising. Above all, I think, our customers came to believe, and do, that we genuinely intended to base our own commercial success on higher quality and lower prices, and had the will and ability to do it. I think we bucked people up. I think we became the people's friend. I think they came to feel that we would go with them into the future, and that in spite of all its hazards the future need not make us afraid.

Whatever it was there must have been something about us that rang a welcoming bell. I do not think it can have been just a matter of prices. It certainly wasn't a question of advertising. Since the second world war we have advertised comparatively little. It is not so much because we feel our goods sell themselves, or that we can rely on word-of-mouth publicity, or that the less we spend on advertising the lower our costs and therefore the lower our prices. The fact is that our problem has never been one of selling. We had only stocked what we knew would sell because we knew the public *wanted* it. The problem has been one of getting the stuff to sell at the right quality and the right price; the problem was of production, not of sales.

We were now well into the fifties, the period in which Britain swung up and away from the deprivations and austerities of war and the immediate post-war society and for the first time in her history entered the Affluent Society. The Conservative Party came to power in 1951 and remained there for thirteen years. The restoration of a relatively free market stimulated business. Not everybody benefited from the new prosperity. Some people were critical of it, believing that the prosperity was not based on sound economic foundations. The problem of the balance of payments continued to plague the country: sections of the community continued to live in poverty. The reduction of the cost of living was sought not only by the aged and the poor, but by the country as a whole, which could not buy its daily bread, most of which had to be imported from abroad, unless the prices of its exports were competitive in world markets. Well, Marks and Spencer did its bit; and it is pleasant to be able to record that we were given full credit for our efforts, by the public and the press. In 1962, the Chancellor of the Exchequer, Mr Selwyn Lloyd, introduced what was in effect a second budget in July of that year with the intention of restraining personal spending. The famous and controversial 'Pay Pause' was established: there were to be no increases in wages for the time being, and a surcharge of ten per cent was to be imposed on all rates of purchase tax and customs and excise duty. Purchasing power at the rate of 210 million pounds was to be withdrawn from the economy. The spring budget had already gone a long way in the same direction: among other measures it had increased the purchase tax on clothing from five to ten per cent. Simon did not hesitate. His response to these pressures was to lower his prices once again. Between February 1962 and May 1963 we cut prices by about two million pounds. One cartoonist described St Michael, the brand image of our company, as 'The patron saint of price pegging'.

I would be very embarrassed if anybody got the impression that these reductions in prices landed us in great financial difficulties. They did not. They might have done, particularly those we instituted in the early fifties. But as things turned out the fifties were a time of great expansion. They were good times for nearly all business: we benefited especially on account of the expansion of textiles and food. In the ten years between 1956 and 1966, our turnover rose from 119,400,000 pounds to 238,015,000 pounds, almost exactly doubling, and our profits after tax were more than tripled, going from 4,955,000 pounds to

18,468,000 pounds. In this period ninety-nine per cent of our merchandise was manufactured in Britain. We more than doubled our share of the national clothing market. At the end of the period our textile sales accounted for about ten per cent of the national total spent on clothing. Today, more than two-fifths of the ladies' briefs sold in Britain are bought in Marks and Spencer; more than a third of ladies' dresses and underwear; one man's shirt in nine is a Marks and Spencer's shirt. Many, many families are almost entirely clothed in the goods we sell, and are pretty well fed by us as well.

There has been a great expansion in food. Ten per cent of Britain's cakes are bought in Marks and Spencer. Food is a great problem; there are many things to be observed, but the critical one is Hygiene. Simon was almost neurotic on the subject of cleanliness. This may have been the reason why in the first place he did not wholeheartedly favour the great expansion in the sale of foods which several of us – above all my son Marcus – wished us to undertake. If Simon found any dirt or rubbish lying around he got quite angry, and rather than see it lie there would have taken a dustpan and removed the offending particles himself. We ran down our catering units for customers in the post-war period, and by 1961 they had totally disappeared. But on the other hand we have vastly built up the sale of foods, largely under the organisation and direction of Marcus. This tremendously important and flourishing department is now under the direction of Simon's nephews, Michael and Gabriel Sacher. I wish Simon had lived to see what we have achieved in this field.

Quite apart from the achievement, and its importance in an era when we are steadily getting into close contact with the countries of Europe, the field itself is fascinating. Marcus prepared a paper for the Oxford Farming Conference in 1966, which involved him in analysis of the demand for foodstuffs – 'the demand for quality foodstuffs is large and unsatisfied' he concluded – and gave us the chance to have a good re-think about what we should do in the future. A few years ago an American writer, in an article entitled 'The Ultimate in Sanitation', observed that 'some British food service managers think that Marks and Spencer have gone too far in its sanitation programme and a few raised eye-brows even on this side of the Atlantic would not surprise this magazine'.

However, as I mentioned earlier, the progress of which we have been proudest is in human relations inside Marks and Spencer. A special role in 'Operation Simplification', as it came to be called, was performed by the Company's secretary (now Vice-Chairman and Joint Managing Director), Bruce Goodman. He has recorded how in the mid-fifties, though business was good, and getting better, overheads were growing even faster than profits, so that profits before tax expressed as a percentage of turnover were being steadily eroded from ten and a half per cent in 1945/6 to eight and a half per cent in 1955/6 – with tax increasing all the time! I have mentioned the initiative taken by Simon and his visit to the store in Slough on his way home. Though Simon envisaged the operation, however, it could not have been carried out if a handful of men had not first thought it out, a larger body had not interpreted it adequately for the men and women who were, so to speak, in the front line, and if they in turn had not put their best into making it work.

Work it most certainly did. What was gratifying, too, was the favourable attention which the experiment produced. In 1966 Bruce Goodman told an audience in South Africa that we were encouraged to see, on the tenth anniversary of 'Operation Simplification', the experience of this campaign still aroused interest outside Marks and Spencer, and, indeed, outside Britain. In 1958, in response to a suggestion, we had opened a permanent exhibition at our head office in Baker Street to illustrate the methods we had adopted to eliminate administrative wastefulness. It was visited by almost ten thousand businessmen representing some five thousand of the largest firms in Britain and overseas. Mr Hugh Fraser said in Parliament at the time, having been to see our exhibition, that if national and local government adopted our methods there would be a saving of four thousand tons of paper and nearly ninepence off the Income Tax. The Civil Service paid a tribute to us by describing our campaign as 'a most refreshing approach to the problem of excessive paper work' and 'a great encouragement to the O. and M. officer (Organisation and Methods Division of the Treasury) wherever he is'. Next to dirt Simon's most nagging obsession was unnecessary paper-work. It combined the ultimate two evils for him: it showed a lack of confidence in people, and, as I said in discussing his father's early days, the fundamental principle of a store is the belief you can trust people to sell your goods for you in delegation; and it was a confession of inefficiency. In a House of Lords debate on technical and scientific manpower and research in 1961, he said:

It has been a bee in my bonnet that the proliferation of papers seems to have a damaging effect on industries, and maybe on the Government, too.

The costs of administration throughout all Government Departments have grown year by year and are probably still growing. An examination would reveal that many thousands of tons of paper could be found to be unnecessary. Tens of millions of pounds could be saved.

Five years later I took up the same theme in the Lords, alas, when Simon was not alive to do it for himself. I took up his theory that the misuse of manpower was not just a matter of bad human relations, but that what was bad business was in some fundamental way immoral: 'If we, as managers, can find the language to explain these matters to the workers, and say not "You, Bill," but just "Bill". . . .'

We were, of course, a peculiar firm in that Simon's father and mine had a distinct sense of obligation to the people who worked for them. To what extent this was an inheritance of their Jewish religion, with its historic emphasis on patriarchal authority and responsibility; to what extent it was begotten in two young men who began business in the bosom of family and friends and fellowship; to what extent it was commonsense and self-interest, or the expression of filial admiration for the personalities of two very loving and lovable fathers, I cannot say. But that is how Ephraim Sieff and Michael Marks were, and their two sons took in their philosophy and example as something they had to further to honour their fathers' memories. In the thirties our concern for human relationships did not give us popularity in all quarters. We were among the small minority of companies who were not only actively interested in the pay and working conditions of their own employees but in those of men and women who worked for the companies that served ours. In the thirties we announced that we were instituting an enquiry into wages in our *suppliers'* factories. One manufacturer told us rather fiercely that this was the first occasion he had encountered on which a customer was asking a manufacturer to raise wages. Simon promised him that it would not be the last.

It certainly was not. In recent years we arranged with a building firm for the construction of a new store. Just after work began a few of us went to have a look at how things were going. It was raining – raining very hard. The tarpaulins which had been put up to shelter the men were not doing a proper job – the men looked wet and miserable. We said to the builder, 'Why don't you put up a shed where the men can come in the morning and change into working clothes, and bring a spare pair of trousers they can change into if they get soaked?' We found the men had no proper lavatory, and that they were eating their midday meal of sandwiches in the shelter of the half-constructed walls. We asked for a temporary building as a dining-room, and we got them lavatory accommodation. Some weeks later the Chairman of the firm, an MP, came to see me. He told me with pride that our store would be available for opening several weeks ahead of schedule: productivity of labour on that site had gone up by some almost sensational proportion, and that the casual labour turnover had dropped significantly. We congratulated him.

When I look back, it is the record of doing, or at any rate trying to do, things for the people who work for us that gave me most pleasure, that and the faith that those who came after us will continue to do the same, and for the same reasons. It is very heartening to know that what we do is appreciated, that warming knowledge not being based on hope or hearsay or even the occasional flattering testimony, but on *fact*. For instance, the national average canteen attendance is about forty per cent; for Marks and Spencer's canteens the figure is eighty-five per cent. The proof of the pudding is in the eating.

The most important pudding, however, is the service which the public gets. We provide hair-dressing service for the girls in the lunch-hour (they can eat their lunch under the drier) and we try to give them comfortable, relaxing rest-rooms where they can feel at home. We do this partly for their personal benefit and partly so that they will be in the best health and temper to stand up after lunch in a busy sales-room and be patient and cheerful to shoppers pressed for money and for time. But it is what we do for the public that sets the limits of what we can do for everybody else. We really have tried to serve the public beyond the limits of what was expected of us and, again, it warms the heart to note how often the public has expressed its gratitude. One occasion in particular stands out in my mind, and I am glad that, though it was in the year in which he died, Simon was alive and well to enjoy it too. In February 1964, in a debate in the House of Lords, Baroness Burton of Coventry, a great servant of the public herself, made a speech in which she dealt with the problem of protecting the consumer from goods that were dangerous. Speaking of inflammable nightdresses, Baroness Burton said:

Marks and Spencer told me that they had for a long time been conscious of the problems of fire hazard in children's nightdresses. They had eliminated children's winceyette many years ago, probably soon after the war. The only children's nightdresses they sell now are of brushed nylon, sold under the

British Nylon Spinners' 'flare-free' ticket. In 1961, and in 1962, they had trials in stores of children's nightdresses and pyjamas in Proban-treated winceyette. These trials were unsuccessful, first, because the public did not seem willing to pay approximately 5/- per garment more, and secondly, because the fabric was harsh and uncomfortable. On both occasions it was necessary to reduce prices to clear. I would stress that, in addition to having the merchandise for sale, Marks and Spencer briefed sales assistants to tell customers – and not only those customers who were interested in the Proban-treated garments, but those interested in any type of nightwear at all – of the advantages.

As a result of this experience, did Marks and Spencer throw in their hands? No, my Lord, they did not. They tell me that they are now looking at further samples of Proban-treated winceyette with an improved finish. Experiments are being made with an alternative fabric to winceyette, vincel-cotton, which may take a Proban finish more successfully. A trial quantity of children's nightdresses in knitted Teklan will be available and will be sent out to stores within the next two or three weeks. I would say to the House, in passing, that this fabric has a 'handle' comparable with that of brushed nylon, but is flame-proof, and most shoppers like the feel of it.

Simon died on 8 December 1964. He had been Chairman of the company for nearly fifty years. He has been dead long enough for me to see him in a perspective I never saw him in when he was alive. While he was alive he dominated me. I always deferred to him; it never occurred to me to do anything else; I grew up in the assumption of his superiority, as a brain, a business-leader, and as a human being. Since he died I have in one sense felt a freer person: my decisions and judgements are not related to those of anybody else as they were to Simon's. I am perfectly ready to revise my estimate of his worth, but in fact, as every year of his absence from my life goes by, I miss him more, and understand better what I owe to his creative genius.

I certainly see him more clearly now, five years after his death than I did before. I see, for example, that his whole life was bound up with the business in a way mine never has been. It was not that he could not relax or give himself to other interests, but that he saw Marks and Spencer as an integration of human life. What I mean is well conveyed in a remark he made after listening to a concert given by Moiseiwitsch: 'You know, his playing made me wonder why we couldn't do better in the business.' He had a sense of harmony and essential human experience which he groped for in his daily work, sensing when enjoying the perfection of philosophy and art how far his work was falling short of his ideal. His failings, and they were slight, were impatience and high-handedness, never displayed to the salesgirl and the salesman on the shop floor – to them no man could be more considerate – but to those around him. He was aggressive in argument, authoritative in manner, and ambitious in outlook; but only his equals or his rivals got the brunt of this. Simple as my nature was compared with his more complex ego, mine was aged and sophisticated in general attitude to life. He could never believe in his own achievements. He spoke of them sometimes like a child at a birthday party wondering if it is really happening after all, and if it is, whether it will go on.

Trying to look at Simon objectively I find that what I admired in him most was the clarity of his purposes and the directness with which he went out to achieve them. He found himself running a chain of penny bazaars and wanted to convert it into a chain of super-stores. He did it. He was egotistic enough to want his goods to have a distinct quality, second to none, and accepted as such by the nation. He got this. The brand name 'St Michael' means something to everybody who shops in Marks and Spencer: if they knew it, they would know it means above all Simon. Above all he wanted to forward his enterprise on a philanthropic attitude to human relations, on the notion of trust and service and progress. He did that too. He had left his colleagues, and, I believe his customers, a great legacy.

It is difficult for me to be objective about him. Not only did I love him: nearly the whole of my adult life was spent in a professional relationship with him, one which he dominated. It is impossible for me to conceive of what my life would have been had our partnership not existed. I brought only two things into his business life – a knowledge of textiles, and an experience of diplomacy as a result of my work with Weizmann which came in useful at various stages in the development of the business, particularly in our relations with suppliers in the twenties and thirties. I think my practical knowledge of British industry as a whole was useful to Simon when he entered the great period of expansion after he came back from America. Simon did not know a great deal about British industry at first hand. He preferred to stick to his last; listen to people he trusted talk about it. I think too that my work with PEP, my articles in the national press and my talks on the BBC, increased the pace at which Simon's philosophy of business and that of Marks and Spencer got across to those who were interested.

The ultimate key to the success of Marks and Spencer was peculiarly Simon's contribution: his instinctive judgement for what the people wanted. Our feats of adaptation to change of demand could never have been so swiftly executed had Simon's sense of how things were changing not been so highly developed and reliable. He rode the market like a jockey rides a great race – sensing what is happening before anybody else does, and boldly and swiftly acting on his judgement. That was the secret of Simon's success with the public. His success within his own company was due to his feeling for his employees. He was too much of a Napoleonic figure himself to regard everybody as of equal ability; but he was enough of a democrat to believe that everybody deserved equal consideration. My brother Teddy expressed this very well just after Simon died. Teddy related that recently there had been a proposal for extra Christmas bonuses, the increase to favour those employees with many years of service with the Company. Simon would not have it: 'No,' he said, 'this applies to a few only and is creating an élite – I would rather improve the lot of all by raising the bonus for all those who have been with the firm for three years and are making their career with Marks and Spencer.' And, developing Simon's democratic approach to decision-making, Teddy described his 'tremendous faculty of criticism and self-criticism' and quoted his so pregnant observation: 'I am the greatest rebel of you all.'

11
Thinking It Over

Even in my full vigour I was never much of a hater, and in the days of my youth felt ill at ease when I was occasionally expected to regard some of my fellow human beings, either individually or in groups, as, to some extent, enemies. Perhaps I have been too easy going. Certainly, my disinclination to hate is not founded on an infinite capacity to love. For example, much as I owed and owe to the German people, I have never since the early thirties made a visit to Germany: I could not risk the embarrassment of the thought crossing my mind when I spoke to some hospitable German I had met in a bus or at a beer-counter: 'Was he one of those who persecuted the Jews?' My daughter-in-law, Daphne Sieff, to whom I and my family owe so much, once said to me: 'You could also wonder if he might be a descendant of Goethe, or Schiller, or Heine, or whether he fought in the underground against Hitler.' I could. That imaginative thought helps me to contain my prejudices, but does not lift me above them. Perhaps it is because I do not expect myself – or anybody else – to love so much that I can live free – so far as I am aware – of hate.

For my personal relationships I can do nothing but express gratitude. My relationship with Simon and with members of my own family is something apart. Outside those, there are three of long standing, the memory of which I would mention if only because I know it would bear fruit in the garden of recollection unto the last. Two of the men are alive. I have mentioned them already: Max Nicholson and Leonard Elmhirst. I have described how I came to know them both: through PEP in the early thirties. Max Nicholson is the cleverest man I have ever met, and one of the most lovable. I may not be a good judge of which men are clever, and which men are not: but many men generally agreed to be clever have been introduced to me, usually in the hope that I might be able to assist them, and Max tops the lot. It was not a case of me being asked to assist him, but of me hoping to be allowed to associate myself with his good works. As for judgement of which man is lovable and which is not, I speak with an authority at least equal to that of any man. Max has been a journalist, a civil servant, a resident brain in government. For many years he has been able to indulge his love of nature as Director-General of the Nature Conservancy. For me he has represented as nobody else quite has what I have always most admired; the application of the intellect to the everyday pressing affairs of men in a steady unsensational attempt to leave them better than they were before: service of one's fellows by planning, not by preaching; blue printing a path to *real* progress, not preaching theoretical pie in the sky. Max could fit my limited practical experiences, my gleanings, my gropings, into theoretical totalities which covered society as a whole. His mind was broad enough not only to see every practical social and economic problem in its complete world context, but to be able to construct viable solutions to them, and then plan patiently to bring them about. He could do it because there was every-day wisdom in his widest calculation; the human element, not the ideal – the planner's opium – was the meat and drink which kept him going. If Max told me a thing could be done, I knew it could be done. However impossible of execution a project looked at any stage in the operation, I could lift my heart with: 'Max says it can be done.' His verdicts never failed me.

Leonard is more my own age. I suppose anybody might glean something profoundly true about Leonard by noting his recreation in *Who's Who*: it is 'care of trees'. That is his recreation: but his vocation has been the care of his fellow men, in which life work he had the partnership of his wife, Dorothy, also my friend of forty years who died, alas, a few months ago. Leonard is a Yorkshireman, the second of eight sons of a West Riding parson. He read history and theology at Cambridge, and nearly became a parson himself, but the first world war took him to India where he became very interested in the relation of village civilisation to the land. After the war he decided to study Agriculture scientifically but in a social and economic setting, and spent two years at Cornell University, in the United States. From here he went back to London to study the Ancient Rural Civilisations which had disintegrated when exposed to Western capitalism, and met the Indian poet Rabindranath Tagore, who had founded his International University (Visva-Bharati) at Santiniketan, in Bengal.

Tagore commissioned Leonard to start a department of rural reconstruction, and train young Indians to take it over. While doing this work, Leonard renewed his acquaintance with Dorothy Straight. Dorothy, born in Washington DC in 1887, was the daughter of William Whitney, an extremely wealthy public-spirited man, Secretary of the Navy under President Cleveland. In 1911 Dorothy had married William Straight, a remarkable man of the greatest promise, who died of pneumonia serving with the United States Forces in France in 1917. Leonard had met Dorothy at Cornell, in 1920. She went there a great deal because her first husband had been there. Now, in Bengal, they found they shared similar specific interests. They got married. They also decided that the problem they had been studying in India existed in Britain. The historic five thousand-acre estate of Dartington, near Totnes in Devon had been run down to 820 acres by the agricultural depression from which Britain had suffered since the 1870s. In 1925 they bought it, together with two adjacent farms, and 190 acres of woodland. They restored the fourteenth-century house, perhaps the finest example of the domestic architecture of that century which can be found in Britain today. They rehabilitated the land, developed the estate, and established local small scale industry: cider mill, sawmill, textile mill and a builder's yard. They built fifty cottages. They integrated into this framework a cultural and educational establishment – schools for dance, drama, music and design, and a progressive coeducational boarding school. Elmhirst land became the life-giving centre of a rural area which had suffered terribly from depression and unemployment; at the height of the slump of the early thirties it was employing six hundred people.

Their project stood for many different things: a revived rural life in which satisfying work and adequate pay would halt the drift to the towns; faith in the concept of intelligent, humane, well-informed and practical planning; a belief in the capacity of people to live in freedom, political, intellectual, religious; the strength of technology and craftsmanship in artistic and moral terms; the essential contribution of the arts to the simplest everyday life; the need to bring up children to be themselves, not admirable copies of their parents. They were liberal pioneers in a dark age. They succeeded not because they were rich but because they were children of light. Leonard was always neat to the point of being dapper, perfectly mannered, efficient, firm of purpose, clear in mind, seeing always where he wanted to try and go, aware of the possibilities of failure, but never accepting them as the slightest reason for not trying. I see Leonard as one of the makers of the way of life, a leader who leads because he really loves the led, a man whose way of loving the Lord is to love his fellow men – and *do* something for them.

I look back with gratitude on my friendship with the third man: Aneurin Bevan. It seems hardly credible to me that he died nearly ten years ago – his presence still abounds in my everyday life. Unlike Churchill, Bevan did not have the long delayed chance to become a great man. He died before his time. A universal tragedy: had he lived he could have done much for his country; and, he could have realised the potential in himself. I am prejudiced: he was my friend. For many years I lived in a house I bought from him. In some respects I found myself more sympathetic to the beatings of his heart and mind than to any other man's. Simon's mind I found complementary: Nye's supplementary. I owe him a great deal.

I did not believe in Nye's politics, or, at any rate, in those nostrums of the hustings, that uneasy electoral combination of prospectuses and shibboleths to which he nominally subscribed. I am not sure how much he believed in them himself. He was profoundly committed in his attitude to human beings and society, he was empirical about arrangements and institutions. This, I think, would have shown if he had become Prime Minister. What a voice and vision would then have dominated the life of Britain! How many dark places would have been illuminated, how many doubts and dangers would have been dispelled. Our problems would not have been waved away by a magician's wand overnight; but the attempt to solve them would have been rendered meaningful and more exciting. And I believe would have been solved. Wherever our proper, realistic level in the modern world lies, Nye would have seen it, and could have led us there. We would have gone there eyes open, tails up, ready to make it not a retreat but a triumph. Men must be led by men who above all can speak to them. There are the prophets, whose reason for being is to point a way ahead and make man able and willing to tread it. What makes an Isaiah is an unconquerable faith that good is not only morally better than evil, but that it is socially stronger too, the ability to get ordinary men to think the same and act accordingly. The first task of political leadership is to get men to lift up their hearts. Churchill did it in 1940. Weizmann did it time and time again. Nye would have done it for Britain today.

As well as admiring Nye's powers, my heart warmed to his nature.

Like all great men he was a simple man, and like them fundamentally a philosopher and a poet. (His wife, Jennie, also my friend of many years' standing, I have always thought of as dedicated to political action as her mode of being.) One day Nye and I were talking together in his house after lunch and I mentioned Spinoza. 'Why do you think so highly of Spinoza?' Nye asked. 'Because he so perfectly expresses the connection between freedom and morality; because he explains God, eternity, and the life here and now in a way that makes sense to me: man's "highest good" is "knowledge of his union with Nature" in the "intellectual love of God" by which, in and through the practising of virtue, he may enter into "blessedness", enjoying it continuously, that state of mind being the part of eternal life which is knowable here, what else there is, if any, remaining unknown.' Nye sat in silence for a moment or two looking not so much as a man pondering what he has heard as a man pondering what he will do. Then he left the room and came back with a sheaf of papers. 'Did you know I wrote poetry?' he asked. 'No,' I said, 'I certainly did not.' I knew he read it: he could recite Shakespeare, Keats, Shelley and Wordsworth endlessly. 'Well, I do,' he said, 'and I want to read you some.' So, rather shyly, especially for a man who was so uninhibited, and so used to hearing the sound of his own voice, he began to read. He read several poems to me. 'So you see, Israel, I too know something about philosophy,' he said, when he had finished, as though something I had said had given him the impression that I thought philosophy was above or below him, or at any rate alien to his way of life. 'Why don't you publish those poems?' I asked. 'Oh, I couldn't,' he said. 'I'm too shy. What would my friends say? There's hardly anybody I'd dare read the stuff to.' And he collected his papers and left the room, taking his poems back to where he had got them from. Neither he nor I mentioned them again, nor to this day do I know any more about them.

Voluble and irrepressible as he was, Nye, like many other men who resemble him, had the gift of silent companionship. Sometimes, after we had been pottering in the garden together, or strolling around my grounds or the fields around his house, we would sit down in his or my sitting-room. Each of us would pick up a book, or a magazine, or a newspaper, and we would read. If one of us came on something that impressed him, he would read it out to the other. Then we would resume our silence. Sometimes we would read to each other in this way for an hour or two. He was not much good at games, but he and I loved playing bowls together. 'If there's one thing I have learned to master,' he said, stooping to deliver a wood shining in the late summer sun, 'it is *bias*. But having mastered it I would not want to live without it.' We both loved good simple food and claret, and talk aimed not at complicating but at simplifying life.

Nye belongs in that gallery of the dwelling-place of my mind in which I keep my private collection of great men, those I think great whether I knew them or not, and whenever or wherever they lived. Nye did not believe that the every-day life that surrounded him was the best that could be. On the contrary, he believed it fell far short of what was possible, that it ought to be better, and that it could be made so – here, now, in our lifetime, this very day. He believed that, and he fought for his belief to the end. His greatness was in his humanity, his essential humility, his sense of the all-human predicament, and his passionate fight to lift his fellow-men out of it. The power of his vision was his conviction that it was simply bound to come to pass.

Beyond the portraits of individuals which adorn the walls of the dwelling-place of my mind are the wider canvases of the communities and the causes I recall with love. I cannot for a moment, and I think it will be understood, take my eyes off the phenomenon of the State of Israel. To those of us who have been Zionists all our lives, the establishment of the State of Israel is the fulfilment of one of these ideals. We have seen in it the future focal point of all Jewish thought and endeavour, both in Israel and in the Diaspora. And, indeed, since 1948, so it has been. But, in the last two decades in Israel, a new Jew is being fashioned by environment, by pioneering, by incredible hazards, by setbacks, as well as successes. We are looking at the Jew who, once again, builds with one hand and keeps the sword in the other, to defend himself against the enemies who surround him.

We, in the Diaspora, are ready for Israel to play a special role in our lives, for we see in the State a sort of guarantee of the survival of our people – physical, spiritual and cultural. Indeed, it is hardly possible in our day for us Jews of the Diaspora to prepare any programme or plans of action unless, in some way or other, we bring Israel into relation with our projects. In all our communities, we look to Israel eventually to set for us the standards which will fit into the new freedom which the Jews are attaining. We look with pride and longing expectation.

However, not everything I am aware of in this brave new state fills me with joy and unconditional hope. I wonder sometimes if there is not a loss of spiritual contact between the Jews of the old settlement in Israel, the *Yishuv*, and us, the Jews of the Diaspora. Are we, in the Diaspora, too complacent about the achievements of the State in the first two decades of its existence? Are we thinking of Israel only in terms of our financial contribution? Do we not sufficiently understand the minds of the Israelis as they contemplate their achievements? Is there something which has changed, not for the better, on the other side, so that the people of the new State have lost something on the way to their achievement? I have found in Israel that many people are, so to speak, ready to skip about two thousand years of our history, most of it in the Ghetto, and live in the present and the future regardless of the special heritage of the past. They see in the new State, the be-all and end-all of being a Jew. Many of the *Sabras* I have spoken to – the Sabras are those born in Israel: the word is an Arab one, meaning 'prickly pear' cactus – often pass over *Galuth* ('exile') history as something which should be forgotten. They want to escape from the memory of its shame and degradation, close their eyes, turn their backs, on the image of the oppressed and vilified Jew. I understand how they feel. But I think they make a great mistake. They attempt something which is as impossible as it is undesirable. They are trying to forget the very core of the Jewish experience. It was in the Ghetto that the Jew evolved his traditional ideas on nature, the Universe and God, his fellow creature, his own heart, and produced that culture and outlook which we call Jewish. The Sabras refuse to enter into the strange but humanising experience of vicarious suffering – suffering in the past as well as the here and now. They do not want to live again in the agony of the evil Hitler committed against their kinsmen. They do not want to live through the pain and anguish of the Jewish martyrdom. They believe that they in Israel are the masters of their fate, that they can bend their environment, and surmount the many obstacles which bar their progress. They believe that knowledge, skill and will-power are all that are needed for them to conquer, and that they have them. Herzl's dictum 'If you wish it, it is no fairy tale' seems to be their motto.

The attempt to achieve the conquest of the Negev is a striking illustration of their outlook. They believe that the Negev is vital to the existence of Israel. For them the Negev is not a desert and a waste, but a part of Israel which shall bloom like a rose. The Sabra is convinced that deserts are a thing of the past in the Middle East, that they have been the burden of indolent people who have not cared for their land or their future, and have left their rich and populous habitations to turn into arid wastes and desert lands. They, these sanguine and determined Sabras, never sparing themselves, ever surging on, have united together to transform the waste places into fields of corn and fruitful orchards. The desert has been pushed back; a settled and self-supporting people have found new life, sustenance and prosperity. For these Jews, cast in a heroic mould, history ended prior to the Roman conquest and resumed again in 1948. The exile – the *Galuth* – ended in 1948. There was then to be no looking back.

Given this mental attitude, it is not surprising, therefore, that these pioneers look with feelings that sometimes border on contempt upon those Jews who remain outside Israel to enjoy the indulgences of the world outside. But while much of the Jewish heritage comes from the experience of the Jews struggling as a modern nation state in the Middle East, much more comes from their historic experience in the outside world. Foremost in the mind of a Jew who believes in his faith are the concepts of charity and justice. The two must be combined – in conscience, the one does not exist without the other. Justice is the action; Charity is the state of mind in which the action is performed. There is no justice without charity, and charity not acted out in justice is a tinkling cymbal. To live justly before God is to behave charitably to one's fellow man. This whether he is a Jew or not. Justice is the condition in which men help each other. This idea is the essence of being a Jew.

I think there was nothing very special about the attitude of the Jews towards charity before they were taken into captivity in Babylon in 587 BC. The leaders of the Jews, the ruling caste, were deported. Only a peasant population was left. But the voice of Jeremiah was lifted. Nebuchadnezzar sacked and destroyed Jerusalem and burned down the Temple which Solomon had built 350 years before. Judah was laid waste. The occupation of their country at that time taught the Jews a profound lesson which others have had to learn since: they came quickly to know that in captivity, and under tyranny, one man depended utterly upon his neighbour – this Jew upon the next Jew – and that no man knew when his turn would come to be in need – for shelter, for food, or for money to save his life. At that time, charity, nationhood and survival went together. To hesitate was to risk losing all. There was one hope – to give when asked and quickly.

Six centuries later the Temple of Jerusalem was destroyed again, this time by the Romans. Again, in AD 70, the Jews were a shattered people: the survivors streamed out all over Europe and the Middle East. Once again Jews had to learn the lesson of suffering. The Jew in Rome was conscious of the Jew who lived in Paris and of their relationship in an international network in which charity, justice and survival intertwined. They discussed with one another the application of their ethical system to the various societies in which they lived. A rabbi in Worms would correspond with a rabbi in Cordova on the problems of interpreting the Talmud in the changing conditions of the world.

Because it was based on a fundamental ethical approach to the survival problems of the race, Judaism became an evolving, not a static, religion, facing and tackling the social problems of the day. And there contained in it, engrained, this profound notion of the dependence of one man on another – not simply as the wish of God, but as the only hopeful lesson pointing away from the tragedies of the past. Distance did not dilute this faith. It strengthened it. Jews may come together by chance from the ends of the earth, but they look on one another as potential friends. The Talmud is full of sayings like 'All Jews are colleagues', 'No Jew must be allowed to go hungry', 'God gives to him who gives', and so on.

One of the most solemn and poetic prayers which we Jews have is recited on the festival of the New Year. The prayer is spoken on the day on which God is supposed to come to judgement on mankind. After the blowing of the trumpets, the prayer goes on to list those who after this day shall live and those who shall die, those who shall be fed and those who shall go hungry, and so forth. And the prayer issues the warning that in ten days from the New Year there will be the fateful day of Yom Kippur, the Day of Atonement. In this span of ten days God will decide whether he should seal His Judgement, and let the sinner suffer the consequences of his sins, or, if he has repented, spare him, and let him live in hope again. The great prayer, the U-Netanneh Tokeph, does not come from Biblical times. About a thousand years ago the Bishop of Mainz ordered a Jew called Amnon to renounce his Jewish faith and accept the Christian religion. Amnon refused. His limbs were cut off. As he lay dying he recited the U-Netanneh Tokeph. In his last moment he cried out that 'only Prayer, Repentance and Charity will avert the evil decree'. Ever after the prayer has had its unique place in our liturgy. Its dynamic comes not from the wanderings in the desert, or from the modern State of Israel, but from the suffering in the Ghetto.

The notion of Charity that comes from his religion and his experience, is fundamental to the Jew's religion. If a Jew faithful to his creed hears a real call for charity he will never refuse. This is the very warp and woof of the nature of being a Jew. And his concept of charity comes from his experience in the Diaspora. It would be tragic, a betrayal of those who suffered in the past, to turn our backs on what being a Jew is really all about, and to behave as if all values are entirely in the present, as if the future depends on what a man does now with scientific brain and resourceful pair of hands. This is the way to the idea that power is ploughshares and bomber-planes; that is not the road forward, but the road back to Hitler and Nebuchadnezzar.

The Ghetto must never go out of the mind of the modern Jew. He must remember it, keep it ever ready in his mind, not in resentment, hate or fear, but in love: love of the wisdom of God which out of evil has brought forth good; out of dark, light; out of prison, freedom; out of servitude, strength; out of suffering, the vision of eternal peace. Out of the Ghetto came the qualities which the Jews can offer their fellow men; not the strength of swords, but the strength of plough shares; not the power to overcome by force but the power that comes of inspiring trust. This comes to a great extent from the Ghetto, from the combination of the Ghetto with the Jew's everlasting religious faith. In the first few centuries after the destruction of the Temple in AD 70, the Jews spread over Europe in their second great diaspora, only to be confined in the cities to the life of the Ghetto. The majority of activities which brought prestige and power to other men were denied to them. The only important trade they were left free to practise was the one which the Christians thought too theologically sullied to be conducted by themselves – the trade in money. The matrix of trust which has been built up among the Jews of Europe on the basis of their political and religious experiences – on the correspondence with each other about the fundamental issues of life and death – became, when the European economy began to move from barter to commercial trading and require a system of international banking, a dynamic social and economic force. Jews who had to make journeys, especially in foreign parts, would ask for money to be lent to them by other Jews at intervals along their routes. Sums of money were deposited by the traveller to be used, months, possibly years, later, when he came that way again. 'You have money of mine. Hold it for me. I may make a journey, or I may send my son.' Jewish agents set up business all over Europe. They charged interest to provide the security. They prospered. Jewish families accumulated large funds. These were large enough for kings to borrow from, to finance wars and bail empires. The loans of the Fuggers of Augsburg underwrote half the kingdoms of Europe in the sixteenth century.

It was not, as is sometimes said, that usury was permitted to Jews and not to Christians; usury is forbidden to Jews – see the book of Leviticus. The point is that because they were confined to ghettos the Jews were unable to expand into property, industry or land, but could only hold and deploy capital in the shape of money. Their acquisition of a dominant role in international finance was the combination of the capacity of their moral and political experience to cover a continent with a network of trust, with the incapacity of ghetto life to provide them with any outlet for initiative, except the field of money.

But what is important is not that Jews made money in the Middle Ages: what is important is how they made it; in what spirit, and to what end. The vicissitudes of the Jews, from the days of the wandering in the desert to the days of the gas chambers in Germany, have accustomed them to live on this earth with an imminent sense of death. A man who knows that he may shortly die is more likely to reflect on how he should live than a man for whom death is a word in an unread book. It is a curious paradox that it is easier for men to survive to the degree that life does not matter to them. Life in the concentration camps was more bearable for the Jews than for many others because Jews had been impregnated by history in the virtue of compassion. Where, as in Belsen, they could only spend their time looking after each other, they flourished. They had learned the lesson that there is no will to live in looking after oneself. The great Christians, as other religious people, have learned the same lesson in a not dissimilar way: 'He who wishes to save his life must lose it.' To my Jewish friends who seem to me to trust too much to life in the present and future, and to neglect, a little, the creative Jewish past, I would conclude by saying: 'It's all in Isaiah Chapter One and Two.' When Isaiah denounces his people, tells them they have forsaken the Lord and profaned their Temple, it is because they have turned to material things and sought them for themselves.

'Oh you evil people, you have forsaken the Lord.' He inveighs against the Hebrew people. 'Why do you think I need your hallelujahs and your prayers! Your blood offerings stink in my nostrils! Your gifts are an abomination to me. What I want from you is to care for the widow, the orphan, and the sick. I want you to do all these things. But first I want you to live by the Law.' And so on. 'This is my will, and your justice. Do this and your nation shall come unto Zion.' Be strong. Let no man put you down. Put not your trust in princes. But do not expect to hold your place by the boast, however good, that you can defeat all comers. Make sure you can defeat all comers: but also love the Lord, follow the ways of your people: remember your past.

Naturally at my time of life my mind turns to the future of the business in which I have lived my professional life and, through which I have enjoyed my most profound personal relationships. Will it continue to prosper along the lines laid down by Simon? I am sure that it will prosper, increase and not diminish. I believe that those who will come after the Simon-Israel generation will do much as we have done, not because they venerate Simon or – God forbid! – myself, but because they are fully seized with the same ideology of business. My dear brother, Teddy, is the present Chairman. He is sixteen years younger than I am, only a few years older than my two eldest sons. Simon asked Teddy to leave my father's business in 1933 and come to join us. For many years Teddy was in Simon's direct tutelage, lived in his house, and was indoctrinated with Simon's views and methods as nobody else has been. It has been a great advantage to have somebody who by the accident of being born between the two generations has been able to preserve a continuity of philosophy and management not always found when the representatives of one generation go and the business must be handed over to leaders thirty years younger. After Teddy there are many able men of both families. My sons, Michael and Marcus, have been, apart from the second world war, in Marks and Spencer all their working lives. They are Sieffs through their father; Marks through their mother. Simon's son, the present Lord Marks, does not have a great part in the business: he is a poet. But my sister-in-law, Miriam Sacher, has two able sons in the business, Michael and Gabriel, and there are grandsons on either side. There is that tower of strength, Bruce Goodman, not in flesh but in spirit a member of our families, casting an all-seeing eye on every aspect of the firm's affairs. For the next two or three decades we have got able young people coming on, from within and outside the family, who will follow our existing ideas through to the end and no doubt improve upon them. We are training our young people, each of whom carries the baton of potential chairmanship on his pedlar's tray, to understand what we understand by good merchandising, good business, good human relations, good profitability, and I hope, the good life which gives all these things meaning. It is a continuous training, and I daresay that if you spoke to my grandsons – I hope to any of the young men of their age who are making their way in the business – they would say a great deal of what I have said, but say it better.

The future of the business depends on two things. First, quick imaginative study of what the people need – not of what the public can be persuaded to buy; but of what the people really *need*. Only in supplying real needs will a business flourish in the long term. Only by giving the people what *on reflection* they continue to want will a business earn the respect of the customer, which is essential to anything more durable than a cheapjack's overnight success. So long as Marks and Spencer continues to study what the people need, and efficiently produce it by means of a staff humanely organised, we can meet any economic trend and any economic challenge. Efficient and humane adaptation to the needs of the people is the first and last principle of Marks and Spencer. It is, in my view, of all really enterprising concerns.

The other guiding light of business enterprise is attention to human relations within the business. Firms, like our own, which study human relations – labour relations, and industrial relations, they are called in some places – are often asked to supply people to lecture on the subject. It is very difficult. How can you tell people to do things which you know they are not doing because they are the way they are? You cannot get the good will of the people who work for you by changing words such as 'canteen' into 'dining-room', 'navvy' to 'worker', 'office boy' to 'junior clerk', and so on, or even just by paying higher wages. In the last analysis good labour relations come from workers approving the kind of people they believe their employers to be.

I look back now on a life, the fullness of whose cup I owe, as few men have, to the generosity of other people. Simon gave me for sixty years what few men enjoy for five or ten, what many men never know: the gift of male companionship. I do not know what my life would have been without Simon: I find it impossible to create it in imagination: it is like trying to write Hamlet without the Prince of Denmark. Of what I owe to him I could sit and write all night. Of what I might have given to him – ah, how less a rewarding and congenial task. All I could be sure of is that I was less anxious to be proved than he was. From the beginning he was desperate to show he could succeed. When I joined him I had done well in, and out of, my father's business. My ego and my pockets were tolerably well lined. I had been to university. I could get on well with people. I enjoyed life. I was ready to smile. I was neither tense nor self-critical. Simon, perhaps, found me a good companion.

Becky was a remarkable woman; good and gifted enough to be Simon's sister; too good, nevertheless, to be my wife. Direct, straightforward, always to the point, she was not an easy ally in the struggle for life. She believed in the truth, and the telling of it, and did nothing to dull its edge. Sometimes she hurt people: but if they could wait a little, they would find that she had realised the impact of her words, and would dress as nobody else could the wounds – not serious ever – which she had inflicted.

It was not easy being brother-in-law and husband to two people of genius. It was more difficult because they were intellectuals and rationalists whilst I was romantic and empirical. Moreover, each of them was conditioned in their attitude to me by their attitude to each other: Simon, the one son, surrounded by vigorous sisters, led by the beautiful and incisively minded Becky, was always somewhat jealous of Becky's hold over his otherwise faithful friend. Becky, sceptical of any male's claim to dominance, and particularly of her brother, always resented the overt awe in which I held him. Not until they were both dead, dying within just over a year of each other, did I realise quite how my life had been influenced by the combination of these two strange strong souls.

At the time I write these words I am in terms of this generation by no means alone. My very dear sister, Miriam, five years younger than I am (Simon's widow, deeply bereaved by his death six years ago) is still alive. So is her elder sister, Pauline, only eighteen months younger than I am. Simon's youngest sister, Elaine, is so much my junior I can hardly regard her as my generation, but her elder sister, Miriam

Sacher, seems to have grown up with me. She is as generous of heart and outspoken of opinion, as I remember her as the amusing seventeen-year-old I once accompanied to Paris: at the last minute Becky could not come with us, so I was Miriam's escort and chaperone; she reported afterwards, 'Israel danced with me a lot and told me all about life. One thing he said I always remember: "Give way gracefully in little things, and you will get your way with the big things".' Miriam and Elaine spend as much time as ever on good works, and find time to support the arts as well. Harry Sacher, Miriam's husband, is still alive – eighty-eight years old. Harry is a great man: leader-writer on the *Daily Chronicle*, and resigning on a question of principle at the outbreak of World War I, then leader-writer on the *Guardian*, colleague of Sidebotham, friend, disciple and trusted adviser of Weizmann, and for nine years in the twenties a successful barrister – and state-builder – in New Israel; father of Michael and Gabriel Sacher, both of whom now on the Marks and Spencer Board. It is a good thing to grow old with a few of one's own generation around one: Miriam and Harry Sacher live quite near to me in the country. Then there are my own children: Judith lives in Israel doing so many of the things her mother would wish to be doing if she were alive. My dear sons, Michael and Marcus, continually delight me by carrying on the good work, particularly in regard to Israel, that Simon and I began.

I am now into my eighties. Chance or fate, or the will of God, put what name you like upon the process, has taken me into interesting places and shown me interesting people. My last years have in many respects been the best. Grandchildren, great-grandchildren, great nephews, great-great-nephews, and the nieces, have proliferated: the descendants of my oldest friends abound. I see in Britain a great society in which the number of those who suffer poverty or neglect is smaller than my father, for all his faith and optimism, would have thought possible: and I have been allowed by God's will and help to make a contribution to this. Over the seas, in Israel, I see a new country which for all its perils, travail and besetting faults, is the realisation of nearly three thousand years of dreams of a Jewish home and refuge on *this* earth; and I was allowed to make a contribution to that. Around me in these peaceful Berkshire fields are my flowers, my cattle, my books and paintings, my children and my children's children. In my old age, I say with Isaiah:

MEMOIRS

    I will look at my dwelling place
like clear heat in the sunshine, like a
cloud of dew in the heat of the harvest. . . .

    I will look upon Zion.

Index

'A National Plan for Britain', *see Week End Review*
Abdullah, King, 127–8
Acworth, Bernard, 169; *see also* 'Letting the Socialists in'
Africa, West, 132
Ahad Ha-am, *see* Ginsberg, Asher
Aldershot, 82
Alexander, Samuel, 37, 84
Alexander II, Czar, 8, 52
Alexander III, Czar, 8–9
Alexandria, 99, 101–3
Alfred Behrens and Company, 46–7
Algeria, 102
Allenby, General, 92, 105, 110, 111, 127, 130
Alliance Israelite, 98
Altneuland, 103
America, *see* United States of America
Amery, Leopold, 87
Amnon, 199–200
Anglo-Palestine Company, 69
anti-Semitism, and 1882 pogroms, 7–9, 11, 70, 108; Ephraim Sieff and, 23–4; Hitler and, 43, 179, 197; and Dreyfus trial, 71–2, 130; and 'Protocols of the Elders of Zion', 105; at University of Munich, 133; Mosley and, 170
Aqaba, 110, 136
Arabs, the, and the First World War, 87, 90, 92, 98; and the Balfour Declaration, 92, 96–8, 120; and the Zionist Commission, 101, 102, 104–7, 110–11, 124–8, 130; and Feisal/Weizmann agreement, 110–20; Britain's attitude towards, 124, 126–8, 130; and creation of State of Israel, 135–7; mentioned, 121, 197
Ashkenazim branch of Jewry, *see* Jews, Askenazic
Asia, 1
Asia Minor, 1
Asquith, 86
Atlantic Ocean, 52, 178, 184
ATS, 181
Augsberg, 201
Austria, 8, 156

Bab-el-Wad, 104
Babylon, 1–2, 4, 70, 198
Babylonian Talmud, 1

Backhouse, Charles, 53
Baku, 75
Baldwin, Stanley, 172
Balfour, Arthur James, 37, 78–9, 84–6, 91, 94–5, 98, 111, 114, 120
Balfour Declaration, 70, 83, 86, 91–105, 113, 120, 124, 128–30
Baltic Sea, 3, 10
Barlow, Sir Thomas, 171
Barran Clothiers, 53
Barry, Sir Gerald, 164–6
Bartlett, Vernon, 165, 166
Basle, 71, 72, 73
Basle Program, 71
Bath, 60
Batley, 42
Bavaria, 45
BBC, 189
Beaumont and Co., 12–14, 20; *see also* Sieff & Beaumont Ltd
Beaverbrook, Lord, 164–5
Belgium, 43
Belsen, 201
Ben Gurion, David, 109, 129, 135, 138, 139
Bengal, 192–3
Benson, James, 45
Berkshire, 205
Berlin, 73, 80
Berlin, Sir Isaiah, 93
Besan, 127
Bevan, Aneurin, 194–6
Beveridge, 166
Beveridge Committee, 176
Bevin, Ernest, 166
Bialystok, 52
Bianchini, Commendatore, 98–9, 130
Bilu, 108
Bir Salem, 104
Birkenhead, 58
Birnbaum, Nathan, 70
Bismarck, 7–9
Blackett, Sir Basil, 166–8
Blackpool, 30, 143–4
Board of Deputies of British Jews, 95
Board of Trade, 177, 178
Boileau, 35
Bols, General L. J., 127, 130
Bolsheviks, the, 105, 128–9
Bonaparte, Napoleon, 2, 104, 190
Bosnia, 126

INDEX

Bradford, 42, 79
Brandeis, Louis, 131
Brave New World, 166
Bristol, 49
Britain, 2, 5–6, 9–11, 24, 27–8, 37, 52, 54–8, 69–70, 72–6, 78–121, 124–30, 132, 135–8, 142–3, 153, 155–6, 163–4, 167–8, 172–85, 189, 193–4, 205
Britain and World Trade, see PEP
British Foreign and Colonial Corporation, 144
British Palestine Committee, 88–90, 94
British Union of Fascists, 170
Brown, Ivor, 165
Budapest, 70
Bunbury, Sir Henry, 175–6
Burton, Baroness, 187–8
Butler, R. A., 175

Cairo, 97, 99, 101–3, 110, 126
California, 52
Cambridge, University of, 131, 192
Canada, 42, 177
'Capitalist versus Communist Planning', 168
Cardiff, 57, 60
Castleford, 55, 58
Central Electricity Board, 175
Chalutzim, the, 99, 106-7, 109
Chamberlain, Joseph, 72
Chamberlain, Neville, 165
Chapman, Sir Sidney, 40–1
Chapman, William, 61–4
Chasidim, 4–5, 25
Che-Chaltuz, 109
Churchill, Sir Winston, 37, 85–6, 194
Citrine, Walter, 166
Clayton, General, 92
Clayton Aniline Works, 78
Clemenceau, 114
Cleveland, 193
Cobden, 37
Cohen, Samuel, 66-8
Cole, Professor G. D. H., 166
Cologne, 76
Committee of Jewish Delegations, 114
Common Market, 139
Commonwealth, British, 132, 165
Conservative Party, 78, 165, 166, 169, 170, 172, 174–5, 183
Cookham, 168, 175
Cordova, 199
Corneille, 35
Cork, 48
Cornell University, 192, 193
Cossacks, the, 77
Courland, 3
Cowen, Joseph, 96, 98, 130
Cox, Colonel, 127

Crimean War, 77
Crossman, Richard, 139
Cunningham, Sir Alan, 138
Curzon, Lord, 170
Czechoslovakia, 156

Dagutski, Rabbi, 15–16
Daily Chronicle, 205
Daily Express, 165
Daily Herald, 169
Daily Telegraph, 172
Damascus, 113
Daniel Sieff Research Institute, 132–5; see also Sieff, Daniel
Danzig, 76
Darlington, 143
Dartington Hall, 166, 193
Dawson City, 53
Deedes, General Wyndham, 105
'The Democratic Faction', 72
Derby Fusiliers, 81
Derby, Lord, 81
Devon, 193
Dewhirst, Alistair, 53
Dewhirst, Isaac, 53, 57, 59, 60
Dewhirst Ltd, 53, 55
Dickens, Charles, 139
Didsbury, 49, 68, 69
Disraeli, Benjamin, 168
Disraeli, Mrs Benjamin, 168
Dizengoff, Meir, 103
Dreyfus, Charles, 37, 78
Dreyfus Trial, 71
Dublin, 15
Duff Cooper, 165, 166

Eckhard, Mrs, 83
The Economist, 169
Eder, David, 98, 110, 122, 130
Eder, Edith, 122
Edinburgh, 79
Education Acts, 175
Edward VIII, 171–2
Egypt, 101–2, 109–10, 129, 136
Egyptians, Ancient, 20
Ehrlich, Paul, 80–1
Einstein, 131
Eiregola, 3, 5, 6, 9, 11, 15, 27
El Arish, 103
El Qantara, 103
Elliott, Walter, 166
Elmhirst, Dorothy, 166, 192–3
Elmhirst, Leonard, 167, 174, 177, 191–4
England, see Britain
English Review, 169; 'Letting the Socialists in' published in, 169
English Women's Zionist Organisation, 122

INDEX

English Zionist Federation, 91, 94, 98; see also Zionist Organisation of England
Exilarch, see Rosh Ha-Golah
Exodus 1947, 135
'Experiments in the Marketing of Agricultural Products', see PEP

Federation of American Zionists, 110; see also Zionist Organisation of America
Feisal, Emperor, 96
Feisal, King, 110-19
The Film Industry, see PEP
First World War, outbreak of, 80, 81, 83; Sieff family involvement in, 81-3; and Balfour Declaration, 92, 97; conclusion of, 112; and Peace Conference of Versailles, 112-20, 124; mentioned, 13, 38, 68, 70
Fisher, H. A. L., 175
Flanders, 81
Forestry Commission, 175
France, 4, 8, 35, 43, 45-7, 82, 85-8, 90, 98-102, 112-20, 130, 139, 156, 165, 193
Frankfurt, 80
Frankfurter, Felix, 114
Fraser, Hugh, 185
Friedenwald, Harry, 110
Fuel and Power, see PEP

Gaitskell, Hugh, 168
Galilee, 127
Gaster, Dr, 90
Gaulle, Charles de, 139
Gautier, 35; see also *Voyage en Espagne*
Gaza, 103
General Strike, 148, 150
Geneva, 74, 77
George V, 97-8
Germain, Herman, 142
Germany, 4, 7-9, 35, 37, 43, 45-6, 68, 72, 83, 85-6, 97, 100, 102, 105, 133, 156, 177, 179, 191, 201
Ginsberg, Asher, 78
Ginsburg, Romana, 122
Glamorgan, 154
Glasgow, 48, 79, 154
Goethe, 35, 46, 191
Goldmann, Nahum, 135
Goodman, Bruce, 185, 202-3
Goodman, Romana, 122
Government and Industry, see PEP
Grand Mufti of Jerusalem, see Husseini, Amin el
The Greater Britain, 170
Greenberg, Hayim, 135
Guggenheimer, Theodore, 45, 46

Haggadah, the, 21
The Hague, 79
Haifa, 135
Halifax (America), 178
Halifax (England), 79
Halifax, Lord, 179
Hall, Noel, 168; see also 'Capitalist versus Communist Planning'
Hallé Orchestra, 20, 36
Hallé, Sir Charles, 36
Halprin, Rose, 135
Hamburg, 135
Hebrew University, 79-81, 106, 110-12, 133
Heine, 35, 191
Henderson, Leon, 179
Herzl, Theodore, 70-4, 93, 103, 108, 112, 197; see also *The Jewish State*
Hibbat Zion Movement, 108
Hitler, Adolf, 43, 126, 156, 162, 171, 173, 179, 191, 197, 200
Hirsch, Baron Maurice de, 108
Holland, 43
Hovevei Zion, 108, 130
Huddersfield, 42, 43
Hugo, Victor, 35
Hungary, 8, 70
Hull, 10, 11
Husseini, Amin el, 121, 126
Huxley, Aldous, 166; see also *Brave New World*
Huxley, Julian, 166

ICI, 156-7
Imperial Chemical Industries, see ICI
India, 83, 85, 192-3
International University, see Visva-Bharati
Iraq, 136
Ireland, 154, 177
Irwell, Henrietta, 122
Irwell, River, 42
Israel, creation of State of, and 'political' Zionism, 70-3; and 'practical' Zionism, 71-3; and 'synthetic' Zionism, 73; and influence of First World War, 83; and Balfour Declaration, 70, 83, 86, 91-105, 113, 120, 124, 128-30; and Zionist Commission, 70, 94-112, 114, 122, 124-31; and Jewish Agency for Israel, 106, 132, 135, 137; and declaration of Israel's independence, 135-9; and the Sabras, 196-8; mentioned, 74, 90, 103, 200, 205; see also Palestine
Italy, 43, 98-101, 130

Jabotinsky, Vladimir, 86, 92, 106, 121
Jaffa, 103, 104

209

INDEX

Japan, 101, 163, 179
Jerusalem, 1, 78, 80, 92, 95, 104, 107, 109, 111, 121, 124–8, 132, 134, 198, 199
Jerusalem Talmud, 1
Jessup, 138
Jewish Agency for Israel, 106, 132, 135, 137
Jewish Colonial Trust, 69, 71, 108
Jewish Legion, 86, 92, 106, 109
Jewish National Fund, 67, 72, 79, 108, 125
The Jewish State, 71
Jews, the, in Babylon, 1–2, 4, 70; Askenazic, 3–4, 27, 37, 77, 102; Sephardic, 4, 37, 66, 77, 102; and Chasidism, 4–5, 25; family relationships among, 5–6, 24; and 1882 pogroms, 7–9, 52, 70, 71; emigration to Britain among, 9–11, 26–8; emigration to Ireland among, 14–15; Manchester community, 2, 5–6, 11–21; 32–3, 37, 74–80, 83–6; Hitler's persecution of, 43, 179–80, 191, 197; Nuremberg community, 46; Leeds community, 53; and beginnings of Zionism, 70–3; and Uganda project, 72–3, 76; and foundation of Hebrew University, 79–81, 106, 110–12, 133; and Sykes-Picot Agreement, 87–8, 90, 92, 110, 112, 113; and *Palestine*, 88–90, 92, 110; and Balfour Declaration, 91–105, 113, 120, 124, 128–30; and Zionist Commission, 94–112, 114, 122, 124–31; and Jewish Agency for Israel, 106, 132, 135, 137; and Feisal/Weizmann agreement, 110–19; and 1920 Jerusalem pogrom, 121; and W.I.Z.O., 122–4; and declaration of Israel's independence, 135–9; Mosley's attitude to, 170–1; spiritual inheritance of, 186, 196–202; mentioned, 44–5, 205; *see also* anti-Semitism, Israel, Palestine
Johnson, Herschel, 136
Joppa, *see* Jaffa
Joyce, Colonel, 110–11
Judaea, 92, 111
Judah, 198

Kaiserman, Joe, 33
Kaunas, *see* Kovno
Kenyon, G. R., 47
Keren Kayemet le-Yisrael, *see* Jewish National Fund
Kerr, Philip, *see* Lothian, Lord
Keynes, Lord, 176
Khan Yunis, 103
Kiriat Ye'arim, 104
Kisch, Frederick, 125
Knowsley, 81

Koenigsberg, 3, 7, 9, 10, 12, 25
Kovno, 3, 7
Kremenetzky, 79

Labour Party, 165, 166, 169, 170, 174–5, 180
Ladino, 4
Lancashire, 30, 43, 57, 58, 59, 81, 154, 156, 163
Lansing, 114, 120
Laski, Nathan, 37
Lawrence, T. E., 112–14
League of British Jews, 95
League of Nations, 69–70, 114
Lee, Jennie, 195
Leeds, 11, 53–8, 60, 79, 144
Leibnitz, 133
Lenin, I. V., 112, 173
Lessing, 35
'Letting the Socialists in', *see English Review*
Leumi le-Israel Bank, 69
Leventin, David, 103
Lévi, Sylvain, 98, 100, 114, 120, 130
Liberal Party, 174–5
Lichfield, 61
Lindsay, Kenneth, 164, 166, 167, 170, 174, 175
Liptons, 57
Lithuania, 2–5, 11, 15, 16, 19
Liverpool, 79, 177
Llandudno, 30
Lloyd George, David, 84–6, 121, 126, 169–70
Lloyd, Selwyn, 183
London, 11, 35, 46, 48–50, 53, 60, 69, 73–5, 78, 80, 84, 86, 88, 94–6, 112–14, 142, 146, 147, 153, 158–9, 167, 168, 192
London Transport, 175
London, University of, 40, 166, 168
Los Angeles, 53
Lothian, Lord, 121
Lydd, 103
Lydda, 109
Lytham St Annes, 91

Maccabees, the, 71, 92
McColl, Andrew, 166
McGowan, Lord, 157
Macmillan, Harold, 172; *see also* Reconstruction
Macy's, 179
Mainz, 199
Manchester, 2, 5–6, 11–28, 33–9, 45, 47, 52, 58, 60, 61, 75–80, 83, 84, 91, 93, 94, 99, 113, 125, 128, 146, 147, 157
Manchester Grammar School, 18, 33–5, 38–9, 46, 82

210

INDEX

Manchester Guardian, 36–7, 42, 49, 83, 87, 205
Manchester Jewish Hospital, 67
Manchester, University of, 35, 37, 39–41, 66, 68, 72, 75, 80
Manchester Zionist Organisation, 66, 69, 76–8
Marks, Barnet, 52–3
Marks, Elaine, 32, 33, 35, 204, 205
Marks, Ephraim, 52, 64
Marks, Hannah (mother of Simon Marks), 48–9, 58
Marks, Hannah (daughter of Simon Marks), 48
Marks, Maurice, 52
Marks, Michael (father of Simon Marks), early life of, 35, 52; character of, 35, 47–8, 59, 186; last illness of, 48, 59, 62; emigration to Britain of, 52–3; early days in Leeds of, 53–5, 144; and 'Penny Bazaars', 56–8, 141, 143–5, 155–7, 189; marriage of, 58; and establishment of Marks and Spencer, 59–62, 142; treatment of his employees, 143, 157, 186; mentioned, 30, 45
Marks, Michael (son of Simon Marks), 48, 202
Marks, Miriam, and marriage to Harry Sacher, 48, 125–6, 202, 204–5; and Daniel Sieff Research Institute, 132, 134; mentioned, 35
Marks, Rebecca, and early friendship with Israel Sieff, 30–2, 34–6, 41, 42; at Manchester University, 41; and marriage to Israel Sieff, 48–51, 123, 204; character of, 51, 123, 204; Zionist activities of, 95, 96, 122–8; and death of her son Daniel, 132; mentioned, 66, 67, 99, 100, 168, 171, 205
Marks, Simon, and childhood friendship with Israel Sieff, 19, 31–9, 52, 59; character of, 31–2, 37–9, 43, 188–9, 203–4; training in France and Germany, 45–7; death of his father Michael, 48; marriage to Miriam Sieff, 48; death of his mother Hannah, 48–9; friendship with Chaim Weizmann, 48–9, 68, 140, 146–7, 181; and Israel Sieff's marriage to Rebecca Marks, 50–1; elected to Board of Marks and Spencer, 62; and struggle for control of Marks and Spencer, 63–4; friendship with Agnes Spencer, 65; Zionist activities of, 87–8, 90, 94–6, 113, 140, 142, 205; made Chairman of Marks and Spencer, 94; in the army, 94–5; and Daniel Sieff, 131–4; and expansion of Marks and Spencer, 141–61, 180–90;

friendship with Edward Sieff, 202; death, 188; mentioned, ix, 1, 18, 40, 69, 177, 191, 194
Marks, Tilly, 35
Marks and Spencer, the initial partnership, 45–7, 52, 59–62, 65; Simon Marks elected to Board of, 62; Simon Marks' struggle for control of, 63–4; Israel Sieff elected to Board of, 64; Simon Marks made Chairman of, 94; nineteen twenties and thirties development of, 141–61; post-war development of, 180–90; speculations on future of, 202–3, 205; mentioned, 14, 18, 38, 43, 167, 177
Marks and Spencer Benevolent Trust, 65
Marr, William, 7
Marschner, 47
Massel, Joseph, 75, 78
Maypole's, 57
Mecca, 110
Mediterranean Sea, 100–1, 120
Melchett, Lord, 166
Melikoff, 8
Mevaseret Yerushalayim, 104
Middle East, 77, 83, 86–8, 101, 102, 120, 132, 135, 139, 198, 199
Mikveh Israel, 107
Milner, Lord, 114
Moab, 111
Moiseiwitsch, 188
Molière, 35
Montague, Edwin, 85, 87
Montefiore, Sir Moses, 75
Morning Post, 172
Moscow, 2, 73
Mosley, Lady Cynthia, 170, 171
Mosley, Sir Oswald, 166, 170–1; *see also* The Greater Britain
Motelle, *see* Motol
Motol, 72, 73, 76
Mount Scopus, 80, 111, 112
Mountain Ash, 154–5
Munich, 75, 165
Munich, University of, 133
Mussolini, 170, 173

NATO, 139
Nature Conservancy, 192
Nazareth, 127
Nazis, the, 133, 171; *see also* Hitler
Neal, Laurence, 166
Nebuchadnezzar, King, 198, 200
Negev, the, 135, 136, 197–8
Nehardea, 2
Netter, Charles, 107
Neue Freie Presse (Vienna), 70
Neumann, Dr Emmanuel, 135
New Party, 170, 171

211

INDEX

New York, 10, 138, 139, 142, 178
Newfoundland, 38
Nicholson, Max, 155, 165–6, 174, 175, 191–2
Nieman, River, 3
Nile, River, 103
Nobel Prize winners, 80, 133
Nobel's, 85
Nottingham, 146, 178
Nuremberg, 45–6, 47

Obendorfer, 47
Observer, ix, 165
Odessa, 108
Office of Price Administration (OPA), 179
Ormsby-Gore, Major W., 99, 100, 103, 104, 110, 114
Ottoman Dominion, 87; *see also* Turkey
Owen, Gail, ix
Oxford Farming Conference, 184
Oxford, University of, 166

Pale of Settlement, the, 4, 8, 9, 52, 58, 76, 77; *see also* Russia, Czarist
Palestine, and early history of the Jews, 1, 4, 73; Weizmann's attitude to, 67, 72–3, 79, 83, 105, 128–31; and Anglo-Palestine Company, 69; British administration of, 69–70, 94, 114, 120–1, 124–30, 135–8; and Balfour Declaration, 70, 86, 91–5, 97, 105, 120, 124, 129; and Zionist Commission, 70, 94–5, 97–112, 114, 122, 124–31; and Peace Conference of Versailles, 70, 112–20, 124; modern settlers in, 70–3, 79, 103, 106–9, 125; establishment of Hebrew University in, 79–81, 106, 110–12, 133; and events of First World War, 83–93, 97–8, 104–6; and Conference of San Remo, 94, 120–1, 124; and Feisal/Weizmann agreement, 110–19; and WIZO's work, 122–4; establishment of Daniel Sieff Research Institute in, 132–5; mentioned, 139; *see also* Israel, creation of State of
Palestine, 88–90, 92, 110
Palestine Bureau, 88
Palestine Office, 106, 108
Palestinian Talmud, 1
Paris, 46–7, 50, 70, 73, 78, 80, 99–100, 112–20, 124, 125, 199, 205
Paten, J. L., 38–9
Pearl Harbour, 179
'Penny Bazaars', *see* Marks, Michael
PEP, 164–77, 189, 191; *Britain and World Trade* published by, 174; *Fuel and Power* published by, 174; *Government and Industry* published by, 174; *The Film Industry* published by, 174; 'Experiments in the Marketing of Agricultural Products' published by, 176
Perkin, William Henry, 37, 75, 80
Perpetual Fund for Israel, 67
Persia, 1, 21, 55
Persian Gulf, 136
Petah Tikvah, 108, 130
Peterson, 64
Philistines, the, 103, 104
Pichon, 114
Pinetti, Dr, 7
Pinsk, 72
Pinsker, Leon, 108
Poland, 2–4, 42, 52, 53, 56, 83–4, 108, 134
Pole, Tudor, 101–2
Political and Economic Planning, *see* PEP
Portal, Lord, 171–2
Portugal, 4
Preston, 94
Priestley, J. B., 165
Pripet Marshes, 72
'Protocols of the Elders of Zion', 105
Prudential Assurance Company, 144
Prussia, 3, 8
Pum-beditha, 1, 2

Racine, 35
RAF, 49
Ramla, 104
Ravensdale, Lady, 170
Reconstruction, 172
Rees, Goronwy, 64; *see also* St Michael
Reeves, 48
Rehovoth, 132, 134, 139
Rhine, River, 4, 76
Richmond, 170
Richter, Hans, 36
Rintoul, Dr, 85
Rishon le-Zion, 132
Romans, Ancient, 1, 132, 198, 199
Rome, 73, 99, 100, 170, 199
Roosevelt, Franklin D., 178
Rosh Ha-Golah, 2
Rostov-on-Don, 77
Rothschild, Baron Edmond de, 80, 98–100, 108, 130
Rothschild, James de, 99
Rothschild, Lord, 95
Rumania, 108
Rusholme, 76
Russia, Czarist, 4, 7–9, 14, 24, 52, 70–2, 75, 77, 83, 105, 108, 128, 159; *see also* Pale of Settlement, Soviet Union
Rutherford, 37

Sabras, the, 197–8

212

INDEX

Sacher, Gabriel, 184, 202, 205
Sacher, Harry, 48–9, 56, 76, 87–8, 90, 113, 125–6, 132, 134, 148, 205
Sacher, Michael, 184, 202, 205
St John's School, 38
St Michael, 64
Salford, 18, 46, 48
Salter, Sir Arthur, 168
Samuel, Edwin, 99
Samuel, Herbert, 84, 85, 95, 126, 127
San Remo, Conference of, 94, 120–1, 124
Santiniketan, 192
Sassanides, the, 1
Saturday Review, 164, 165
Scandinavia, 43
Schiller, 35, 46, 191
Schuster, Lord, 173
Scott, C. P., 37, 83–5, 87, 113
Second World War, 48, 126, 156, 177–80
Sephardim branch of Jewry, *see* Jews, Sephardic
Sereni, Angelo, 100
Shaar, Hagai, 104
Sharett, Moshe, 135
Shefelah, 103
Shrirow, 75
Siady, 3, 14
Sidebotham, Herbert, 87, 88, 90, 113, 205
Sieff, Chaim, 5–7, 9, 15, 24
Sieff, Daniel, 131–2; *see also* Daniel Sieff Research Institute
Sieff, Daphne, 191
Sieff, Edward, ix, 14, 18, 35, 50, 190, 202
Sieff, Ephraim, and early life in Russia and Germany, 1–3, 6—9; and emigration to England, 2, 5–6, 10; and residence in Manchester, 11, 17–28; and Beaumont and Co., 12–14, 20; and Sieff & Beaumont Ltd, 13, 41–5, 49–50; marriage of, 15–16, 24; character of, 20–8, 39–40, 186; as a Zionist, 69, 95, 124–5; and First World War, 81–2; mentioned, 128, 147–9
Sieff, Israel, birth of, 17; childhood, 18–28; early friendship with Rebecca Marks, 30–2, 34–6, 41, 42; childhood friendship with Simon Marks, 19, 31–9, 52, 59; at Manchester Grammar School, 18, 34–5, 38–9; at Manchester University, 40–1; joins father's business, 41; marriage to Rebecca Marks, 48–51; elected to Board of Marks and Spencer, 64; friendship with Chaim Weizmann, 66–70, 139–40, 146–7, 167, 181, 189; first visit to Palestine, 103–6; and Daniel Sieff Research Institute, 132–5; and expansion of Marks and Spencer, 147–61; and PEP, 164–76

Sieff, Judith, 205
Sieff, Marcus, 48, 184, 202, 205
Sieff, Michael, 48, 50, 202, 205
Sieff, Miriam, birth of, 18; childhood of, 19, 36; marriage to Simon Marks, 48, 96, 204
Sieff, Pauline, 18, 20, 35–6, 204
Sieff, Sarah, 3, 14–24, 26–7, 49, 82
Sieff, William, 18, 35, 82–3
Sieff & Beaumont Ltd, 13, 42–3
Silver, Dr Abba Hillel, 135
Simon, Sir Leon, 98, 130–1
Sinai Peninsula, 90, 110
Slough, 159, 185
Sokolow, Nahum, 114, 120
Solomon, Flora, 158
Somme, River, 102
South Africa, 185
Soviet Union, 3, 136, 165; *see also* Russia, Czarist
Spain, 4, 77
The Spectator, 88, 89
Spencer, Agnes, 65
Spencer, Thomas, 53–4, 59–61
Spencer, Thomas, Jr, 48, 61, 62, 64–5
Spencer Trust, 65
Speyer Institute, 80
Spinoza, 195
SS Canberra, 100
The Statist, 174
Steel, Bernard, 62–3
Stein, Leonard, 92, 101
Stettin, 10
Stockton-on-Tees, 58
Strachey, John, 166
Straight, William, 193
Strauss, Jack, 179
Success, Lake, 136
Suez Canal, 83, 85, 90, 103, 110, 136
Sussex, 96
Sutcliffe, 43–5
Swansea, 177
Switzerland, 72, 139
Sykes-Picot Agreement, 87–8, 90, 92, 110, 112, 113
Sykes, Sir Mark, 87, 88, 90, 92, 95–8, 110
Syria, 111, 112
Syrians, Ancient, 21, 92

Tagore, Rabindranath, 192–3
Talmud, the, 1, 3, 5, 21, 27, 199; *see also* Babylonian Talmud, Jerusalem Talmud, Palestinian Talmud
Taranto, 99, 100
Tardieu, 114
Tel Aviv, 103–4, 107, 126, 130, 132, 133, 138
The Times, 42, 169

213

INDEX

Titus, Emperor, 1
Torah, the, 1, 3, 33
Totnes, 193
Tout, T. F., 37, 41
Trans-Jordan, 110
Treitschke, 7
Trieste, 109
Truman, Harry S., 136–8
Trumpeldor, 92
Tunisia, 120
Turkey, 71, 83, 87, 91, 92, 98–9, 103, 104, 106, 110

Uganda, 72, 73, 76, 78
Ukraine, the, 4–5
'The Ultimate in Sanitation', 184
United Nations, and UNSCOP, 135; and creation of State of Israel, 135–9
United States of America, 7, 8, 42, 49, 52, 57, 77, 86, 91, 96–7, 99, 101, 106, 108–9, 113, 114, 120, 124, 131, 134–8, 141–3, 147, 153, 157, 165, 177–80, 184, 189, 192, 193
UNSCOP, see United Nations

Versailles, Peace Conference of, 70, 112–20, 124
Victoria I, 27–8
Vienna, 70, 79
Vilia, River, 3
Vilna, 2–3, 75
Visva-Bharati, 192
Voyage en Espagne, 35

Wadi Musa, 110
Wadi Waheida, 110
Wakefield, 55, 58
Wales, 30, 57, 154
Waley, Arthur, 99
Warrington, 58
Washington, 179
Washington DC, 193
Waterford, 14–15
Wauchope, Sir Arthur, 133
Week End Review, 165; 'A National Plan for Britain' published in, 165–6
Weisgal, Meyer, 134, 138
Weizmann, Benjamin, 76, 91
Weizmann, Dr Chaim, friendship with Simon Marks, 48–9, 68, 140, 146–7, 181; friendship with Israel Sieff, 66–70, 139–40, 146–7, 167, 181, 189; character of, 66–7, 194; early life of, 72, 76–7; author of *Trial and Error*, 78n; and 'practical' Zionism, 72, 78, 79; and 'synthetic' Zionism, 73, 79; and move to England, 73–80; and Hebrew University, 79, 80–1, 111–12; and outbreak of First World War, 83–5; and issue of Balfour Declaration, 86–93, 128–30; and Zionist Commission, 94–112, 124–6, 128–31; and agreement with Feisal, 110–19; at Peace Conference of Versailles, 112–30; at Conference of San Remo, 120–1; and Daniel Sieff Research Institute, 131–5; and declaration of State of Israel, 135–9; elected President of Israel, 138–9; friendship with Harry Sacher, 205
Weizmann, Michael, 49, 132
Weizmann, Vera, 49, 66, 73–7, 79, 80, 83, 96, 111–12, 122–4, 135
Weizmann Institute of Science, 134–5
White, 114
Whitehaven, 154
Whitney, William, 193
Wholesalers' Association, 153, 154
Who's Who, 192
Wigan, 32, 58, 60
Williams-Ellis, Clough, 166
Willstätter, Professor Richard, 133
Wilson, Woodrow, 99
Wingate, General, 102
WIZO, 122–4
Women's International Zionist Organisation, see WIZO
Woolworths, 57, 141–2
World War I, see First World War
World War II, see Second World War
World Zionist Organisation, 68, 71, 108, 131
Worms, 199
WRNS, 181

Yavneh, 132
Yorkshire, 43, 53, 54, 56, 57, 59, 61, 156, 192
Youth Aliyah, 123
Yukon, 53

Zakkai, Yochanan Ben, 132
Zalman, Elijah Ben Solomon, 3
Zerubbabel Society, 108
Zichron Ya'acov, 108
Zionist Actions Committee, 68, 76
Zionist Commission, 70, 94–5, 97–112, 114, 122, 124–31
Zionist Congress, First, 71; Seventh, 72; Eighth, 79
Zionist Executive, 106, 110, 125, 128
Zionist Organisation of America, 131, 134; see also Federation of American Zionists
Zionist Organisation of England, 66, 69; see also English Zionist Federation
Zoppot, 76
Zurich, 77, 82